18.92
Royal
1993

COME HERE

COME HERE

A MAN OVERCOMES THE TRAGIC AFTERMATH OF CHILDHOOD SEXUAL ABUSE

Richard Berendzen

Former President of American University

and Laura Palmer

VILLARD BOOKS

New York

1993

Villard Books is a registered trademark of Random House, Inc.

Library of Congress Cataloging-in-Publicaton Data

Berendzen, Richard.
Come here: a man overcomes the tragic aftermath of childhood sexual
abuse / Richard Berendzen and Laura Palmer.—1st ed.
p.   cm.
ISBN 0-679-41777-X
1. Adult child sexual abuse victims—United States—Psychology.
2. Berendzen, Richard.   I. Palmer, Laura.   II. Title.
HV6570.2.B47   1993   362.7'6'0973—dc20   93-6924

Book design by Richard Oriolo

Manufactured in the United States of America

9 8 7 6 5 4 3 2

First edition

For
Natasha,
Deborah, Seth, Max,
and Gail

Through many dangers, toils, and snares,
I have already come;
'Tis grace that brought me safe thus far,
And grace will lead me home.

"AMAZING GRACE"

CONTENTS

PROLOGUE

By the time I was eight years old, my childhood felt like a prize. I had buddies, a bike, and a baseball bat. I went to school every day and then came home to our white frame house on Fairview Avenue and played outside until it was time for dinner. For the first time in my memory, I was like everybody else. It felt like a miracle.

I had been in bed with rheumatic fever and asthma from the time I was four years old until I was seven, when we moved from the rainy dampness of Portland, Oregon, to the dry heat of East Dallas. The dramatic change in climate and new antibiotics made it possible for me to be active instead of bedridden.

One Sunday afternoon when I was eight years old, I ran inside to get a drink of water. Odd noises were coming from the middle bedroom. The panting, staccato sounds were unlike anything I had ever heard. The door was slightly open, and I saw my parents inside. Their naked bodies twisted and lurched together in a deformed arabesque.

"Come here."

So, with nothing more than that two-syllable summons by my mother, the sexual abuse of my childhood began. "Come here." Its simplicity was as stark as the terror it unleashed.

My mother told me to undress, which I did, leaving the carefree part of my childhood on the floor with my clothes. At age eight, I did exactly what my mother said. My parents were having sex, and so, for the first time, did I. I remember my father's face gripped in a frenzy, but I couldn't tell if it was one of agony or pleasure. My parents were naked, their hair disheveled. They were breathing so hard it sounded like a race. I was baffled and bewildered and between them and under them; they were big and I was small and everyone was moving and fast. My involvement was slight but indelible.

Once it was over, it was erased. I got up, got dressed, and got out of there. It hadn't happened. I couldn't know what I knew. In fact, I didn't know what I knew. What had just happened? And why? Why?

Later, we all sat down for Sunday supper at the kitchen table. We ate simply. My mother cooked from cans rather than recipes. My father never talked much, and when he finished eating, he cleared his plate and went into his bedroom to read, as he did every night. I asked to be excused and went out to play. My mother did the dishes. No one said anything about that afternoon. Maybe it never happened. Or if it had, maybe it never would again.

But three years later I heard the words again: "Come here."

In the decades that followed, I became an astronomer, and the origins of the universe billions of years ago became more comprehensible to me than my own childhood. For forty years I suppressed what had happened to me in the middle bedroom, once with both parents, and then, repeatedly, for many months with my mother. In space, time is a measure of distance. For me, as years passed, memories of the middle bedroom drew farther and farther away, like a receding quasar. I knew I was now safe because I was in control. I was sure of that.

COME HERE

One

THE BOY

T he hardscrabble town of Walters, Oklahoma, was where I was born in 1938. This dusty hamlet is on the southern edge of the state, not far from the Texas border. The land is open and wide, and the lives it supports are caught in a time warp from small-town America decades ago.

My grandparents owned the general store in town, and my father, Earl Berendzen, worked there from the time he was a boy. He was a devout Methodist, conscientious and reliable, a decent guy in a town where the men had Skoal in their cheeks and shotguns in their trucks.

My mother grew up on a farm a few miles away, in the plain and unforgiving land that had to be pummeled into productivity. Her parents were elderly when she was born, and her brothers, nearly grown, soon moved out of the house. She had to leave school in the fifth grade to work as her parents' sole farmhand, picking cotton until her fingers bled from the thorns on the low, stubby bushes. When she was twelve, her mother died, and for the next two years she ran the farm and took care of her father. Baptized Florine Adora Harrison, she called herself June. When she was fourteen years old, she took off to see the world.

It is hard for me to imagine what gave my mother the courage to venture alone into the world beyond the farm. Barely literate, she had never lived a day away from the farm when she suddenly ran away in 1922. Was she daring or desperate, following a dream or fleeing from demons? Had something happened to her, a beautiful young girl alone and vulnerable on a farm with her aging father, and big brothers nearby? She left with only her dog, Laddie, a medium-sized collie that she said was the smartest dog in the world.

She was gone almost fifteen years. When she finally came home, she said she had been moving from one military base to another, taking pictures and making maps for the government. She claimed that she had traveled to every state.

In her youthful photographs my mother is a stunning brunette with blazing eyes. She was too much for her times, too daring, too spirited, too demanding. She was a woman who wanted to set the world on fire and ended up only consuming herself.

She came back to Walters when she was thirty and rented a room from the mother of the man she eventually married. She had traveled the nation; Earl Berendzen had never left Walters. He was smitten with her immediately. They dated, and he soon asked her to marry him. She refused. He kept asking and she kept refusing until one day she changed her mind.

I don't know what finally made her say yes, but I do know it was a marriage with a secret, right from the beginning: Earl, June, and the Secret. Ever since I was a child I knew that something powerful had prompted her to leave home and something else momentous had occurred during those missing years, but I never could find out what had happened.

My father knew. Once when they were fighting, he almost blurted it out. My mother tore into him like an enraged bear. "I told you never, ever, ever to mention that, Earl Berendzen! I'll kill you if you even think of saying anything!" Decades later, toward the end of his life when he was old and deaf, my father tried to tell me about it, but

4

his voice was too distorted and his thoughts too tangled. Even then, with my mother far away, I think he still feared her, such was her domination.

My mother was severely mentally ill for most of her life and all of mine. As a child, all I knew was that she was wildly unpredictable. Labels like manic, paranoid, delusional, and psychotic came years later. Sometimes she would be furious for no apparent reason; then, in a snap, she could suddenly become incredibly loving, supportive, and fun.

When I was four, she became convinced that the good life awaited us in Oregon. The good life was always where we were not. So, despite my father's protests, we moved to Portland. There I developed asthma and rheumatic fever. For three years, my temperature hovered between 100 and 103 degrees. My mother seemed to take care of me around the clock. She fed me, talked to me, and read to me. Except for a few minutes in the evening with my dad, she was my only companion, my only friend.

Like other children of that era, one of my favorite books was *The Little Engine That Could.* I pestered my mother to read it to me over and over. I loved the story of the tiny steam engine that had to chug over a mountain to carry Christmas toys to the children on the other side. The engine was too small, and the mountain, too big. But what it lacked in power it made up in determination. It chugged along with the words "I think I can, I think I can, I think I can."

All I wanted in life was to get better. I yearned to belong to the world beyond my bedroom. Kids rode tricycles, laughed, played tag, and kicked balls. Sometimes my mother would ask them to play outside my window so I could watch, which I greatly enjoyed. I don't know why she never invited anyone in to visit me. Perhaps she feared I might catch something and get even sicker, or perhaps she wanted me secluded for herself.

My father would visit me for a few minutes at night when he came home from the shipyard where he worked as a painter. For the most part, during the years when children my age went to nursery school, kindergarten, and first grade, I was alone, with only my mother and my imagination for friends.

I learned to live in my mind. If I was going to have fun, it had to be my own invention. I made mountains with my knees for my toy soldiers to march over and hide behind. Shadows on the ceiling became airplanes. I moved the sheets around to make forts.

After dozing on and off in the morning, I waited until I could turn on the radio to listen to soap operas like *As the World Turns* and *Stella Dallas*. Before it became a television show, *Queen for a Day* was an afternoon radio program, and I remember clapping for the woman I thought had the most tragic life and deserved to win the dinette set. The programs I liked the best were *Sergeant Preston of the Yukon, The Thin Man, The Shadow,* and *Captain Midnight.* I followed the plots intently and begged my parents to let me send for a Captain Midnight decoder ring.

I was thrilled when it arrived and I could decipher my own secret messages, even if they were as banal as "Drink your Ovaltine." It didn't matter. For the first time I interacted with the world outside my bedroom window through those magic words, "Okay boys and girls, this is a message just for you, it's from Captain Midnight and the code is seven, fourteen, eight, twenty-three . . ."

My mother was determined to make me well. In keeping with the World War II spirit, she assigned weapons to each mouthful she fed me. "Now this is a bomb. Here comes a fighter plane." Carrots became soldiers to fill the ranks of my army, and they fired corn kernels for bullets. Grapes were bombs I dropped from my fantasy plane straight to their target—my mouth. I was a warrior all right, feverish, listless, and five years old.

World War II was not the only combat I knew. My parents fought all the time. My mother did not need a reason to be furious with my father. She accused him of everything. She said he caused my illness. She claimed I got rheumatic fever from strep throat that I caught from him. "It's all your fault, Earl Berendzen. Because of you, Richard's sick. If he doesn't get better, you're to blame." She said that over and over, like the devil's rosary. I finally tuned it out, the way people who live near airports stop hearing jets.

My mother kept insisting, like a jackhammer, that my father was a Nazi. I knew from the radio that the Nazis were the enemy. My mother assumed the name Berendzen was German. She would yell at my dad, "We're fighting the Germans and you, Earl Berendzen, are just like all those goddamn Nazis—pigheaded and disgusting."

I don't remember my father responding. He would retreat downstairs to his basement workshop. On rare occasions he would carry me down to see his tools. This was one of the few things I remember our doing together during the three years I was sick.

He might have wanted to do more for me, but I know my mother wouldn't have let him. Only she was good enough to take care of me. She wove me into her obsessive web. "Oh my son, my son, I'll take care of you. I love you so much, you don't know how much I love you. You are so perfect. You are my life. . . ." She would go on and on like that, her words binding me to her and excluding my father.

I now know I lived two childhoods, the one I remembered and the one I repressed. The one I remembered was the one that made it possible for me to survive. I was fifty-one years old before I remembered some of the repressed parts, like the Christmas Eve when I was five. Because I had spent nearly all year in bed, it was an extraordinary, incredible moment when my mother allowed me to come into the living room.

I had looked forward to Christmas for weeks. My mother had told me I could help decorate the tree, but my joyful moment ended when my mother insisted that I sing Christmas carols.

"Sing 'Silent Night.' " I couldn't because I didn't know the words. "Sing, damnit! Don't you know that all children sing Christmas carols on Christmas Eve? That's the way families are supposed to be. Sing 'Silent Night'!"

I couldn't even hum it. I didn't know the melody. Suddenly she hit me so hard that I smashed into the wall. The shock and surprise hurt more than my bloody lip or bruised head. The pattern was set. I was her passion and her prey.

Finally, when I was six, on the advice of our pediatrician, my family moved to a warm, dry climate—Dallas. My health improved dramatically. Whatever the cause, I was freed from my sickbed. And I discovered the great Texas outdoors.

In Dallas, I found the stars. I would lie on my back in the grass at night and stare at the sky. It was magical. After staring at my bedroom ceiling in Oregon, I was captivated and awed by the grandeur of the Texas sky. While I was sick I had invented imaginary worlds to amuse myself, but here was a real world, a universe, full of wonder. I didn't need to imagine a thing to make the heavens more interesting. Besides, the sky was always there. I could always rely on the stars. How far away, mysterious, and noble they seemed.

Because my health had improved substantially, I was able to enroll in school. I started in the second grade and felt blisteringly self-conscious because I was seven and had never been to school before. I felt that the other kids knew much more than I, so I worked hard to catch up.

Childhood was a code I was determined to crack, but it could be perplexing at times. The teacher would say things like "All the red birds go to one side of the room and all the blue birds go to the other." I had no idea which bird I was. When the class sang, the other children knew the words and when to clap. Although I sometimes felt painfully awkward in the classroom, it didn't matter. I was glad just to be there.

From the start, my mother was obsessed with my academic achievement. The hard part for me was that she couldn't stop. She wouldn't just help me with my homework—she did it. Sometimes I got into trouble in elementary school for turning in work that was hers instead of mine.

From my earliest years my mother tried to mold me. I would be educated, poised, and classy, not some blue-collar guy like my dad. I'd work in a high-rise office building downtown, not in the neighborhood hardware store.

I wasn't allowed to dress like the other boys. I always had to wear laced-up leather shoes, even when I played baseball. Sneakers were forbidden. The other kids wore blue jeans to school; I dressed in khaki pants with stiffly ironed creases. Even my lunches were unusual. No bologna or peanut butter and jelly for me. Every day I had the same thing: two sandwiches, thick with meat, lettuce, tomatoes, and gobs of mayonnaise. Most of my lunch would end up in the garbage. There was just too much. And no one would trade.

My father was as passive as my mother was dominant. Dad got up at six every morning to work at the hardware store. He stayed until closing, when he swept the floor and counted the money.

He came home at the same time each evening, ate dinner, and then retreated to his bedroom, where he read *Reader's Digest*, *Coronet*, *Field and Stream*, and the Bible. At times, my father and I would go to the garage. Wearing an old-style undershirt, with his wavy hair soon sweaty from the workout, he would dazzle me with his skill with a punching bag. And he showed me how to do it. These rare father-and-son moments would last only a few minutes before my mother inevitably would appear, ask what we were talking about, and order me elsewhere.

I think she was afraid he and I might become too close. The few times he wanted to take me to a ballgame or target shooting, my mother always had reasons why we shouldn't do it. The game would be too noisy; the gun too dangerous; or the day too hot. Besides, she said, I didn't really want to do any of that anyway. We didn't challenge her; we knew it never worked. Most men would not have put up with the abuse my dad did, but I didn't have most men for my father. Or most women for my mother.

My parents had a strange relationship. They had separate bedrooms and rarely communicated without quarreling. Except for that Sunday afternoon, I have no memory of seeing any affection between them. I never saw them laugh, tease, hold hands, or hug, much less as I found them that day. I only heard them fight, or more to the point, I only heard my mother berate my father for being a stupid bore and an inconsequential failure.

My dad became exhausted from her verbal abuse. She never relented. With seemingly endless ability, she could find ever more vicious things to call him. "Earl Berendzen, you are the stupidest human being who ever walked the face of the Earth." "Your mother is a toad of an ugly, squat German woman." "You have no brains and no balls. You're nothing."

He would get up from the table and quietly say, "Have it your way, whatever suits you. Just leave me alone. Quit harping, and just leave me alone." Most nights he was like a boarder you take in to help pay the rent; he ate supper, picked up after himself, and then went back to his room. Yet, no boarder would have accepted the verbal assault he passively took, over and over.

My parents were destined to have nothing in common. Ideologically, my father was the conservative, and my mother, the liberal, which gave them something else to fight about. She thought FDR was a savior and Eleanor Roosevelt a saint. My dad thought FDR was a socialist who'd ruin the nation. Politics and current events never came up without a battle. The only topic they didn't fight about, surprisingly, was race. Both of them always supported civil rights, which was unusual given their roots in the segregated South.

I would get annoyed with my father for not standing up for himself. Occasionally, when he'd make a feeble attempt, my mother would only scream louder and louder until he gave up and retreated in sullen silence to his room. It was his bunker, piled high with stacks of magazines. How could he argue with a cyclone? Wild, furious, dangerous, and unpredictable—it can move anywhere at any time. It has no reason. When it approaches, prudent people hide. They don't try to fight it. In fairness, what could he do? She was mad, or at least profoundly mentally ill. Even as a child I sensed how futile it would have been if my dad had fought back, but it gnawed at me to see him so beaten down and helpless.

Oddly enough, we did do things together as a family. On Sundays we sometimes went to the Methodist church together. My mother always drove, because she said my father was a stupid driver. She drove as wildly as she acted. When he complained about her driving, her screaming in the enclosed car became unbearable. So he stopped complaining.

I loved to go to the movies, and occasionally the three of us went together. We saw Abbott and Costello films, and Roy Rogers was my favorite cowboy. Even at the theater, my mother insisted on sitting between my dad and me.

It may sound odd, but I loved both my parents. I looked at my father as a hard-working and honest man who tried his best. Even though he never expressed his feelings to me, I knew he cared about me. It was love by deduction: He worked hard to provide a home, food, and clothing for me, so I knew he cared about me and wanted me to succeed. But I don't remember him ever hugging me, reading me a bedtime story, or patting me on the back and saying something like "Good job, Son" or "I love you, Son" the way dads did in movies. He never took me aside and tried to explain my mother's behavior. It would have meant a lot if he had said something like, "Your mom means well, but she has a problem. She can't help herself. She attacks me all the time. I just ignore her. Let me know if she ever goes after you. We'll figure something out. You can count on me."

As a boy I did love my mother, but tangled up with the love were feelings of resentment, hatred, and remorse. Sometimes she would be gentle and loving; other times she would scream at me and hit me for no reason.

I used to look forward to getting my haircut. The barbershop was the one place where I could immerse myself totally in a masculine world. As the barbers snipped, I listened to men chew over sports and brag about hunting. They talked about baseball and cars and the deer they bagged. I thumbed through gun and motorcycle magazines as I eavesdropped. I couldn't get enough of this world.

One day after my haircut, my mother came into the barber shop, grabbed me by the arm, and yanked me to the doorway. She screamed in my face and slapped me repeatedly, snapping my head back against the red, white, and blue barber pole. I cried more from humiliation than hurt. I never knew when my mother would turn on me, hit me, and tell me I was bad. Worst of all, I never knew why. If I had known why, perhaps I could have protected myself. In moments like that, I felt confused and ashamed. Why couldn't my family be like everybody else's? I envied the normalcy I saw in my friends' homes. People spoke to each other in ordinary voices without being cruel or frightening. I knew life was supposed to be like that.

I kept hoping it would be like that in my house someday. Sometimes, for a few days or a week or two at a time, it was, which enabled me to keep hoping. Life was tranquil when my mother was calm. Then her mood would shift and unpredictable hell would break loose.

I knew my mother was unusual, but that was all. In the absence of insight, I just had to adapt. If you are stranded on an island, you learn to live with the weather. You put up with it. So it was with my mother. She was all I had. I got used to her emotional climate and never complained, because deep inside I thought that even an unpredictable mother was better than none at all.

Her manic outbursts made me feel submerged in a lava flow of hot madness. Volcanos at least release smoke and sparks before they blow. Not my mother. Without warning, it could happen in the grocery store or the front seat of the car. Suddenly, she would screech and slap me. Or she'd bury her nails into my arm until they drew blood. Or she'd dig her high heel into my foot. I'd freeze, as silent and still as the nineteen-hundred-year-old silhouettes of dead children in Pompeii. I let my mother hit me because I just wanted to survive. That's what my father did with her verbal hits. When he did try to resist, she destroyed him. I watched and learned. In that sense, he may have helped me survive.

My mother never allowed my father to discipline me. I don't know if he knew about my mother's beatings. I never told him. If he couldn't save himself, how could he save me? If I did tell, I was sure she would only become more enraged at me and a bad situation would become intolerable. Some of the worst times occurred when she ordered me to the middle bedroom and made me bend over and pull down my pants. She whipped me with a yardstick that had LINDOP HARDWARE written on it. Sometimes she would make me find a branch from a tree so she could hit me with it. If I came back with one that wasn't strong enough, she would shake me until my vision blurred and send me out to get another one. To keep from crying, I concentrated on counting the strokes.

One time the pain became so intense that I burst into tears and started hiccuping uncontrollably. I coughed and gasped and tried to breathe between hiccups. One of my friends came to see if I could play. My mother told him I would be out in a minute, but I couldn't stop crying or hiccuping. So I waited inside for what seemed an eternity. He kept shouting, "Hey, are you coming?" I couldn't get a sound out. Further enraged, my mother gritted her teeth and snarled, "You're acting just like your asshole father. Stop that. Act like a man."

Sometimes her attacks came from nowhere. Other times they arose from my failure to match her expectations. I hadn't straightened my room to her satisfaction. I hadn't vacuumed the carpet well enough. I had forgotten to put something away. She would whip me raw. It was like peeling off strips of bark from a young birch. My backside would be crimson and felt like I had sat on coals. I tried to distract myself until it stopped hurting and then just forget about it, too ashamed to tell my friends.

Physical pain heals quickly, but never being safe in your own home is corrosive. My mother's irrationality and unpredictability meant part of me always had to be on guard. She was like a Texas rattlesnake the same color as its desert surroundings. You don't see it until you step on it, and then it is too late. So it was with her mania. In many ways my mother looked the part of an ordinary housewife, devoted to her son and fastidious about her home. She was invisible in the context of her East Dallas surroundings until that ugly moment when she turned in a venomous assault.

The flip side of mania, however, was a mother with an *I Love Lucy* zaniness. When she decided to landscape our yard, she went to a nursery to buy trees, but decided they were too expensive. So one night after my father and I were asleep, she went to a park and dug up small trees and shrubs. When we woke up, they were planted in front of our house.

With more force than he usually mustered, my amazed father demanded, "Where did you get those plants at night?"

"I got them from a park. They've got lots of them there."

"But Florine, you can't go steal plants and trees from the park. It's illegal!"

"Earl Berendzen, you're a stupid, dull fool, a pathetic excuse for a man. Nobody will miss them. All you ever do is ruin things. So shut up! Shut up!"

My father, with an Eagle Scout's morality, was outraged by her theft. They had an explosive fight. As always, my mother prevailed. So did the shrubbery in our yard.

My parents, like nearly everyone who survived the Depression, were cautious with money. Dad earned it, and mother controlled it. My father would cross town to a market that sold peaches at two cents less a can. He would buy dozens of cans and stack them on the back porch. We'd have peaches for months.

My mother's sense of saving money was, characteristically, more bizarre. Once she decided that V-8 juice was nutritious but too expensive. She had a new blender and thought it would be easy to make her own. So she bought several dozen bags of each vegetable listed on the label. She knew everything except the proportions to use. Nor did she realize how much liquid a stalk of celery or bunch of carrots would make. She ended up filling every container in the house with the ersatz V-8 juice, which was not red but a dull, stagnant green. She scrubbed out the bathtub and poured in the juice. She filled buckets, glasses, pitchers, and cups. For weeks, we drank the stuff, which tasted like muck from a pond.

One day when I was about ten, she took my friends and me for a picnic at the zoo. We didn't sit off in a quiet, grassy area. We spread our blanket in front of the lion's cage. People walked around us while we munched and drank. Escapades like this amused my friends. Certainly there wasn't another mother like her on Fairview Avenue. When she was in the mood, she could be charming. In her sane periods, she had a rapier wit and acid tongue worthy of an untutored Cyrano de Bergerac. No one could withstand her verbal dueling—my dad, shopkeepers, my teachers, or me. That same mad energy could propel her into wildly unconventional but amusing adventures.

No one dared to do the things she did. When kite flying was popular in my neighborhood, my mother decided her son would have the best kite of all. So she purchased a kite replica of an airplane from an Army-Navy store. The military used such kites for aerial target practice by pulling them behind planes. I tried to fly it myself, but it was so big that I couldn't get it off the ground. Not deterred, my mother tied it to the rear bumper of the car and took off down the street. The kite rose about twenty feet and immediately crashed. That didn't matter. It was still high adventure. She wanted her son to have the ultimate kite. After all, he was her son.

When I found my parents in the middle bedroom that fateful Sunday afternoon, I was amazed that they were doing anything together, let alone anything possibly pleasurable. I had never seen anyone naked before, certainly not my parents. I was kicked off guard, like the surprise wave that topples you when you glance back toward shore. I felt confused and submerged in an undertow I could not control. I was relieved to get out of there and come up for air. It felt good to be outdoors again in a safe and normal world. Since nothing like the middle bedroom had ever happened before, I had nothing to compare it to and no reason to think it would happen again. It was an aberration.

When I think of my childhood, I see a mosaic of images. The photographs my mother took were stage-set. Often she would have me stand outside facing the sun to avoid shadows on my face. In the bright glare of the Texas sunlight, I could scarcely see. My eyes would tear and I would squint. My mother would bellow at me to open my eyes wide and smile. With the early morning sun's rays directly in my face, I simply could not see. Out of the blinding glare, I would feel the slap of her hand even before I heard her shout, "Damnit, I told you to open your eyes and smile. Do what I tell you. Now look happy." She slapped me until I looked happy.

For the photographs, I always had creases in my pants and bright clean shirts. Sometimes she would stand me in front of my toys, which looked like a display in a trade show. She kept them lined in precise rows. The other kids were supposed to marvel and conclude who had the ultimate mom.

On my birthdays and at Christmas, my mother would photograph the presents before I could open them. She would record the vast number of packages. But she cheated. She would take a game apart and wrap the board separately from the deck of cards or the game pieces. When she gave me a croquet set, she wrapped each ball, mallet, and hoop individually. All gifts were always from her; nothing was from Santa or my dad. She wouldn't allow it. I never got a gift from my father until my twenty-first birthday.

In books, I found the ideal families and role models. My mother had taught me to read when I was sick, and the richness and vastness of the world I discovered in books never disappointed me. I relied on them for my heroes and a sense that life was worth living. Biographies of Abraham Lincoln and the explorers engrossed me. I knew all about Vasco da Gama and Cortés and Magellan. My favorite was Sir Francis Drake. Although not as famous as Magellan, he seemed more creative and daring. I had started to make a model of him for a class project when my mother took over, obsessively making him a velvet jacket with detailed stitching and tiny buttons and a feather in his cap. He looked gallant, and unlike anything a child could make.

One of my treasured possessions was the *Volume Library*, an encyclopedia compressed to the size of an unabridged dictionary. I loved that book. One section was called "The One Hundred Most Influential People in History." I read the vignettes about men like Aristotle, Leonardo da Vinci, and Franklin over and over. I realized they were mortals just like me. They were not mythic gods, but real people with real problems and shortcomings, who struggled and chiseled out their lives with determination and a sense of purpose. Here I learned that life mattered and that if you were steadfastly loyal to yourself and your dreams, you could be anything, anything at all.

These men inspired me in a way my father never could. I saw that many individuals in the *Volume Library* came from humble origins. They set the standards and drew the mark in the sand that the next jumper tries to surpass.

Lincoln's life mesmerized me. His lonely and impoverished boyhood, his determination to succeed, and his dogged pursuit of excellence was a story I took to heart. He had a breakdown, was defeated several times, but finally went on to become our greatest president. His life taught me that adversity can be survived—and must be survived—to achieve success. Great men never give up.

When I think back about those stories, I see themes they all had in common: an intense work ethic, triumph over adversity, and the exhilaration of the unknown. It thrilled me to read about explorers setting off for years to go over the horizon to places no one had been before. The thought of never knowing what you will find, the potential for discovering something that has never been known before, was an idea that captivated me as a boy and remains with me today.

I compensated for the distorted parts of my childhood by immersing myself in books that were evocative and stirred the blood. I read everything I could find by Arthur Conan Doyle, Edgar Allan Poe, Edgar Rice Burroughs, and Zane Grey. The novelist I admired most was Charles Dickens.

My mother also bought me *Compton's Encyclopedia*. I would pick a different letter each week and gladly spend hours reading that volume. I hopped around the alphabet, skipping sections I didn't understand. There I learned about the great wars.

With my chemistry set I made gunpowder and set off a huge quantity of it on the walk in front of our house. It blew a crack that still remains.

Sometimes, in her erratic way, my mother would attempt to extend my education. One day she announced that she'd signed us up for detective school. I don't know what prompted this. It might have been my reading Sherlock Holmes. Another time she enrolled me in a Dale Carnegie–style public speaking class. In a class for adults, I was the youngest person by thirty years. These activities were like fireworks that went up in the sky and then fizzled into the emptiness of the night. We would go a few times, and then, poof, she'd have us drop out.

Learning to fence was like that, too. She came home one day with two masks and foils and announced that I would learn fencing. Of course, I had no instructor. But she read that youngsters of privilege learn such things in fancy British boarding schools. So I looked up fencing in my encyclopedia, and my friends and I tried to teach ourselves.

She decided we would learn about religion by going to a different faith's service each week. One week it would be with Christian Scientists; the next, Catholics. We went to Lutheran and Baptist churches and visited a Holy Rollers' service. We went to synagogues and Greek Orthodox churches. I found this odd escapade of my mother's perplexing but interesting.

My mother had intermittent jobs when I was small. Most were inconsequential but out of the ordinary, such as counting the cars that crossed a busy intersection. Another time she placed a penny on the sidewalk and counted the people who would stop to pick it up. She then replaced the penny with a nickel and then a dime. Maybe she invented that job. It's hard to imagine someone paying for research like that then in East Dallas, but that's what she claimed.

I was always relieved when her focus was directed on something other than me. One of her longer-term jobs was working in a darkroom, processing film related to medical studies. I went with her once, and remember being fascinated as the images seemed to float through the developing solution from blur to precision. As if by magic, a detailed picture could emerge from a plain piece of paper. As usual, my mother was the sorceress.

When she called me one Saturday and told me to meet her at the darkroom, I was excited. I was eleven years old and could travel by bus myself. She told me exactly which bus to take and insisted on the route to follow. She wanted me there by late afternoon. I didn't know why. When my mother told me to do something, I did it. It was like blinking. I didn't have to think about it.

When I got there, I knocked on the door and she let me in, locking the door behind us. She said she was going into the darkroom and did. I could see nothing in there but darkness, a void. Since I couldn't follow her with my eyes, I had to follow her voice. From out of the total blackness I heard her say, "Come here."

Everything was black. The walls were black, the floor was black, the ceiling was black. My eyes were wide open, but I could see nothing. I had just come from the bright Texas sunlight. The heavy darkroom door slammed shut behind me. Now I was in the darkest dark. I was afraid to move, but afraid not to.

"Come here."

My mother was nude, or almost nude, on a metallic counter. She started undoing my belt. I remember more of what was around me than what happened to me. I remember how cold the metal was on the countertop. The room was abnormally cold, and I remember shivering. I remember that the counter, floor, and walls were hard, and the chemicals stank. I remember the lock of her hands on my body, trapping me in the dark. Like a great horned owl that searched out its prey in the blackest night, she had me locked in her talons.

Stunned and repulsed, I found myself being consumed by my mother. Now there was something else to fear. Clumsy, insistent, she soon finished with me.

Nothing was said. I stumbled back into my clothes in the darkness and headed for the bus. I was momentarily disoriented by the heat and the lingering brightness of the day. The sudden jolt of light both reassured and startled me. My eyes slowly adjusted as I tried to blink my way back into the mainstream, joining others waiting for a bus. I wanted a life that had nothing disgusting in it. "Why? Why? Why?" I didn't want a life with answers so much as I wanted one without such questions.

At that age, I had heard about sex, and girls were just beginning to interest me. My buddies and I wondered sometimes what it would be like to neck with a girl. All that seemed quaint compared with what had occurred between my mother and me, which I knew was as dark as the room where it happened.

She got home shortly after I did, and made dinner for my father and me, just as she did every night. She gave no sign that anything had happened. This brought a gravity and quiet terror all its own.

It is hard to describe the confusion I felt. I had no idea why my mother had insisted I meet her at the darkroom. Was this supposed to be pleasurable? Instructive? Was this an aberration? If I knew why it had happened, I might figure out if it would happen again.

I became acutely aware of my mother's moods. My body had learned to read her as well. Sometimes I would see her arm pull back the way she did before she slapped me, and my arms instinctively would go up to protect my face. Nothing made her more furious than that, especially if I reflexively did it in public.

I thought I had figured out what to do to survive. I could navigate around my mother. I had been confident of that. I could take my own soundings and steer clear, but the encounter in the darkroom had changed the compass and shaken my confidence. Now my world became distorted, all the angles too acute or too obtuse. I needed to figure out the geometry of my life all over again and find the equation to put it back in balance. If she ever called me back to the darkroom, maybe I could think of a reason not to go. Ultimately, though, thoughts like that took me nowhere. No one stood up to my mother and won. Certainly my whole life had proven that to me.

The only comforting thought was that it had been a long time since the episode in the middle bedroom with my parents. I made myself think that it would be a long time until it happened again. And in a long time, maybe things would change; maybe my mother would change.

She remained unpredictable, however. One day I came home and found the dining room table missing and in its place a regulation-size Brunswick pool table. It filled the room so completely that the cue sticks bumped into the walls.

When my father came home, he was livid. "Holy God, how much did this cost? Why did you get it?" They argued in the kitchen for a long time.

"Richard will enjoy it. It was the right thing to do."

"He might enjoy a child's toy pool table, not this!"

A few days later our minister called to say he would stop by. My mother panicked at his seeing the pool table, so she covered it with sheets, which of course looked even crazier. The minister came, stared at the strange sheet-covered dining room table, and never said a word. Maybe he didn't dare.

My mother certainly professed to want only the best for me. For several years, before air conditioning, children would stay indoors during the scorching Dallas summer afternoons. I don't know what other kids did then, but my mother read me Emily Post's *Etiquette* and the Bible out loud from one to four P.M.

She prepared me for the life she wanted me to live—one of class, refinement, and elegance far surpassing her own. She drilled me relentlessly on etiquette. "What do you do when you have six forks, two spoons, and four knives? Which spoon goes on the right? Where do you put the oyster fork?" She shrieked at me if I made a mistake, so I dutifully tried to get everything right. Undoubtedly, I was the only kid in East Dallas who understood the correct way for a butler to announce guests and when gentlemen should return to a drawing room.

This seemed more boring than ludicrous. I didn't care about Jim Smartlington going to a Toplofty's afternoon tea at Mrs. Three-in-One's, but I obeyed my mother. If she said I needed to know this, then I learned it. Rebellion was not an option.

When my mother read the Bible, she read everything. She marched through every name—the Ha'nochites, the Pal'luites, the Hez'ro-nites, and all the begatings. We laughed over the begatings.

Some of my loyalty and trust for my mother remained, because I never forgot how she had cared for me when I'd been so sick. She was all I had, and I thought, as a little boy, that without her I might have died. I thought my father was a good man who worked hard to take care of us. I wasn't much more analytical at the time than that. When you're a child, your parents are the boat that carries you across the ocean. It might not be the best boat or the strongest boat, but it's the only one you have to protect you from the perils of the sea. I did not look for ways to sabotage the voyage.

It wasn't long after the experience in the darkroom until I heard the words again.

"Come here."

It was in the afternoon, always in the afternoon, that my mother called me into the middle bedroom. The gray stucco walls of the Spartan room were bare. There was a space heater on the floor. The mirror over the dresser had had a crack in it ever since I hit it throwing my pirate's sword. The imitation art deco bed matched the dark wood veneer of the dresser. The badly worn floor creaked slightly. Venetian blinds that rattled going up and down hung over the two windows.

"Come here."

When I heard those words, I pulled still and deep inside of myself. If I were silent, maybe she would forget, forget that she heard me come into the house, forget that she wanted me in her bed.

But it never happened that way.

"Come here."

I stopped and felt an overwhelming stillness, the silence that negotiates between the living and the dead. The predator had found its prey.

Even after more than four decades, I still feel a cold shudder when I remember those words, "Come here." And I feel that same shudder when I remember her eyes from the middle bedroom—unblinking, unswerving, uncompromising.

Even in the dim light, I always could see her eyes. Charged with a ferocious hunger, those eyes followed me as I took off my clothes and hung them in the closet. My nakedness embarrassed me, her eyes contaminated me even before she touched me. Instinctively I knew this was wrong, that what my mother demanded was evil.

What happened after that came in a dizzying blur, feelings of confusion, disgust, and terror slamming into each other, toppled by momentary convulsions of nausea, excitement, and shame. A hurricane overtook my small boat. I tied myself to the mast, closed my eyes, and tried to survive the storm.

I felt a deep revulsion, a revulsion buried under my skin. My body knew a secret, hidden from the world. Yet within this awful revulsion, I experienced momentary pleasure, ripples of tingling sensation. To experience pleasure and disgust for the same reason and almost simultaneously created overwhelming confusion and torment. If I knew I hated what happened between my mother and me, how could my body respond as it did? Arousal led to pleasure, which capsized instantly in shame and disgust. It sickened and bewildered me to hate my body for making me feel good. Paradox does not fascinate a child.

My body was me. I didn't understand a response as reflexive as a sneeze, something uncontrollable and separate from the thinking and feeling part of me.

Confusion corrodes. Was I a traitor to myself if I felt shame and pleasure simultaneously? In this internal guerilla warfare, I fought with myself over my own emotional terrain. In an instant, the most intimate connection one can have with another human became the most dehumanizing and degrading.

I had felt humiliated and ashamed when my mother slapped me but that was externalized and less confusing. I hated her. I hated being hit. That brought no pleasure, only fear. Her fingernails would dig into my flesh and then she would hit me for no reason. I didn't want my friends to know about it. Boys are supposed to stand up to bullies. You don't get points for surviving your childhood. Only in my *Volume Library* did strength over adversity count for something.

When my mother beat me, she beat my body. It only burned on the outside. My soul remained mine. But incest cut to the quick. Her heart of darkness ravaged my heart of hearts. I burned from the inside out, incinerating my sense of self.

Once her abuse began in the middle bedroom, it continued for many months. It happened every few days, or once a week for a while, or not for a month. When it didn't happen for several weeks, I became increasingly vigilant, always alert for a change in her eyes that might soon beckon me to the middle bedroom. I sensed the slightest shifts in her mood and learned to read her as the Chinese read animals to predict earthquakes.

I listened intently for the sound of her heading my way or those two awful words. I associated "The Tennessee Waltz" and the "Third Man Theme" with those hideous afternoons because she left the radio on in the living room. The only sound I remember from the middle bedroom was of mockingbirds chirping just outside the windows. They sounded pure and clean, an affirmation rather than a violation of nature.

I don't know what my mother felt as she stole the childhood she had struggled to keep me alive for. She stayed silent, her body just as mute. I didn't know if these encounters gave her pleasure or were supposed to be good for me. Was she trying to teach me something? I kept waiting for any explanation, any clue that might explain what had happened between us. None came.

She never said, "Look, about this afternoon . . ." At first, I expected her to say something. My mother had reasons for everything. When she gave none for this, I desperately wanted her to explain. After a few days had elapsed, I would wonder if I had imagined the whole thing.

The chaotic helplessness I felt intensified because I didn't know why these bizarre episodes were happening. Knowledge equals self-determination, and I didn't have either. I knew it was over when my mother bolted from the bed, taking her clothes to dress in the bathroom. She didn't look at me afterward, and I didn't see her face. With trepidation, I then would get up and dress, fearful that if she weren't finished, I'd be in greater trouble. If I passed her in the hall and was lucky, she would walk right by. If she said anything, it would be something like, "We need a quart of milk." She went about the rest of the afternoon like Harriet Nelson, tidying the house and preparing dinner for her family.

Sometimes, though, she'd stay in the kitchen muttering to herself. She would scowl angrily at the utensils and talk to them about evil Earl or UFOs or CIA experiments on her. She became absorbed and animated in her monologues. Then she might be calm for a while, only to scream at me at dinner because I hadn't set the table right.

As I looked at this raging mother of mine, an image of her from the middle bedroom an hour and a half earlier would flash through my mind. Her violent shifts in mood convinced me that she was sick, different. That awareness did not eliminate my confusion, for thinking she was sick only made me feel guilty for hating her. It would have helped if my father had explained things to me, if he had told me about mental illness. I fantasized about running away from home, and once started saving my allowance in a sock. I had nowhere to go. If I'd had a close aunt and uncle with an extra room in Kansas, I might have told them my problems and seen if they'd take me in. But there wasn't anyone like that.

For many reasons, I never told anyone about the sexual abuse. I was deeply ashamed. I thought I was the only boy who'd ever had this happen. And I wanted no one to know, ever. If any of my friends had come to the house and seen us, I would have snapped. More degrading even than being with my mother, the ultimate humiliation would have been for a buddy to have witnessed it.

Also, I feared I wouldn't be believed and my mother then would make my life far worse, a true Dante's *Inferno*. My fear of being beaten prevented my telling anyone.

Besides, I felt I had no one to tell. My father, the logical person to confide in, had never confronted my mother about anything and won. Moreover, he had been in the middle bedroom the first time she ordered me to her bed. He didn't stop her. He never said anything about it afterward. He never indicated any disapproval or regret. My grandparents were dead, and I scarcely knew my other relatives. How could they defend or rescue me? My parents never socialized with friends of their own, so I knew no adult friends of the family. I knew the neighborhood kids, but I didn't know any adults other than their parents. Never would I have confided in them, for they might have told my friends. Although my parents and I sometimes went to church, few people knew us because we always left immediately after the service. Even though my teachers were friendly, what could they do? Either they would do nothing or they would confront my mother. If they did the latter, she would detonate, and I knew they couldn't stand up to her. I was sure she could beat them down, too.

The only person I ever considered telling was my pediatrician, who was a good doctor, a warm and caring man. When I went for my check-ups, my mother always remained in the examining room; I was almost never alone. Once she left the room briefly, and I started to confide in him. But her return was faster than my courage.

No 800 numbers existed in the late forties and early fifties, nor were there lectures about "good touch and bad touch." Child abuse was virtually never discussed, and when I did hear about it, the cases invariably occurred far from where I lived and involved girls. I felt absolutely isolated, with no place to turn but to myself.

As a young boy, I found that if I worked hard, I could forget about my feelings. The switch that gave me mastery over my situation was denial. If I didn't think about the trauma, I could forget it—perhaps forever. And if I forgot it, it effectively hadn't happened.

I believed in the power of my own will. Self-determination I learned about later by reading about leaders I admired. Man is master of his own fate. Whenever the abuse came into my mind, I would say, "I'm not going to think about this." It was my way to fight back. I couldn't stop the abuse, but I could, through force of will, stop myself from thinking about it. Denial became synonymous with survival. How could it hurt me if I didn't think about it?

I kept my equilibrium by living on the outskirts of the abuse and reducing its importance in my life. I minimized it. I learned to live from moment to moment and to compartmentalize my life. I split myself up like a house with many rooms. On some days at two in the afternoon, my mother would slap me with a vengeance. At three-thirty she would say "Come here." By five-thirty I'd be playing football with my buddies without a hint of anything that had gone before. Emotionally, I was on remote control, and switched from room to room or feeling to feeling as easily as blinking.

I was determined to survive, and minimizing the abuse helped. Also, I searched in books for answers. I went to the Dallas public library and tried to read about sex. I wandered in the stacks and found a few reference books in the card catalogue, but they were textbooks way over my head.

As my friends and I approached puberty, we started talking about girls. We traded lots of information back and forth, much of it wrong. I listened, never letting on how much I really knew. Ever since the rheumatic fever, I had tried never again to be an outsider. Ironically, when I finally felt like an insider, it came in a way I hated. I already knew adult sex, while my buddies still talked about kissing and which girls wore bras.

My friends were the oxygen in my world. They sustained me and gave me life. When I came home from school, I always looked forward to seeing them. I relied on them more than they ever could have known and more than even I realized at the time. Their saneness and acceptance enabled me to keep my faith in myself.

We would stage great battles with our toy soldiers by re-creating historical ones that I eagerly researched in the encyclopedia. One time we restaged Hannibal's battle with the Carthaginians. We figured out where the mountains would be and how he would lead the elephants through. We re-created them with human-scale battles, too. We used sticks for swords and garbage can lids for shields. Persimmons became grenades, which, although not historically accurate, improved the intensity of our combat. We clobbered each other in games of "Kill the Guy with the Ball." When we weren't figuring out ways to maim each other, we put on plays on the garage roof. We invented creative board games, our improvised versions of *Clue* and *Monopoly*. We shot tin cans with our Red Rider BB guns and terrorized the neighborhood cats. We were a rough-and-tumble bunch of eleven-year-old boys, twentieth-century Hucks and Toms, brimming with energy and full of mischief.

Much in my life was happy. My parents provided clothing, food, and housing. It could have been much worse. I could have been totally alone.

During the period of the abuse, I had the only nightmare I've ever had. In the dream, I suddenly became an orphan. Totally abandoned, I was forced to be completely self-reliant. The dream so terrified me that when I woke with a start, I couldn't believe it wasn't real. I remember sitting bolt upright in bed and staring at my moonlit room with visceral, pulsing fear. Ironically, while I could endure the beatings and survive the middle bedroom, the thought of being without parents—of being solely on my own as a child—horrified me. My passive father and destructive mother had abandoned me emotionally, yet it didn't feel that way to me as a child. I believed they wanted the best for me and in the end would keep me safe.

But during the period when my mother intensively abused me—when I heard those terrifying words, "Come here"—nothing that my parents might have wanted for me mattered. My mother's vigilance when I'd been sick became pointless; my father's hard work, irrelevant. Although I appreciated what they'd done, my mother's abuse and my father's obtuseness to it all pushed me away from them both. I just wanted to flee.

As soon as an episode in the middle bedroom ended, I would get dressed, get on my bike, and ride away. I would have pedaled off the planet, but my mother said I could go only a certain distance from the house and no farther. If I cheated and she found out, she might throw away my bike, and then I would have no escape.

Pounding nails was another way to diffuse my anger. I had started building a soapbox car in our backyard. My dad kept all kinds of wood in the garage. From that treasure trove I nailed planks together for the frame, which was about six feet long and three feet wide. I could have assembled the whole car with a few dozen nails; instead, I used a hundred times that many. I pounded nails for hours straight.

From the library, I had read about cars and engines and studied diagrams to see how to make the steering system work. I got the wheels from an old lawn mower. My friends and I went to a junkyard to get a drive shaft and gears. I spent months and months on the car. It was a project that never ended. I put an old license plate on the front. I found a horn. And I dubbed the car Richard's Hotshot. I rode it a few times, down a hill, of course. The brakes were lousy and when I tried to stop, the car spun in a circle.

Where the car really took me was away from my mother. I vividly remember leaving the middle bedroom, going to the back yard, pounding nails as hard as I could into every inch of my car. I pounded with a vengeance, staring straight down at the nail. The concentration, energy, and noise of pounding nail after nail after nail blocked out everything. Nothing else mattered to me except one nail, one hammer, and one board.

By the time I was twelve and taller and stronger, my mother stopped hitting me. She may have quit when she realized that I was physically more powerful than she. The sex ended, too. It ended by just never happening again. There was never any explanation. I didn't know if she was disappointed in me, if I had done something wrong. Had something been completed? Did I know everything I was supposed to know? I had no idea. This also brought a baffling sense of rejection. She used me and then discarded me, and that felt both crude and cruel. Many months lapsed before I felt safe enough to conclude that it had ended.

As I entered my teens, my mother became increasingly delusional and paranoid. Her mutterings became longer, louder, and more dis-jointed. I tried to live around her, not venturing too close. My father did the same. If he noticed her disintegration, he didn't say anything. He was as rigid as my mother was irrational. He set his alarm clock for the same time each morning, and ate the same thing for breakfast. He took the same route to work and left the same time every day. His arrival home never varied by more than a minute or two. He not only marched to a consistent drummer, each step was the same size.

I cherish one memory of my father because it was the only time I ever saw him in another context. To my surprise, he told me that he had signed up for a public speaking course. Why, I don't know. I am surprised my mother allowed him to do it. By then, though, her mental state was deteriorating rapidly, and so, too, was her domina-tion.

At the last class, he had to give a presentation. He invited me to be his guest at the graduation. This was one of the few times we did anything alone, and the first time I had seen him in a suit except for on Sundays.

My father stood behind the rostrum, a tall man with a high fore-head. I don't recall what he said, although I remember well how the audience responded—with laughter and applause. He was pithy, poignant, and funny! My dad! Earl Berendzen, shining on his own charm and wit. I had never known he had a sense of humor until that evening. Amazing! I admired him without having to think up reasons why. Perhaps that evening I glimpsed the real Earl, the one my mother had suppressed and hidden for so long, the man I had never gotten to know.

One day, out of nowhere, my mother told me to get in the car. I was about fourteen. Convinced that UFOs were controlling her life and that people were spying on us, she drove faster than ever as we headed south on the highway. She careened wildly between lanes, trying to elude the spies that surrounded us. The spies sped equally fast, she claimed, in cars both behind and in front of us. They were after her on all sides. Bracing myself against the dashboard, I pleaded with her to slow down. She only drove faster.

Eventually, she swerved off the road, and our car skidded sideways on the gravel. She pulled up beside a motel and I panicked, wondering what she now had in mind. This time, I resolved the motel would not become the middle bedroom. I'd hit her if I had to. I was big enough and strong enough. If necessary, I was ready to strike out on my own. But instead of sex, she wanted to hide from spies and aliens. I called my father. I told him he *had* to come get us, and he did. We talked about whether to take her home or to a hospital. I said she had to go to a hospital because she needed help. Besides, if we took her home, the same thing could happen tomorrow as soon as my father went to work.

So we drove my mother to a private mental institution, where she was admitted immediately. My father couldn't afford it for long. So after a few weeks, she had to go to a state facility. It was a massive old brick building, vintage 1930s, with bars on the windows. To me, it seemed as severe and hostile as a maximum security prison. It felt like we were throwing my mother into a cage, and that made me sad because it seemed so cruel.

My father and I didn't talk much on the way home from our first visit there. How odd it was to see him in the driver's seat, and strange for it to be just the two of us. The loud silence rattled. We weren't used to talking together. I felt awkward, like on a blind date. We didn't know what words to use. I don't remember my dad explaining anything about her illness. I knew the hospital was for people with problems like my mother's, but I didn't know what happened once they got there.

Back home, we settled into our same quiet routine. The pendulum swung back and forth from day to day as it always had. I went to school, he went to Lindop Hardware, and we had supper together every evening. I became extremely self-sufficient, a conscientious, responsible latch-key kid. I came home, had a snack, did my chores, and studied. I began to come into my own, as I felt safe just to be me. I felt wonderful, at times overjoyed finally to be free from my mother's mania and abusiveness. In a way, my mother didn't exist anymore. My father and I thought about her silently and separately, but we also had closed a door in our lives, even if it remained slightly ajar.

We visited her regularly. What we saw so shocked us that maybe we both were too stunned to express what we felt. For many months my mother was treated with insulin shock and electroshock. In the early 1950s such procedures were more experimental than therapeutic, often with brutal consequences for the patients.

When we went to see her, my father first had to fill out forms to certify we were family members. Each step required waiting and approval and delays as we negotiated our way into bedlam—to my youthful eyes, into a dungeon of writhing misery and pain.

To reach my mother, we passed hallways with people shouting through tiny windows: "I'm sane! I'm sane! Let me out! Call this number. My friend will get me out. People just want my money. That's why I'm locked up. Help me, please help me. I'm not crazy." The pleading and crying and wailing ripped at my soul. I knew about quiet anguish, but these screaming hallways were corridors of hell.

My mother looked pitiful, even ghastly. Her hair was stringy and her clothes in disarray; she was stooped and uncoordinated. Her once blazing eyes now were hollow holes, with no thought or spirit behind them. The electric currents had vaporized my mother. She was not the living dead but the dead living.

Every time we saw her she was the same. She begged to come home. She pleaded and purred, "Oh, Earl, I've missed you. I'm perfectly fine, Earl. I'm sane now. I'm fine. If I come back home, I'll feed you so well." My father would say that we had to listen to the doctors. They knew what was best. "Don't listen to them! Listen to me. Take me home. I want to go home. I'll behave now. I'll be so good to you. Please!"

Tears flooded down my mother's cheeks when she spoke to me. "Richard, I love you. I always have loved you. Let your mother come home. I want to take care of you. I'll be good. I promise. I haven't always been good, but I'm well now."

Seeing her like this brought a sadness beyond anything I had ever known. I had hated her so much. The things she had done made me furious. When she abused me in the middle bedroom, I would think, "Make her stop! Make her stop!" I prayed for her to stop, and at the time it wouldn't have mattered who stopped her or how they did it. If someone had said a machine could have sucked the passion out of her and crushed the fire in her eyes, I would have said put her in it. But seeing my wish fulfilled in such a destructive way made me feel guilty. My mother looked like refuse on a rotting human dump. Since I had pleaded with my father to take her to a hospital, I felt responsible for her being there.

On one visit I saw my mother in a straitjacket. Apparently her sedation hadn't worked or the doctors feared giving her any more. The image jolted me. I had wanted her bound so she couldn't harm me, yet when she actually was, I wanted her freed, the way one yearns to release a trapped and scared animal. Pity can overwhelm hatred. Pathos can replace pain. Eventually, insight can supplant remorse. But that came decades later.

For my father and me, the immediate issue was whether my mother was well enough to come home. How could we know? Had she truly changed? Certainly she'd become passive. But had she become sane? Did the doctors know? For that matter, did they truly understand her treatment?

She would show us her gums and say the hospital was hurting the roots of her teeth. She hated the hospital so much that if the walls had been wood, she would have tried to chew her way out. She was beyond desperate. I felt like I was looking at someone in a five-hundred-foot well and trying to decide whether to get a ladder.

Once after visiting her, my father and I stopped at a café. He and I rarely ate out, so even stopping for a chicken fried steak was a big deal. He asked me what I thought about my mother's coming home.

I told him the issue wasn't whether she was happy or unhappy, but whether she was well or sick. We knew her behavior had changed, but was that the same as getting better? I knew I didn't want to punish her, and I felt uncomfortable thinking that she might be there for her whole life. At the same time, I wanted her away from me. I didn't want the burden of deciding, either.

This one time my father and I could have shared our secrets. I could have told him about the middle bedroom, and he could have told me about what happened to her in those missing years. Secrets were the noose that tied us to Florine Adora Harrison. Even with slack in the rope while she was hospitalized, neither of us dared cut the noose.

I was afraid. I was afraid if I told my father, he would tell her doctors, and they would keep her hospitalized indefinitely, maybe forever. I didn't want to be responsible for that. It was bad enough the way it was. Or, if I told, they might increase the electroshock treatments. She might get worse, or even die.

What could my father have told me? If there was something that made her madness understandable or acceptable, why couldn't I know? Had she been raped on the farm before she ran away? Did she have a baby out of wedlock? An earlier family that had died? My imagination probed every possibility.

For whatever reasons, we didn't stray past the boundaries my mother had seemed to set. Maybe she still had that much control. Or maybe we knew the perimeters were landmined; if we crossed them, our lives would explode.

Sometimes we could take my mother to lunch. We picked her up at the hospital at noon, and had to have her back a few hours later. We ate somewhere cheap and fast. Then we took her to a park and sat on the grass. Even with her memory hazy and fading, she kept promising us how good she would be if we'd only take her home. But we didn't. We waited until her doctors released her.

When we brought her home, it was like scooping up a jellyfish on the beach, a body without bones. She had no personality. She had no form. She wasn't defeated and she wasn't destroyed—both would have been kinder. She was cinders left after her personality had burned out. A bag of scraps no one could use, a string too short to be saved, she sat silently in a chair and stared blankly out the window. She had been reduced to ash and stubbed out.

Gradually, over the next many months, she regained some of her personality and a fraction of her sense of humor. Even so, her dynamism never reached more than one percent of what it had been. Despite this, her delusions remained. She imagined things and still believed that UFOs controlled her. I was dismayed: Her paranoia continued even though her personality had ended. It made me distrust doctors, especially psychiatrists. Her creativity, imagination, and wit were gone. I wasn't sure if she was better off this way or the way she'd been before. It was better for me, but was it worth it?

By then I was a teenager. I certainly wasn't afraid of her. I knew she couldn't hurt me any longer. If she ever said "Come here" again, I would simply refuse. I knew I was now strong enough to say no. When I was about fifteen, I thought about the abuse and felt ashamed for not having been man enough to say no or fight back. Feeling that power then as an adolescent, that heady sense of self-defense, made me embarrassed that I had ever been so weak.

At first, dating seemed awkward to me. I felt self-conscious and unsure. Going to the movies and holding hands with a girl felt strange after what I had learned so young. But I knew this was a normal rite of passage, not the last voyage of the damned.

How I felt with girls was totally different from how I'd felt in the middle bedroom. My emotions, my desires, were all different, and after some initial self-consciousness, I felt fine. I relaxed and let myself have fun. I never forgot my desire to be like everybody else.

I worked hard to convince myself that what had happened between my mother and me was over, finished, and behind me; it now could cause me neither pain nor harm. When I tried to understand what had happened, it led to confusion rather than clarity. I tried to sort it out, got mixed up, and decided to close that chapter of my life and put it behind me. If it didn't affect me on a day-to-day basis, then in effect, it hadn't happened. My memories of the abuse were like a spot on the highway behind me, which I watched recede in the rearview mirror; it became smaller and smaller until it vanished.

By the time I was fifteen, my mother was pathetic, not even a shadow of her former self, more like a ghost. Her eyes now blank, her stare vacuous; instead of a mother to fear I now had one to pity. I did pity her, but I also went on with my life.

I became engrossed in hot-rod cars with loud mufflers, drive-in hamburger stands with roller-skating waitresses, and the Platters and Buddy Holly. I cheered at pep rallies, where our school's opponents turned into barbarians, and our team, gladiators. And I bopped at sock hops and danced dreamily in the school gym, transformed into a romantic wonderland for Valentine's Day.

As I progressed through high school, I studied more and more. Never had I enjoyed a subject so much as I did geometry. As I approached my senior year, I found my way out. In effect, I now could ride my bike out of the neighborhood or drive my hotshot car past the base of the hill. I could leave Fairview Avenue and my passive father and pitiful mother, and I could make my own life. To do so I needed two keys: hard work and education. The first came naturally, perhaps a legacy from my dad or an extension of my coping mechanism for the abuse. So, then, I resolved to concentrate on education.

Much of my interest focused on high school. I enjoyed my Latin class, and became absorbed in building a Roman fort for a class project. I studied reference books to learn how forts had been constructed and built mine to scale. When finished, it measured about ten square feet and weighed sixty-four pounds. It was my version of one on the Rhine River that Caesar's forces used to battle the Gauls and preserve Roman culture.

Work on it consumed me for months, the way building my car had. I had no trouble drafting the plans. Making the bricks, though, stymied me. I made my own mortar, which wouldn't stick together. I had built gates from balsa wood with hinges so they would open and shut, but I couldn't figure out how to keep the bricks from crumbling. Working with plaster of paris and sand, I could not arrive at a formula that would prevent them from falling apart.

My father would ask about my progress and occasionally watch me work when he came home from the store. I had experimented to make bricks that would bond, be strong, and hold up. One night my dad came by, and I told him about the problem. Immediately, he said, "Try linoleum cement." The next night he brought me a big can of it. It worked! My dad had provided the missing ingredient to make my cherished project strong and durable. None of my friends knew the key, nor did my teacher. It was my dad, of all people. How odd.

When I finished the fort, I put a time capsule in the cornerstone to be opened in a hundred years, and the Dallas public library put the fort on display.

By the beginning of my senior year in high school, I had a steady girlfriend. Barbara Edwards was pretty and bright, and I was proud that she was my girl. We soon were going steady and decided to marry after she told me she was pregnant.

This was sudden and a surprise. But Barbara was my first love, and with unwavering certainty, I was devoted to my unborn child. That child was my responsibility. I was determined to do right for the baby and right for Barbara. Besides, as two seventeen-year-olds, Barbara and I cared deeply for each other. Getting married was an easy decision.

Ironically, my mother was the only adult who supported the idea from the beginning. My father, in his peaceful compliance, went along with it. He only wanted to know when to show up for the service.

Barbara's father, who opposed the marriage, refused to come to the church or give his daughter away. So she came down the aisle alone. Her mother, although not thrilled by the teenage wedding, supported her daughter.

Having been out of the mental institution for several years, my mother had regained a measure of energy and motivation. She helped plan the marriage. She arranged for the flowers and the reception. It was a traditional wedding, and all of Barbara's friends and mine attended.

I remember feeling proud and convinced that we were doing the right thing. I wanted my wife and child to have a secure life, and I would provide that by working hard in school so I could get a good job.

Two

THE STUDENT

I won a scholarship, which helped with my tuition at Southern Methodist University in Dallas. The college interviewer asked my intended major. I replied, "What's the hardest subject? What do most people flunk out of?" Physics, he replied. So physics it was. I wanted to test myself, to scale the mountain, to climb the heights. If he'd said Japanese poetry, I would have picked it.

Barbara and I couldn't afford an apartment. She worked and I had a part-time job, but we would need what we earned for the baby. My mother said we could stay at my parents' house, which we did. We had no other choice. She had attained some equilibrium, and except for her eccentric taste in clothes—always dressing totally in red—she seemed erratic but stable.

The library at SMU was unlike any I'd seen before. It thrilled me to sit in a special reading room with leather-bound editions of Plato and Emerson. I went to the library between classes or whenever I had free time. Fascinated by the lives of the great men, mortals just like me, I felt like a diviner looking for water, determined to find the origins of excellence. The answer seemed to be discipline, hard work, and drive.

Just to make something out of myself wasn't enough. I wanted to provide for my child. Deborah Carol Berendzen arrived on December 1st; I had a test and paper due that same day. I remember walking into my English class and announcing the birth of my baby daughter. Everyone applauded and then the class went on as usual, with the professor perhaps wondering about this first-term freshman father.

Looking at my beautiful baby daughter the first time, I felt the happiest I'd ever felt. By age eighteen I had known pain, confusion, despair, hatred, and loathing. Now I knew perfect joy.

For the first time, I felt the serenity of unconditional love. I didn't think such goodness could exist in the world, let alone my world. Her innocence was my salvation; she was the cornerstone on which I would build the rest of my life. I wanted her to grow up in a home of peace and tranquility, and never know dark secrets, disgust, or shame. I was determined to provide for her and to be the loving, supportive father that every child deserves.

By then I had become fascinated by astronomy and awed by the scope of time. I was eighteen years old, and the cosmos had existed for some fifteen billion years. I was a tick in time. Time fascinated me. My desire for achievement was linked to my sense of time. I computed how many minutes make up a life span of seventy-five years. At my birth, roughly 39.4 million minutes lay ahead of me, and I'd use them up at the rate of 526,000 per year. I've never stopped hearing the ticking of that clock.

Hard work became as automatic to me as breathing. I hoped to transfer to MIT at the end of my sophomore year. Someone told me it was the best, the hardest, place to study physics. So I tailored my SMU curriculum to fit MIT's, and I tried for good grades.

Hard work—my way to shut out memories of the middle bedroom—became the fulcrum of my emotional survival. It also could ensure my daughter's future. Slowing down never occurred to me. To do so would have been both risky and reckless. In addition to my classes, I worked part-time at Lindop Hardware and at the Dallas library. After returning home from SMU, I routinely worked until two or three in the morning, slept for a few hours, and then started classes at nine. It set a pattern I was to follow for the next thirty years.

The school had no place for me to study, because I stayed up long after the labs and libraries closed. With no extra room in the house, certainly not with the five of us living there, I had to find somewhere else.

My mother had built a small darkroom for home film developing off our back porch. Since she had quit doing photography, we decided to convert it into my study area. The darkroom was no bigger than a closet—about four feet wide and three to four feet deep. The walls, floor, and ceiling were all painted dull black. A metal counter at one side became my desk. For two years, I studied in that black box.

I detested working in a darkroom. It was like returning to death row after being acquitted of all charges. But what was the alternative? Somewhere I'd heard that in the struggle between stone and water, water always wins. In time, the smallest stream will wear through or go around the biggest boulder in its path. My desire to succeed academically and my desperate need for a quiet place to study overrode the images that flashed through my mind.

I willed myself not to think about the other darkroom. That was then; this was now. I was a married man with a family. Memories were a nuisance that I had long since learned to control. If I worked hard, I could forget, and night after night in the darkroom, I did just that. I was determined to get to MIT.

When MIT's thick acceptance envelope arrived, I was elated. Since I couldn't afford multiple application fees, I had applied only there. I had done fine in high school and had a good record at SMU, but now I felt as if I had made it to the major leagues. Now I would compete with the best and brightest students and study with premier scientists. I was both thrilled and apprehensive, and knew I would have to work harder than I'd ever worked before.

Barbara and I packed, bundled Debbie into our 1956 turquoise Oldsmobile with a white top, and told my parents good-bye. As I backed out of the driveway, they stood silently and slowly waved. My mother burst into uncontrollable sobbing. I turned the car away from the house and toward the highway to Boston, to the East, to our future, to a new life. As we drove away, I prayed that I was leaving the terror and trauma of my childhood and was entering a fresh, pure adult life of my own. With the past dead, only the future counted. Against any odds, my little family and I would make it productive, loving, and right.

We didn't know what to expect in New England besides covered bridges and steeples. I pictured men puffing pipes, women wearing wide-brim velvet-trimmed hats, and everyone sipping tea at four o'clock with Beethoven sonatas in the background. I'd even heard that proper Bostonians hung their underwear inside pillow cases on the clothesline to avoid embarrassment.

On the outskirts of Boston, I stopped at a gas station and went into the smelly men's room to put on my only suit and tie. You should enter the Athens of America in proper style. After all, this was the hometown of my heroes Emerson, Longfellow, and Thoreau.

On my first day at MIT, I felt like an awning salesman with my polyester suit and vinyl briefcase. The MIT students came from Exeter, Andover, and Bronx Science High and from families of education and class. They carried scruffy green book bags and wore hiking shoes. I may have known about oyster forks, but I had no idea what to do in this real social milieu. In a lecture hall with 250 students I felt like the outsider, starting all over again, unsure if I were a red bird or blue bird.

The only way I could keep up, much less excel, was through hard work. Emerson said, "Every wall is a door." I reminded myself of that and earnestly believed that determination was the only key I had. I could hold my own academically, I felt, only if I persevered. So I did. I had classes and labs in the day and then went home for dinner with Barbara and Debbie. Then I secluded myself in my small home study and worked until well past midnight.

I gained academic success, but I lost my marriage. Untended, my relationship with Barbara withered without my even noticing. I had rationalized that I was working hard, not just for me, but for them. Like so many teenage marriages, we grew apart as we grew up.

One April day I came home from MIT and found an empty apartment and a brief note. My family was gone. Barbara had left me and returned to Dallas with Debbie. She said the marriage was over. Never had inevitability been more shocking. It caught me completely by surprise. I cried until I choked. I had to do something. So in my desperation, I drove straight through, night and day, to Dallas.

I thought maybe Barbara had met another man at work. It would have been easier for me if there had been someone else, but there wasn't. Barbara had never seriously complained about our marriage, and we never quarreled. Debbie was almost three and the center of joy. I could not believe or even begin to cope with her being gone. I was overwhelmed, impaled upon an agony unlike any I had ever known before.

I thought that if I talked to Barbara, she might give our marriage a second chance. This was my only hope as I made the long, lonely drive south. But when I arrived, I found she was as certain it was over as I hoped it was not. She told me the marriage wasn't working and she didn't love me anymore. What could I say to that? With no room to negotiate or compromise, I felt worse than rejected. I felt broken, shattered. I spent an hour with my parents and then drove back to Boston, physically and emotionally exhausted.

For the first time in my life, I felt truly alone. Despite the horrors of my childhood abuse, I always had a home; my family stayed intact, and my parents never abandoned me. Now I had an apartment as silent as a monologue of death, haunted with echoes of Debbie's laughter. Her rocking horse sat motionless in her room, and Mickey Mouse leaned against the wall. I hated being there. I would come in late at night and get into bed without turning on the lights so I didn't have to be reminded of what I missed most. I got up early in the morning and left for the library.

I counted on my work to save me, just as it had in the past. This time, it didn't. I studied late into the night. Sometimes I would drive to the beach and sit on the chilly, damp sand and watch the sun come up while seagulls jabbered like small-town gossips. The gray, forlorn ocean matched my mood. Being there gave me a way to lose myself in something larger than I was. With my family gone and no chance to get them back, I found no answers. Instead, I found nature. The steady thundering of waves and the dreamy flight of gulls gliding along the shore on gusts of wind buoyed my spirits and reminded me of the stars. For the ocean, like the sky, offered a beauty and vastness that could transport me beyond my own travail. When you love nature, you are never truly doomed.

The little things hurt the most. I hated eating alone. Sunday mornings were the worst, because I would wake up alone, read the paper, and it would only be eleven in the morning. In those days, with Boston's blue laws, virtually everything was shut. I would try to study. Soon growing weary of that, I would pace the apartment, making a small loop from the bedroom through the living room and back, for an hour or two at a time.

I felt dead. My heart beat, my blood pulsed, yet part of me had died. Part of me died in the darkroom, part of me died in the middle bedroom, and more of me died in Massachusetts. When the sum of the dead parts became greater than the sum of the living whole, I'd finally be gone and that would be a relief.

Too devastated to take my final exams that May, I asked for postponements. Eventually, this delayed my graduation from MIT by a year. I had never felt more like a failure. Paradoxically, my reason to die and to live became the same—Debbie. I still had a daughter, even if she were growing up thousands of miles away from me. How could I provide for her if I quit school? I wanted her to have opportunities I never had. Debbie remained my reason for living. I didn't have much hope; nonetheless, giving up was not an option. That lesson I had truly learned from my *Volume Library*.

Left with the most profound longing I'd ever known, I felt a yearning, a pulling that I would have followed in an instant if there had been any place to go. I wanted to go home, to a family that was glad when I walked in the door. I mourned the family I'd lost and the one I never had growing up, the family like everybody else's.

Ironically, my life seemed so hopeless that it became easier for me to hope. Hope was all I had. Hope was something no one could take from me, so I clung to it. If I stopped hoping, there would be no reason to go on. All of this was emotional and irrational. I couldn't prove scientifically that I should keep hoping. I just knew that I must.

The days became monotonous. I went to classes, studied, worked at my part-time jobs, and studied for a few hours after that. Eating was an afterthought; I had few friends and little social life. It startled me if the phone rang at all, but never more than the call that came one evening from my mother.

"You're in Cambridge?"

"Yes."

"Where's dad?"

"He's in Dallas."

"How did you get here?"

"On an airplane."

"But I don't get it. Why are you here?"

"I just wanted to see you."

"Where are you staying?" I asked, expecting to hear the name of a local hotel.

"In an apartment."

Gradually, like a game of twenty questions, I put the pieces together and realized that my mother had moved to Cambridge to be near me. She had arrived a few days earlier and settled into an efficiency apartment before calling me.

I called my father, who said he knew she'd left but had no idea where she'd gone. He said he didn't know what to do, but agreed, at least, to come to Boston and talk to her. This proved unsuccessful, as anyone could have predicted. My mother refused to budge.

I told her over and over that she had to go home. "There's nothing in Dallas. You're all I live for." My father went home defeated. Although he regretted her interference in my life, I'm sure it was much easier for him without her.

She stayed for nearly two years. Weeks and months would go by without my seeing her. I blocked her from my mind with intense concentration on my studies. Then she would call and badger me, and I would meet her for lunch. I was always afraid she might do something truly embarrassing, especially when I sensed she was becoming delusional again. Would she call my professors or show up in my classes?

She knew I studied science at MIT but that was all she could grasp. She knew MIT's address: 77 Massachusetts Avenue. She linked that in her mind with a popular TV show, *77 Sunset Strip*. As she became increasingly delusional, she thought TV controlled her mind and MIT controlled TV. And my interest in astronomy and space confirmed her belief that UFOs monitored her.

When she eventually became seriously psychotic, my father and I conspired to get her on a plane to Dallas. We fabricated a story about the house, inventing a crisis severe enough to convince her to return. After meeting her at the airport, my father took her to a psychiatric clinic where she was admitted.

I never considered therapy for myself. In the early 1960s, therapy was not nearly so accepted or widespread as today. Psychiatrists were for crazy people. Given the devastating effects of my mother's treatment a decade earlier, I was especially cynical and suspicious of therapists and mental hospitals. Also, my scientific culture at that time rejected and even ridiculed therapy *a priori.*

As a physics student at MIT, one of the gods in my field was Richard Feynman, a Nobel laureate at the California Institute of Technology. To this day, he stands as one of the towering figures of twentieth-century science. To me, as a young student, he was the ultimate authority—Moses from the mountaintop with the laws of God written in stone. Feynman's now classic lectures were published just as I entered graduate school. They influenced me and a generation of aspiring young scientists. Before discussing physics in his lectures, Feynman offered terse comments on related fields. About psychology he wrote:

> Psychoanalysis is not a science: it is at best a medical process, and perhaps even more like witch-doctoring. It has a theory as to what causes disease—lots of different "spirits," etc. . . . Psychoanalysis has not been checked carefully by experiment, and there is no way to find a list of the number of cases in which it works, the number of cases in which it does not work, etc.

I found therapy dubious; leaders in my profession found it absurd.

As time blunted the immediacy of my anguish, I resumed working intensively. I graduated from MIT, but I didn't attend the ceremony. In fact, I've never gone to any of my graduations. My parents never came and I didn't want to go by myself, so I picked up my degrees from the registrar's office or got them in the mail.

At the urging of one of my professors at MIT, I enrolled at Harvard for graduate studies. In the early sixties, Harvard was exhilarating for a young scientist. My studies before had motivated me, but never so inspired me. MIT students at that time compared studying physics to drinking from a fire hydrant. Brilliant professors, more passionate about graduate research than undergraduate teaching, flooded the students with information. By good fortune, I had as my advisor at MIT George Clark—a wonderful man and a sensitive scientist. From him I learned you can be both.

Clark had seemed a rarity at MIT. At Harvard, however, I found many professors who stood out not only as scientists but also as enthusiastic and enthralling teachers. I now had real role models. Bill Liller, the chairman of the astronomy department, taught with stunning clarity and deep respect for his students. He gave me unprecedented responsibility and opportunity as his teaching assistant. I felt like his professional colleague. That changed my life, for I learned how dearly I loved teaching. Research remained a key interest for me, but teaching became my passion.

Leo Goldberg, a world-renowned astrophysicist, loomed like one of the people I had read about in *Volume Library*. Despite his gentleness, he totally intimidated me. I would prepare for hours before I went to see him. Nonetheless, he always knew more than I did. So next time I would prepare even harder. A kind man, he became a real father figure to me, as did Donald Menzel, the director of the Harvard Observatory. With white mane and impeccable grace, he fit my image of a Harvard professor. For us graduate students, the Christmas reception at his home was the highlight of our year.

Cecilia Payne-Gaposchkin—brilliant and eccentric—was another of my professors at Harvard. She chain-smoked through her lectures, often with two cigarettes going at once. That didn't matter; she had pioneered in stellar atmosphere research. She was a person of firsts: the first person to get a doctorate in astronomy at Harvard, the first woman to advance to full professor and department chair in any field at Harvard, and the first person to understand the physical conditions of stellar atmospheres.

To study with such a constellation of superstars challenged and inspired me. My previous intellectual life had been acutely isolated. I had studied alone, gone to lectures, and then studied alone again. At the Harvard astronomy department, that changed. I became part of a caldron of learning. I learned in the classroom and out, from hallway discussions and dinnertime conversations. I learned from professors, research scientists, visiting scholars, and my fellow graduate students. In short, I found myself in the place I had yearned to find for so long—a caring environment and a vibrant intellectual community.

The youngest, most charismatic professor was a newcomer named

Carl Sagan. He broke the mold. Most of his professorial colleagues were serious and ponderous, but not Carl. Only in his late twenties, outrageously funny and oblivious to creature comforts, he drove a car in worse repair than mine.

I became his teaching assistant for the first course he taught at Harvard. He'd never taught it, and I'd never taken it. We made a dynamic duo! Never had I seen a professor make a lecture come alive the way he did. Fresh out of graduate school at the University of Chicago, he was studying the surface temperature of Venus. He concluded that Venus had a mammoth greenhouse effect; its thick atmosphere absorbed solar energy and prevented infrared radiation from escaping. His theoretical predictions later proved true observationally.

Then he collaborated with a Soviet scientist on a book about extraterrestrial life. In those days, this topic lay outside mainstream academic science. With a twinkle in his eye, Sagan would bound into the lecture hall radiating enthusiasm. He might begin by saying, "Do you realize that you are made of star stuff?" He made learning irresistible.

He showed me that teaching could be fun and that a professor can be imaginative and daring. He threw away the script and wrote his own. This made a lasting impression on me.

After a few years in astronomy at Harvard, I branched into the history of science and other fields. There I met still other professors who helped me chart my course. Gerald Holton had done everything: He had headed the American Academy of Arts and Sciences, had helped found a national project to improve high school physics teaching, and had written superb textbooks on the history of physics. For sheer intellectual acumen, he became my role model.

And there was Owen Gingerich, probably the foremost historian of astronomy in the world. Books grew in his small office like stalagmites—piled on the floor, on window ledges, and out of drawers. They weren't ordinary textbooks but sixteenth-century leather-bound volumes that he had found in flea markets in Prague or Rome. My predictable paint-by-number world became as expansive and glorious as a Matisse. Professors like Gingerich showed me that I could create a life from things I loved most in the world, whether practical and current or not. And he showed me the joy and reward of painstaking

research, often a pursuit that requires decades, and that persever-
ance pays off.

Days never really ended at Harvard. Graduate students would go to
the observatory and talk and argue and laugh all night. These students had a vastly wider range of interests than people imagine when
they think of scientists. With my astronomy friends, the discussions
ranged from debates about world politics and the economy to discussions on literature, foreign films, the Vietnam war, and just about
anything else you could imagine.

I shared a house with four other guys, and we also debated everything—everything from Immanuel Kant to Barry Goldwater to how
much ice cream you could compress into a quart container.

As photography aficionados, we talked at length about F-stops and
Nikons and Canons. One of my roommates built a harpsichord from
a kit and then routinely played Bach on it. Another roommate, an
avid sports fan, could recite every baseball statistic ever compiled.

Never before had I known such an intellectually stimulating life.
While I was growing up, my parents couldn't talk about anything
without fighting. My childhood friends and I had discussed the world,
but at a child's level. As an undergraduate, I simply studied. In
graduate school, I lived a life that before had existed only in my
imagination. I loved it; I reveled in it. And I decided that academia
would be my life.

By then my interests had broadened outside of astronomy. I was
doing research in the history of science and was engrossed in peda-
gogy—the art and practice of education itself. My interdisciplinary
PhD dissertation, which linked astronomy with education and other
fields, required advisors from several departments and a dissertation
committee of some dozen people from different teaching units. This,
I found, was not the most efficient way to get a degree, and my
dissertation turned into more than I had expected. In 930 pages, it
attempted to answer: Why do people become astronomers? What
motivates them to pursue this most other-worldly and seemingly useless discipline? What is their education, and how do their careers
develop? To find out, I asked them. In fact, I asked all the astronomers in the nation why they chose this field.

The deep despair I felt about my divorce finally lifted during my
first year in graduate school. I had been devastated, emotionally

shipwrecked and adrift. For too many months I could see nothing but the wreckage of my life. Finally, at Harvard, something new began to appear and the loneliness of my past seemed put to rest.

While still in graduate school, I met a woman named Gail Edgar, a sophomore at Wheelock College. We met by accident. After having just moved in to my newest low-rent apartment, next to the Cambridge city dump, I went to dinner at the Harvard graduate dining hall. There for another function, Gail was waiting by the door for a cab. A real head-turner, she caught my attention as I passed her in the hall. I turned around and went back to talk. Her laughter and gentleness drew me to her. I knew I wanted to see her again.

We made a date to go dancing. When I arrived to pick her up, I asked if she would like to go to the Harvard Observatory instead. Anyone can go dancing, but I had an unusual adventure in mind. Gail assumed we would go to the facility in Cambridge. The one I meant, however, was about twenty-five miles away. I just didn't think to tell her this.

Newspapers at that time gave gruesome details of the Boston Strangler. His latest victim had just been found, and the whole community pulsed with fear, especially coeds. Rumors claimed the Strangler wore black leather gloves; so did I as I drove. I had no idea of the dread Gail felt as we headed away from Cambridge and out of town. We went from a four-lane highway to a two-lane road to a dirt road to a tire path in the woods. Then, while still driving, I shut off the headlights, a standard gesture of courtesy among astronomers to keep from ruining someone's observation. Gail didn't know this, and I failed to explain. So we slowly drove up to the observatory in darkness.

Observatories are unheated because heat ripples would distort the image seen through the telescope. To keep warm, an observer wears a padded, electrified suit. As I shut the ignition, the observatory door flung open and a friend came to greet us, looking like Big Foot or worse. Gail huddled by her door. Sensing her fear, I assured her, "You're all right. Believe me."

We went inside the observatory, I opened the dome, the telescope rose, and there before us lay the universe. On that crisp, clear night, we looked at the heavens and back into time, and things changed quickly for us. For Gail, the evening had a frightening beginning; for us both, it had a wonderfully romantic ending. Never before had I had a date like this, and I knew it must not be the last we would have. My cosmos changed that night.

After a few months, Gail and I knew we wanted to marry. I had never met a kinder, more loving woman. Or one with keener insight. Her blue eyes were as clear as her sense of purpose, and her integrity stood as durably as a seventeenth-century New England stone fence.

A divorced stranger with a child did not match her parents' hopes for their only daughter. They felt our marriage wouldn't last.

Gail's family was as traditional and nurturing as mine was bizarre and estranged. When you hear the song "I'll Be Home for Christmas," you imagine a family like the Edgars. Gail grew up in a comfortable white colonial house brimming with love, mutual respect, and harmony. Her mother exudes decency and values, and her stepfather is a model husband and stalwart dad.

Marrying me became an act of defiance for a young woman who never wanted to rebel. Gail will not compromise her beliefs, and she believed in me as deeply as I believed in her. We were married in the Harvard Chapel on Thanksgiving Day in 1964. Since Gail's parents would not attend, I had a good excuse not to invite mine. In fact, we invited no guests, and the entire ceremony cost twenty dollars. For poor students, that's all we could afford anyway. What the ceremony lacked in grandeur it made up in warmth and love. That's all we cared about.

In the months that followed, her parents saw our happiness and gave their blessing. Their willingness to accept me impressed me as much as Gail's courageous decision to suffer their disapproval. At last the secure and loving world just outside my window or just beyond my grasp became my own.

With Debbie's birth, I felt unconditional love for the first time. With Gail, I found the love, the steady affirmation, that became the core of my being. And that has never changed. I was blessed and I knew it.

From the start, Gail was my best friend. We began the first of many great adventures together. While I finished my graduate studies, she taught school. We furnished our small apartment with whatever we could scrounge. Our homemade brick bookcases overflowed and our Goodwill sofa had a broken spring. It didn't matter. We were happy and we were preparing for the rest of our lives. She would meet me at my office after work, we'd have sandwiches for supper, and then she would stay with me, making lesson plans while I studied, often into the early morning.

Shortly after we married, we drove to Dallas. Gail had never been to the South, and we were excited about driving across the country together. This would be Gail's first encounter with my mother. Thankfully, it turned out more comical than destructive.

When we arrived, we found the dining room table covered with wedding presents in an incredible array of glittery paper and curling ribbon. Once we unwrapped the presents, I saw that my mother, true to form, had dismantled a flatware set and wrapped each knife, fork, and spoon individually.

The day we started our return trip to Boston, we found the car packed with canned goods—cans of hominy, tamales, Tabasco sauce, pickles, Potato Stix, okra, and black-eyed peas. The dozens and dozens of cans filled the back of the car to the height of the front seat. In astonishment and exasperation, I said to my mother, "What have you done?"

"Well, this is what you used to eat. I thought you'd like to take some with you." It was easier for us to drive back to Boston with the cans than to unload them. We found, though, that if we sped up or turned, cans rolled all over the car. Once, going down a hill, I had to stop suddenly, and cans of hominy and bottles of Tabasco sauce jettisoned over our shoulders. Gail and I laughed so hard I could barely drive.

For weeks beforehand we planned for Debbie's visits with us in Boston. She came at Christmas for two weeks and then again for the summer. I would work feverishly in advance so I could spend all my time with her when she arrived. For about an hour when Gail and six-year-old Debbie first met, she eyed Gail cautiously. That awkwardness soon dissolved, and they became deeply devoted to each other from then on.

The three of us had marvelous escapades together. One night we all got up at two A.M. and took a bike tour of Boston. I wanted to show Debbie what the city did while she slept. Boston had little crime then, and almost the only people on the street that late were police. We had the streets to ourselves. We rode to a bakery and watched bakers sliding trays of dough into ovens. We biked over Beacon Hill and to the *Boston Globe* building and saw the early edition being loaded onto delivery trucks. We pedaled to the harbor and saw fishermen returning from the dark ocean with the morning catch. We stopped for hot chocolate and muffins and knew, in our hearts, that life didn't get better than this.

Three

THE ACADEMIC

In 1969, I finished graduate school at Harvard with a master's degree in astronomy and an interdisciplinary PhD and became an assistant professor in physics and astronomy at Boston University. Gail and I moved into a nearby fifth floor walk-up. Only newlyweds could have found our small, noisy apartment synonymous with heaven.

When we had visitors at home, they always rang the bell. So an insistent, urgent knock on the door one evening startled us. When we opened the door, Gail and I looked at each other. There stood my mother.

"What are you doing here?"

"I'm just here." She shrugged. "I can't be off in Dallas."

"When did you get here?"

"A few days ago."

"Where are you staying?"

"I got a room."

The horror was repeating itself. My mother had rented a room a few blocks away. I was furious; Gail was polite. I told my mother she couldn't stay. Her life belonged in Dallas; mine, in Boston.

"This is not your place. It's mine. This is my home, my family, and my time. You can't stay."

I might as well have spoken to a stone. My words had no impact. I went to another room and called my father. He didn't know what to do. He said he hadn't called me when she disappeared because he didn't know where she'd gone. He feebly said maybe she would come back on her own.

As my mother left, she said she'd be back in a few days. I was livid. Gail, who had no inkling of how destructive and degrading my relationship with my mother had been, tried to be upbeat about it. "It might not be so bad. We'll only have to see her once in a while."

"You don't understand. She is an albatross. I can't get her off my neck. I'll never be free of her until she dies!" I was seething. Gail had never seen me so furious. She didn't understand, and how could I explain?

I didn't know what to do. My father, who never influenced my mother when he was younger and stronger, certainly could not do so now.

Legally, I had no option. She broke no law for wanting to live near her son. Stable enough to function on her own and smart enough to keep her crazier thoughts to herself, she soon found a part-time job. She did her own cooking and shopping. I despised her, but she now was more annoying than psychotic.

I decided to ignore her. I did not call her or initiate any contact with her. When she showed up on our doorstep, I chatted politely for a few minutes and then encouraged her to leave. A few times Gail suggested that we invite her to dinner. I acquiesced, but my mother behaved so strangely that even Gail concluded that we couldn't deal with her. For the most part, I lived, as I always had, despite her. By making my own life brighter, her shadowy presence dimmed, until I scarcely noticed it.

My father sent her money to live on. Nonetheless, she got part-time jobs, jumping from one to another, sometimes lasting for only one week or one day. I never knew how she occupied her time until after the fact. When I asked her, she gave nonanswers. Even when I tried to erase her from my mind, I worried about what she might do. Occasionally, I would hear that she'd called the university. Or someone would ask, "Are you related to a woman named June?" When I said she was my mother, the person would politely pause and quickly change the topic.

If she followed or spied on me, I never saw her. But I was never free from the fear that she might. My mother remained in Boston for several years, until we found another way to convince her to return to Dallas.

The contentment I found in my marriage gave me reason to work even harder; I had more to preserve and protect. Work also kept my trauma sealed in the past. "That was then; this is now. That was then; this is now." That became a mantra I repeated if memories ever crept into my consciousness.

When memories did creep back, I never considered telling Gail about my childhood sexual abuse. My new life mattered more to me than anything else. Even my mother's arrival did not prompt me to tell Gail about the abuse. Why should I? I saw no possible gain, only risk—risk that Gail might love me less or see me as damaged.

I never thought something so remote in my past might bear on my behavior in the present. I believed that the individual, not circumstances, determines character and behavior. If you worked hard enough, you could be anything and do anything, no matter what. Ultimate freedom came from discipline and self-control. I would have dismissed as a fool anyone who tried to convince me otherwise.

At Boston University I found teaching so stimulating and fulfilling that it never seemed like work. I was happy when I got up in the morning, eager to get to the classroom, and challenged to find ways to make science come alive for my students.

Each semester, the students and I set off like explorers on a journey. Even though I'd traveled the route before, my students' curiosity and insights made each trip a new adventure. To meet their expectations and answer their questions required me to know the material as if it were part of me. I spent hours preparing for each class. Teaching truly provides unparalleled learning for the teacher.

Professors should both impart knowledge and create it. Although teaching remained my highest professional priority, I also delved into research, particularly on the history of astronomy. My graduate students and I ferreted out old letters and workbooks from observatories and archives to piece together the story of how, early in this century, astronomers achieved two Copernican-style shifts in thinking. They found that our sun lies far from the center of the Milky Way star system, and that hundreds of billions of other galaxies—each consisting of more than two hundred billion stars—sprinkle across the universe. With support from a National Science Foundation grant, the grad students and I documented this saga. I also continued my research on the career development and education of astronomers.

The deeper I plunged into astronomy, the more compelling it became. The oldest science, it also was the youngest. Throughout the late sixties and early seventies, astronomical breakthroughs and discoveries came at a dazzling pace. This era became astronomy's Golden Age, as new windows to the universe opened. Astronomers began to observe in all parts of the spectrum. And I was privileged to live, study, and teach during a special epoch, as humankind left cradle Earth for the first time and stepped onto another world.

Even so, my deepest sense of belonging remained with my family, which became complete when Gail became pregnant. Although already in my early thirties, I felt like my life was just beginning.

When Debbie was born, I was a teenager. Because of her, I molded myself into a father and a man. She gave me a reason not just to live but to try to excel.

By the time of my second child's birth, my life had far more security, focus, and purpose. Nonetheless, that child became a defining part of my life. As an adult, I reveled in every aspect of her development, from birth on. I was in the delivery room as a nurse handed me the life I'd help create. I witnessed a miracle I could see and hold and touch with a kiss. The miracles of astronomy lie well beyond the human hand. We can see them and ponder them, but we rarely can touch them. Mostly, astronomers embrace the beauty and wonderment in their minds. In studying the origin of the universe, they try to fathom the miracle of birth. There, on the fifth floor of Boston Hospital for Women, I did the same thing, as I watched a universe begin—all eight pounds, four ounces of Natasha Karina Berendzen.

I never have found religion to be antithetical to science. My views have jibed with Einstein's observation that "science without religion is lame, religion without science is blind." My own spirituality has deepened with time and been enriched, rather than diminished, by astronomy and physics. I never have had an easy time, though, with literal religion. The miracles of loaves and fishes, walking on water, and making blind men see seemed to me more like folklore and symbolism than fact.

That, nonetheless, has not intruded on my faith. Even before I understood much about the universe, I stood in awe of how huge, how staggeringly immense, it is. I see in the vastness of space and time a wisdom that far transcends my transitory being and knowledge. The beauty by which the universe works is just too great to have arisen by chance.

When I look at photographs of the most distant realm of the universe and see the ghostly image of quasars billions of light-years away—objects that died eons before Earth even formed—I sense an order and intelligence vastly greater than our own. Some call it nature; others call it God. Whatever the word, the mystery and the majesty remain. And I know Emerson was right: "If the stars should appear one night in a thousand years, how would men believe and adore."

I believe that something supremely intelligent set the laws of nature in action. They're too precise, too elegant to have arisen randomly. Something caused the Big Bang at the beginning of time; something made the original radiation that ultimately produced matter. My fascination with cosmology, the study of the origin and structure of the universe, began in college, and remains as compelling to me now as it did then. Astronomers spend lifetimes chipping away at the remote edge of cosmic questions, but the more answers they find, the more questions they provoke. The answers are there—as if set ages ago by a supreme intelligence. Our task is to find them.

The universe, which can appear violent and random, actually is incredibly ordered. If probed sufficiently, an equation can be created to explain almost anything to some degree of accuracy, from the return of Halley's comet decades from now to microsecond interactions of subnuclear particles. To find order behind reality is to find poetry in action. And from the heartbeat of an infant to the throb of a distant pulsar, I found a special precision and orderliness and grandeur.

With my own full family at my side, my years at Boston University burst into action. I taught large classes, obtained research grants, wrote articles and books, directed graduate students, gave professional talks. I became the quintessential young man on the move.

This provided the opportunity to serve on committees headquartered in Washington, D.C. There I first entered the temple of science—the National Academy of Sciences building. It felt like hallowed ground. The Library of Congress impressed me even more. Books, the mainstay of any academic, are sacramental to me. And there I found the greatest scholarly treasure trove ever assembled. Before my own family had taken root, I had found a life worth living through books.

I found the nation's capital city as fascinating as Boston but in a different way. The ebb and flow of power in Washington courses through the city like a tide that, although capable of being predicted and anticipated, runs on currents that change in both intensity and direction.

After seven years of teaching in Boston, I had the opportunity for a sabbatical, and Gail and I decided to go to Washington. We packed Natasha, ourselves, boxes of books, some clothes, and a four-foot-tall Oriental vase into our VW bus and moved from Boston to an apartment in Alexandria, Virginia. I worked at the National Academy of Sciences and the American Council on Education for two days a week each, and then holed up for three days a week at the Library of Congress, writing a book on the discovery of the galaxies.

The chemistry department chairman at The American University and I both served on an editorial board. He called one day to urge me to apply for a deanship at AU. He chaired the search committee. Although I had real reluctance about leaving full-time teaching and research, I was intrigued with the possibility of both living in the capital and helping to develop a first-rate university there.

I felt so secure in Boston that the search committee did not intimidate me. I was young and just confident and brash enough to end up interviewing them as intently as they grilled me. Why should AU survive? What made the school unique? What were its strong points?

Its weak ones? What were the university's goals and how could they best be achieved? What planning was under way and what needed to be initiated?

For its last question, the search committee asked me what I thought the university needed most. They expected me to say a new library or a sports center or more money. To their surprise, I said, "AU needs a simple five-letter word. It needs pride." I explained that when the university is proud of itself—the caliber of its graduates, its high standards and exemplary integrity—it will have come of age. A university without pride is like a family without love.

Despite my candor—or perhaps because of it—I was offered the job and in 1974 became professor of physics and dean of the College of Arts and Sciences. At thirty-five, I was younger than many of my faculty colleagues.

In the early 1970s, AU had a well-deserved reputation as a party school. Academic standards were low, and the most popular T-shirt on campus showed the ZigZag man, a symbol of pot smoking, above the words CAMP AU.

When the Methodists founded the school in 1893, they wanted it to be a national university in the nation's capital, one that reflected its name—The American University.

Over the decades, that founding dream dissipated in the struggle for budgets and in the university's search for an identity. In coming to AU, I hoped to re-ignite the founders' original vision and work toward building a great university in the nation's capital. Although Bostonians call their city the Athens of America, I think Washington can justifiably claim the title. Socrates supposedly said, "It is not I who teaches, but Athens." So it is with Washington.

No educational resource in the world excels Washington. It's not just the government, but everything that is there because of the government—the museums, the libraries, the think tanks, the embassies, and the extraordinary concentration of decision-makers. A city with such incredible facilities and resources should have outstanding academic institutions that reflect the capital they represent.

In 1976, after two years as dean, I became provost. Second in command in the university, the provost is the chief academic officer.

My life reached a new level of contentment. I relished my work, which daily brought new challenges and opportunities. Our marriage only grew stronger and better. And Natasha was a delightful toddler, funny and sweet, curious and energetic, a dynamo. I loved to walk in the door and hear her gleefully shout "Daddy!" and come running. I had missed this age with Debbie, which underscored the pleasure I felt in watching Natasha grow and change day by day.

One evening there came a frantic knock on the door. Only one person knocked that way, and I felt immediate dread. When I opened the door, there stood my mother.

"What are you doing here?"

"I came because I miss my son."

She came inside.

"When did you get here?"

"A few days ago. I want to be near you. You are the be-all of my life. You are all I live for."

As in the past, she did not appear on my doorstep until she had gotten a studio apartment nearby. She had left Dallas a few days before. I called my father, but by then, with his near deafness, we could convey almost nothing by phone. I didn't know what to do. My father couldn't keep her in Dallas. The past returned.

We never knew when she might appear. Besides worrying about my family, I now worried about AU. As provost, I had special responsibilities and high visibility. I did not want her to cause any disruption. I told her not to come to campus, but she did. I told her not to call my office, but she did.

At age sixty-five, she was self-contained. She had three or four red dresses and switched among them. We would see her occasionally. Then weeks would pass without seeing her at all.

I felt guilty that she lived in a small apartment with sparse furniture and no friends, guilty that I did not help her more, and guilty that I could not accept her into my family. My pleas with her to go home always failed.

Sometimes we would take her for a Sunday drive. After one outing, I dropped Gail and Natasha off and drove her to her apartment. She hung onto my shirt. Without hyperbole she said, "You're all I have. You are my air, my everything. I will *never* leave you." Mental institutions may have electrocuted the madness that made her abuse me as a child, but just as fingernails can grow after death, her obsession with me continued. When I stopped in front of her apartment building, I had to peel her fingers from my shirt.

I walked her to the door, but she turned to follow me. I demanded, "Go back. Go back." She just stood and stared. When I looked in the rearview mirror from a block away, I saw her still standing there in her red dress, transfixed. In those moments, my pity outweighed my anger.

Even though Gail's tolerance for my mother was steady, it snapped one day. My mother had come over. Gail asked her to watch Natasha while she ran to the car to get something. When she returned minutes later, she heard my mother telling five-year-old Natasha, "Your mother is a slut and a whore. You should hate her. Just love your daddy and me."

Gail, who rarely gets angry, this time erupted. When I heard what had happened, I, too, lost my temper. My mother had endangered my daughter, my wife, my family. No, this I would not tolerate. Standing a foot away from her, with my eyes welded on her like a steel laser, I seethed: "If you ever again try to harm my family, I swear I will have you committed until the day you die!" She turned whiter than death. It was a terrible thing to say, but decades of rage had exploded in me, and I was desperate. What did it take to get her out of my life, to keep her from hurting my family, to block her self-centered and maniacal obsession? Up to that point, I saw her as a threat only to me, and for decades she'd been only a nuisance, not a danger. From that moment, however, we never allowed my mother to be alone with either daughter, and restricted all her visits.

Absent good solutions, we simply lived around her. She had just enough pluck and sanity to manage on her own; without it, she might have become a bag lady on a grate.

As it was, she fell into a psychiatric twilight zone—seriously delusional, yet not certifiably self-destructive. If we sent her to Dallas, she would torment my father and undoubtedly find her way back East. We couldn't prove she was a danger to herself or others. She went shopping, had a checking account, paid her bills. But when she lost control, she would still shake furiously and spit out obscenities about UFO's, the devil, and God.

She adamantly refused to see a doctor, take medication, or return to Dallas. With no other viable option, we ignored her. Although we made no effort to hide her, only a few of our friends knew about her. As months eased into years, my mother's presence evolved into a secret to which we were unconsciously tethered. My mother had that way about her: Secrets were the spinnerets that drew you into her web.

I focused on my responsibilities at the university. My first goal as provost was to raise academic excellence by improving the caliber of our students and faculty and the efficiency of our staff and administrative support. I was also determined to create a more serious and competitive institution and make the curriculum more rigorous.

To raise academic standards presented an exacting challenge. It required cooperation and backing from professors, deans, and many others. Fortunately, I got it. We worked as a team and raised the level of education throughout the institution. We emphasized the importance of high quality teaching. We reviewed the curriculum vigorously and expanded the contact time between the faculty and students by 25 percent.

We introduced math and English competency requirements, along with a new core curriculum. We stressed creative ways to use Washington's unique resources educationally. We established a cooperative education program and expanded the university's internships throughout the city. In short, AU's academic standing began to improve apace.

Money became the obvious key to much of what we hoped to achieve. Our plans about standards meant nothing without appropriate facilities and competitive salaries. By 1979, AU's academics were on the move, but much more needed to be done. Then, in 1979, at age forty-one, I was elected university president, to take office in January of 1980.

Even though I knew it would be a demanding post, I reveled in the challenge. My quieter, more profound feeling was one of honor. I was honored to lead the university I loved; honored to work with faculty I respected. While dean and provost, I had taught astronomy. I felt I belonged to the faculty as well as the administration.

My parents came to see my inauguration as president. My father flew up from Dallas. He and my mother had not been together for several years, but they quickly settled back into their bitter ways.

Then in his seventies, my father was almost totally deaf. While waiting in my office before the ceremony he announced in a loud voice, "I'm going to the men's room." My mother yanked down on his pants' leg and shouted, "Earl, sit down! You don't need to go to the bathroom. I'll tell you when you need to go." People stared in amazement as he sat down.

I pleaded with my mother and father to move to a retirement village, which could provide care and security. They refused. My mother would not move outside my radius, and my father wanted to manage on his own, although diabetes was making him increasingly feeble. He returned to Dallas, she stayed, and I went on with my work.

With zeal I sought for AU to realize its potential and become a significant national university. Since high school, I had worked long hours. Now, however, I pushed further. I stayed on campus until evening, sometimes dashing home for dinner with Gail and Natasha before rushing to an evening function or back to my office to work until midnight. In the early morning hours, I'd walk across campus heading home and unwind by reading. I learned to get by on four or five hours sleep a night, with an occasional yawn.

None of this would have been possible without Gail. Shortly after I became president, she said she would leave her job as a school curriculum coordinator to help me. She loved her work, but saw the opportunity for us to work as a team at AU. She stressed that she wanted to help on substantive issues, not just by hostessing.

Gail, who excels at bringing people together, coordinated programs to link the university closer with the city. She ran lecture programs at which professors spoke to influential Washington audiences. She arranged our annual Black Leaders' Night, at which AU's top black students came to our home to meet distinguished black professionals. She organized programs specifically on women's issues, and others designed to enable students to meet Washington leaders and potential employers. And she arranged countless functions to build a sense of community among the university's diverse members—trustees, donors, professors, students, administrators, staff members, alums, parents, and others.

The president's residence is located next to AU in Spring Valley, one of Washington's premier neighborhoods. Originally built in the

1930s as a private residence, then given to the university, AU has expanded and remodeled it many times over the years. From the outside it appears handsome yet unimposing; from the inside, however, it sprawls over many thousand square feet, with nine bathrooms and one of the largest private swimming pools on the East Coast. Gail and I estimated that all of our prior apartments combined would fit into only a portion of the house, if not the pool. Although ideal for university entertaining, the cavernous place did not immediately feel like a cozy home for a child. For Natasha, this hotel-like structure became home from age nine to nineteen. Gail and I faced a dual challenge: how to use this unique facility to best advantage for the university and how to make it a warm childhood home for Natasha.

What the house lacked in privacy, it made up in liveliness. It had a huge open room, suitable for lectures for 120 people or dinners for 80, plus a carriage house, and the pool. Best of all, two magnificent old pin oak trees towered behind the house. A matched pair, they stood strong in winter storms and blocked the summer sun. To me, they became symbols of beauty and endurance. Residents of the house come and go, but these proud trees remain. Late at night, I would stroll in the yard and stand beneath their limbs. Not in the house but under those majestic trees I found solitude and peace and strength. Their long branches became like a vaulted cathedral ceiling.

Natasha grew up at AU. When she was young, Natasha and I walked the campus and talked things over. I told her real management problems at AU, and explained how we handled them. She developed remarkably sophisticated thinking for a youngster. At our kitchen table, she and I sketched a seal and flag for the university. We studied architects' drawings for a new gateway to the campus. And we made our design for distinctive academic regalia for AU graduates to wear at commencement.

Despite my dreams for AU, the 1980s got off to a difficult start. The 1981–1982 recession hit the university hard. It had almost no financial reserves. With a small endowment, it always had been tuition dependent. In the midst of the financial crisis, I met with the faculty and other campus leaders. I gave them the grim facts and asked for their support. Almost to a person, they rallied. We cut expenses and aggressively sought new resources. At the same time—against many people's advice—we continued to raise standards. By 1983, the national economy had rebounded, and AU began an unprecedented era of growth and change. We emerged from the edge of the financial abyss better in every way. The university family had worked together and had succeeded. Adversity can build strength and camaraderie.

When I became president, some people feared I would bankrupt the school with my zeal for change and higher standards. But we built a real team who shared the same goals. The trustees, administrators, staff members, faculty and student leaders became a large, extended family. Like all families, we had disagreements and tensions, but at base we developed a mutual commitment.

I urged that we set long-term plans and goals, something often missing in academia. Too often universities plan today for tomorrow, and hope it will resemble yesterday. The entire university community discussed and debated the school's long-term goals. We framed a vision, set goals, and then worked to make the vision real.

We put our plans in writing; we stated precisely what we intended to do. We set exacting yet achievable goals for 1985, five years after I took office. From the start I wanted to stress shared decision making, high aspirations and goal setting, and responsibility and accountability.

During the 1980s, the university's finances improved dramatically. New donors and former donors with a new level of commitment made this possible. I worked closely with the admissions office to recruit students. They, too, constitute revenue. Likewise, we tried to retain our current students. Satisfied students don't transfer, and they become loyal and supportive alums.

Gail and I went out almost every night to dinners, student basketball games, faculty lectures, or meetings with potential supporters. Neither of us drinks or enjoys formal wear. We, who preferred books to parties, now found ourselves in Washington's consuming social whirl.

I knew that without money my dreams for AU would come to nothing. Moreover, in 1976, the trustees' search committee told me that it picked the president then primarily for three reasons: He might be a good fund-raiser, he knew Washington, and he had access to the media. When I became president and the chief executive officer, I assumed many responsibilities, including fund-raising, linking AU with Washington, and increasing press access to AU.

For a few years, Gail and I wove ourselves and the university into the Washington scene. I learned to work the crowd and even to make small talk, which in Washington can be lilliputian. Our focus, however, was always on AU. I sought donors. Before people will give, they must become believers and share the dream. I had the real responsibility to tell the AU story and convince people that by supporting AU they would underwrite excellence and invest in achievement.

This placed relentless demands on my time. Before leaving for one event, I remember Natasha looking at me with big eyes and softly saying, "Daddy, please stay home tonight." At the time it seemed overwhelmingly important for me to give the speech or attend the function. Now I can't remember the event, but I do remember the look on my daughter's face. If I could redo those years . . .

As arduous as the demands were, they felt worth it because the university was progressing rapidly. Best of all, I did not work alone. In addition to Gail, I had the faculty, the staff, the trustees, and my key officers. I appointed Milton Greenberg as provost, Don Myers as vice president for finance, and Don Triezenberg as vice president for development. The university became a team, and the successes were the team's. I was privileged to be the coach.

We brought back formal academic requirements. We recruited outstanding new faculty and sharply raised admission standards. We expanded the physical plant 40 percent, increased the endowment 400 percent, and built up the financial reserves 1600 percent.

I wanted employers and graduate schools to seek out AU graduates. To achieve this, we tried to recruit first-rate students and educate them well. Then we tried to let the world know about the new AU. In short, I wanted to improve the lot of our students and the future of our alums. My Holy Grail for AU was not money or standards or even academic excellence. It was what I told the Dean's Search Committee in 1974 that AU needed most: pride.

This meant pride in who was admitted, in who taught at AU, in what was taught and how, in the quality of the physical plant and the efficiency of services. Pride comes in many forms and from many sources. It might come from a provocative lecture or a winning team or a new campus building. Piece by piece, during the 1980s, AU improved standards, raised funds, won games, developed traditions, received grants, did research, published books, stressed service, linked with the community, educated a generation, and placed fine graduates in good jobs. Most of all, it came of age. It truly became The American University.

We started with the students. Convinced that we could get superb students if we tried, I felt that one-on-one contact with the university president was important for prospective students and their parents. Conversely, it was important for me. We got to know each other, even if briefly. A university, after all, is defined by more than libraries and laboratories, bleachers and books. It is defined by people—the ones who teach the students and the ones who enable that teaching and learning to occur. The president is but one person out of this vast network. Nonetheless, in the eyes of many, the president becomes emblematic of the institution.

So I traveled the nation, not only meeting prospective students, but also speaking at conferences of educators, civic leaders, and business executives. Rarely would conference planners ask me to speak about AU. Instead, they would want an address about education in the U.S. generally or astronomy or workforce readiness for the next century. My being on the program brought AU some visibility, and the hallway conversations brought more. My goal always was to have AU known and respected. Since the best way to reach large audiences is through radio and television, I became a frequent interview guest on topics ranging from outer space to the inner city.

As my pace accelerated over the years, I adapted to it. On paper, it seems like an impossible way to live—hundred-hour weeks, no real vacations—yet it became normal to me.

Ever since Gail met me, I had worked hard. She, too, grew accustomed to my tempo. But she knew it had accelerated from strenuous to excessive. She urged me to slow down. I refused. Then she pleaded with me. Still I continued and even added more, agreeing to give another speech or chair another commission.

It pains me now to think how I shortchanged my family. I would return to my office on Christmas Day, after opening presents and having lunch, to work until midnight. If I had to travel to a conference, Gail and Natasha might come along and we'd take an extra day together, but we rarely took traditional family vacations. The focus of my orbit always remained AU and my work. Nonetheless, I never felt that we were deprived.

Meanwhile, my aging father continued to deteriorate. It became increasingly clear that he no longer could live alone. The old family house needed repair, far more than he could provide. Ironically, this prompted my mother to return to Dallas. She went back to save her house, not her husband.

Like a neutron bomb, she destroyed people and relationships, not things. She wanted to preserve the house. Even though she had not lived on Fairview Avenue for years and loathed her husband, she went home.

Time triumphed where their hearts had failed. My parents finally needed each other in their declining years. As they became increasingly feeble, they had to depend on each other to survive. My mother lost the energy to scream, and my father lost the ability to hear. His deafness forced her to write out her tirades, which took time and effort. Besides, he could just throw them away. At last he won arguments with her, not through logic or loudness but through silence. In that silence and with the needs of old age, these two old adversaries ceased fighting and begrudgingly began to help each other.

Both of them utterly opposed going to a retirement home. I tried reasoning with them, but to no avail. Their individual and joint reply: No! How about having a visiting nurse? No! Someone to help out with the shopping and cooking? No! A retirement home for just one day? No!

I worried about my parents. Give them another few months, I thought; maybe they will change their minds. Either Gail or I went to Dallas several times a year to check on them. My mother was mentally fragile but physically strong. My father was a diabetic and his doctor monitored his condition closely. The doctor phoned after his most recent physical, and said my father's health was the best it had been in some time. I felt reassured.

Just days later, another call came. It was June 1, 1987. I was in my office. Joan, my assistant, came in, her face tense, her voice quiet. I knew something was wrong. "It's your father's doctor, line two." My father had died from a heart attack.

The news stunned me. I was shocked and unprepared. Days earlier, he had appeared fine. Now he was dead. His doctor explained that diabetes often triggers heart attacks. It happened quickly and he didn't suffer. He was already dead when the paramedics arrived. The doctor said he was sorry.

I called Gail and we left for Dallas at once. On the plane, we made mental lists. Neither of us had ever planned a funeral or dealt with undertakers. Our focus had been on getting my parents into a retirement community and making their late years comfortable. My father's death caught us by complete surprise; I didn't even know if he had a will or, if he did, where it was. I had heard about a family plot in Walters, Oklahoma, but I wasn't sure if it still had space. Also, I worried about the impact of my father's sudden death on my mother.

She was angry and confused. "Earl up and died! He left me. He just died!" My mother repeated those words over and over during the next three days. An hour later she might say, "When is Earl coming home?" We patiently explained what had happened. If she felt any grief, she did not express it. For her his death was a profound inconvenience. She hadn't lost her loving partner after a half century of marriage. She had lost her psychological punching bag.

I located my father's body at Parkland Hospital, contacted an undertaker in Walters, and signed a release so he could take the body to the funeral home. Graciously and professionally, the undertaker reassured me and helped me make necessary but absurd decisions. Which lining did I want for the casket? Did I want the standard model or the deluxe? Choosing a coffin reminded me of buying a car, except the options meant nothing.

The undertaker asked me to give him a suit for my father to be buried in. We had decided on an open casket service because relatives would attend who had not seen him for a long time.

Hardware salesmen don't need lots of suits. My father only had one. It was one of mine that I had given him a year before. He wore it every Sunday.

The suit hung in the closet of the middle bedroom. When I was growing up, my father slept in the back bedroom. When my mother went to Massachusetts, he moved into the middle bedroom. He was alseep there when the heart attack struck. He managed to grope his way to the bathroom, where he collapsed and died.

Gail, Natasha, and my mother sat in the living room as I went into the middle bedroom to get the blue suit. I had been in that room over the years and never felt anything. Instead, when I came home, I tried to remember the good times I had growing up—funny moments with my friends, my teachers at school, the work I had done, the sports I had played. When I would think of the abuse and remember the confusion and pain, I would say to myself, "That was then; this is now."

On the day before the funeral, I wasn't in a reflective mood. I raced through my mental list, checking off chores, obsessed with getting as much accomplished as possible. After I gave the suit to the funeral director, I planned to finish arrangements for the service.

When I walked into the middle bedroom, the first thing I saw was the unmade bed. Like an echo of death, the sheets still held the indentation of my father's body. Seeing that shape was the shout that brought down the avalanche.

Come here.

That bed, those words. An outline on the sheets where someone had died. Suddenly everything that ever happened in that bed compressed into the outline of my father's body. He had his fatal heart attack where part of me died. Like under a thundering mountainside of snow, I was smothered by feelings I thought had ended forty years before. Panic, fear, confusion, helplessness, anguish, and desperation jackknifed inside me. This time, I could not escape. Every emotion I had ever buried, every thought I had ever suppressed, came back with unimaginable force and intensity. I leaned against the wall and gasped for breath. My legs buckled. I thought I would vomit. From the other room I could hear my mother talking with Gail. But in my mind I saw her dark eyes from decades ago in the middle bedroom and heard her command, "Come here."

My bones felt hollow, incapable of supporting weight. My heart raced. I held my chest. Never before had I felt such throbbing, thundering pain. My face flushed. The room spun. As images sped around me and through me, I choked on silent screams. I wasn't remembering, I was reliving the abuse by my mother. Over the years, I had trained myself to handle memories. But this was different. This was cataclysmic. Like entering a warp in space and time, I catapulted back more than four decades. Trapped between the shadow of a boy and the shell of a man, I relived every sordid afternoon all at once.

On one side of me sat the bed where I had been abused and where my father had his heart attack. On the other side, hung his suit—my suit—in which he would lie for eternity. I felt like I was dying, and maybe part of me was. As I struggled to breathe, I staggered around the corner to the bathroom and threw cold water on my face. I sat with my head to my knees, desperate for my blood to do what my mind could not: get me energy, get me air, and get me back in control. My heart then nearly imploded inside my chest, for I realized this was how my father died. He, too, had staggered around the corner to the bathroom, sat on the toilet gasping for breath, and finally fell to the floor dead.

I did not fall, and I did not die—not physically anyway. "Gain control," I told myself. "Hold on. You must hold on."

The voices of Gail, Natasha, and my mother sounded remote, far away, a parody of my life on some other channel. I tried to tune them out and bring myself back to reality. Like a paramedic hoping to keep an accident victim from losing consciousness, I kept repeating facts. "This is 1987. I'm forty-nine years old. I'm married. I have two daughters."

I tried to breathe evenly and steadily. Think about my father, not the little boy. That was then; this is now. Inhale, "That was then." Exhale, "This is now." Gradually I brought myself back to reality. The cold water I splashed on my face felt chilling and refreshing. I regained composure from moments earlier, when long-buried memories had torn through me like vaporous demons.

If I could get back to the living room, I'd be all right. Gail took one look at me, jumped up from her chair, and said, "Richard, what happened? Are you okay?" I claimed I was fine, in a meager attempt to convince myself. I could not explain what had just happened even to myself, and certainly not to them. So I muttered something about being tired and how much still must be done. Was the cemetery ready? Would the florist deliver a wreath?

I coped, as I always had, by working hard. I returned to the survival strategy I had relied on since childhood—leave no time to think about anything else.

At my father's funeral, a Methodist minister from Walters led the graveside service and delivered a simple eulogy. We sang hymns and said prayers. A gentle breeze blew across the flat Oklahoma fields. The sunny skies and dry heat of early June seemed a stark contrast to the dark, narrow grave about to sheathe my father's coffin.

The ceremony touched me, but I kept my emotions in check. I was sad that I hadn't been able to say good-bye to my father, and upset that he died alone on a bathroom floor. I loved him and he loved me. We never said those words; we spoke them in our hearts.

Standing at his grave, I thought that finally he had found the peace that eluded him in life. I thought of him in a velvet-lined coffin of smooth polished wood, wearing my dark blue suit, more dressed up in death than in most of his eighty years of life.

My mother stood there confused, distracted, and oblivious to everything around her. Florine Adora Harrison. I tried to imagine her as the dynamic young woman my father fell in love with half a century ago. For fifty years she had buried him in angry tirades and scathing deprecation. Now, when he was being interred for good, she barely noticed.

When the funeral ended, I dropped a white chrysanthemum into his grave, turned, and walked away with Gail, Natasha, Debbie, and my mother. I hoped my father had been proud of the way I turned out.

I was relieved to get back to Washington, and eager to return to the university. Although Gail and I had been gone for only three days, it seemed much longer. Missing a day of work disconcerted me because of my frantic pace. I only knew one speed: fast forward. Immediately, I began replying to mail and catching up on meetings I'd canceled.

In the following months I felt anxious and agitated, which I attributed to pressure at the office, not to my father's death. Gail, who sensed a change in me, too, thought I had not dealt adequately with my grief. In fact, I hadn't dealt with it at all, and changed the subject whenever she brought it up. Sure, I felt sadness about my father's death, but grief? What would that accomplish? Besides, I had to get back to work.

Why dwell on how I felt? That seemed like a waste of time. Why do it? Gail quietly decided that I hadn't grieved sufficiently or fully come to terms with my father's death. She thought it might help me if she brought out old photographs of my family. I glanced at them, but found them more troubling than therapeutic. How would dwelling on the past help?

What should have been a warning to me became, instead, a challenge. With an arrogance bred from decades of self-control and self-discipline, I believed I could handle anything. The powerful feelings that seized me as I stood where my father died stunned me. I slammed to the ground like a jet caught in a wind shear. I was convinced that once I regained control, everything would be fine; after all, I had proved that for decades. This time, however, the crash destroyed the jet's navigation equipment, and I didn't even know it.

If I had had a different attitude toward therapy, I might have recognized the flashbacks in the middle bedroom as a warning to get help. If I had told Gail about the experience, I'm sure she would have urged that. But I had only one strategic weapon in my arsenal of coping skills: suppress the feelings and work. I coped with stress by working harder and harder. It made me feel safe and secure. Work was wonderful! With it, I could get things done while making my feelings subside. If they resurfaced, it meant I hadn't worked hard enough.

Some time after my father's death, I read a long, detailed newspaper article about the McMartin preschool case in California. A mother and son who ran the preschool were charged with numerous counts of child sexual abuse. I remember reading the chillingly graphic account word-for-word many times, and found it highly disturbing. Although I didn't connect this situation with the abuse in my own childhood, I sensed the fear of an abused child. Their confusion and pain started troubling me.

Sometime after that, I was bothered by a strange new curiosity. I don't remember exactly when it began, or what initially went through my mind. I didn't understand it. But I wanted to know about the abuse of children and, most importantly, why adults did it. This impulse, this urge, seemed to come from nowhere. After my father's death until 1990, this unsettling feeling came perhaps six or eight times—suddenly, abruptly, compellingly. With thoughts of the McMartin case lingering in my mind, I began to read child-care ads in the newspaper and called someone who provided daycare. Women always answered. I made up a story that my wife and I had young children, and that we were looking for child care. After routine conversation, I obliquely suggested something about sexual freedom in my family with the children. I gave this fictional account in hopes of prompting the other person to talk about such matters. But the person on the other end of the line wouldn't express knowledge or interest. When she didn't pick up on the lead, that ended the conversation.

I put down the receiver; the compulsion ended; I returned to reality. I turned to my desk and focused on the next item on my day's agenda. For a few moments, I would close my eyes, as if trying to find myself in an opaque fog. I would reopen them, blink, and dash out to my next meeting. I threw the switch, cut off the feelings, and returned to my usual life. I didn't think about what had just happened. How could I even contemplate having done something so strange?

When I made a call, I was myself but not myself. I felt intent, driven, single-minded in my search. Nothing else mattered for those moments. My mind closed out the world, and I focused only on the call. When nothing came of it, this aberrant part dissolved like smoke. I felt nothing—not satisfaction or relief, remorse or revulsion. These were moments outside of time.

My time and attention centered on AU. The university, by the late eighties, had hit its stride. Our earlier efforts began to reap thrilling rewards. We had worked to recruit highly able and promising students; in fact, I think we raised our admission standards faster than almost any other university ever had. The changes became quite noticeable. Juniors and seniors, who had been admitted under different criteria, began to feel the pressure, and maybe some pride.

We worked to recruit and retain first-class faculty. The faculty responded to the increasing standards, and a vigorous intellectual atmosphere grew on campus. After several years, we could see real improvement in academic standards and in the university's reputation in Washington and around the nation.

We saw changes in other areas, too. Our soccer team came in number two in the nation against UCLA in the eighth overtime—one of the longest games in collegiate history. The long-awaited Sports Center finally opened and our basketball team began to improve, adding more spirit to the campus.

Our achievements brought us pride, which in turn made us try harder and aim higher. I thought about AU's progress on the evening of December 31, 1989, as I went to my office to work for a few hours. On my way home to celebrate with Gail, I stopped by the campus security office to say hello to the guards and wish them Happy New Year on this dismal, rainy night. It was a perfect time to build a fire and stay indoors, but Gail and I wanted to go outside on this symbolic evening.

We decided to go to the Jefferson Memorial, that jewel among Washington's many monuments. The statue of Jefferson, luminous in a halo of white light, is breathtaking at night. For me, it always has been a special, meditative place. Jefferson, perhaps our most intellectual president, fused government and scholarship. When I am at his memorial, I reflect on how precious democracy is, how vital education is, and how Jefferson's transcendent words guide us even today.

We parked our car and walked toward the memorial as midnight approached. My glasses fogged in the thick mist. Then, out of nowhere, came a downpour. Sheets of frigid water turned the lawn to mud and the sidewalk to a glaze. From a distance it might have looked like a scene from a French movie, if we'd had a baguette: a man and a woman, running arm-in-arm through the dark night and pouring rain to the marble monument. But there was no romance this night—just gravelike cold, and gloom.

As we climbed the dramatic stairs to the monument, we fell repeatedly on the slippery stone. Gail bruised her knee; I gnashed my knuckle. Finally we made it to the top only to find a few heavily drinking people blowing horns and shouting. Rather than a place for contemplation and reflection, the scene inside was rowdy and raucous, while outside, driving rain surrounded the memorial in an icy shroud.

At midnight we kissed and looked out at the gray wall of water that imprisoned us next to Jefferson. After a moment, Gail trembled and said, "Let's go home." We locked arms as we inched our way back down, falling several times. "If New Year's Eve is a portent for the year," I said, "this one is beyond ominous." I glanced up at Jefferson, a symbol of reason and knowledge, and then down at the remaining slippery steps and said, "We're heading into a freezing hell." I wondered if we were shivering more from cold or dread.

In hopes that I would exercise regularly, Gail had given me a treadmill for Christmas. I had promised to get a stress test before using it. She had tried for years to get me to exercise, without success. After my father died, she renewed the campaign. I told her I walked a lot, and I did, but not in a way that encouraged cardiovascular fitness. I'd amble across campus, stopping to chat with a professor or student or drop by a dorm or an office unexpectedly, just to test our system. As long as I wasn't seriously overweight, I saw no need to exercise. I thought of stress more as an ally than a villain. Since the treadmill was a major investment, I scheduled a stress test for January 9th. It seemed like a nuisance.

The cardiologist rigged me with electrodes and started me jogging on a treadmill. Intently, he followed the blips on the screen. Part way through the exam, he suddenly stopped it and said I should get dressed. The abrupt halt startled me.

We went into an office and he shut the door. Frowning, he spread out the cardiogram. "I'm not certain what's happening here," he said as he pointed to the tracing. "It could be an anomaly or a spurious tracing. Your heart pattern may be completely normal, but this tracing isn't right. You may have a severe blockage in part of your heart. I can't say based just on this test. I suggest that you go at once to Georgetown University Hospital. It has a superb cardiac unit. Have them do an echocardiogram."

I asked what would happen if there were a blockage, and he said surgery might be necessary. He said the sooner I checked this out, the better. "Don't be alarmed," he said. "But do take it very seriously."

Suddenly I saw a little boy with a heart problem in Portland and my father dead of a heart attack in Dallas. Open heart surgery? This couldn't be happening to me. I resolved that until I knew something conclusive, I would not trip myself with fear. What would that accomplish?

Besides, I had an important evening ahead of me. Some months earlier the mayor had asked me to chair the Commission on Budget and Financial Priorities for the District of Columbia. We had put together a distinguished, bipartisan group of local and national leaders. The group was to meet that night. The next evening, Gail and I had invited them to dinner at our home, so I didn't get to the hospital until the following day.

Gail and I were worried, probably more than we admitted to each other. We didn't tell either daughter; we didn't want to alarm them.

At the university, only my assistant, Joan Leach, knew. I didn't want people at AU to think my health might be bad. That might arouse institutional uncertainty. If I found that, in fact, I needed surgery, we planned to tell our daughters and the AU community immediately, but I needed to find out first.

I didn't feel right. Gail worried because I constantly looked tired. Although I couldn't label it, even before I took the stress test I had thought something might be wrong. I tried to ignore it by telling myself that if I did what Gail suggested—slow down, sleep, and exercise more—I'd be fine.

When I arrived for the echocardiogram, the machine was broken. The test had to be postponed for two weeks. By then the spring semester was beginning, and there was much to do. Even so, hard as I tried, apprehension never left my mind. Because of my fear, the positive moments during those weeks of waiting had an even deeper resonance.

One of those moments took place at the entrance to the university itself. After years of planning, we finally completed the renovation and landscaping for a new main entrance. I wanted it to be dignified, inviting, and classical. AU personnel, outside architects, and I had spent months designing beautiful curved stone gates for both sides of the entrance. We went over every detail: the height and width of the stones, the size and style of the lettering, and how to light it, which had turned out to be a challenge.

On a nippy January night, I went out to see the lights lit for the first time. The lighting crew moved the lights around until the gates were evenly illuminated. Finally, after the adjustments, I crossed the street and looked at the entrance from a distance. It was stunning. Simple, yet dignified, graceful and traditional, the entrance suggested a university rooted in the past and confident about the future.

With the students still away on winter break, the campus was quiet as I stood on Massachusetts Avenue and looked at the entrance. I realized the gates were only a symbol, but a fine one indeed. In the tranquility of the moment, I hoped that everyone who came through those gates—students, professors, parents, alums, and visitors— would feel as proud of The American University as I did that night. I was beginning my tenth year as president—the happiest and most fulfilling decade of my life and a period of great change at the university.

Two nights later, Gail reminded me that the former chairman of the board of the university had invited us to a black tie dinner at his home. I hadn't seen the invitation and Gail was uncharacteristically vague about the purpose of the evening. As I put on my tux, I asked her what she knew about the evening. She said she wasn't sure.

When we arrived, so many parked cars lined the curbs I thought there must be another function in the neighborhood. But when we walked in, I heard a chorus of "Surprise!" To my astonishment, the party was for me, in honor of my ten years as president.

Nearly three dozen trustees attended with their spouses, as well as the officers of the university and the general counsel. Debbie was there, too, although Natasha was away at college. Everywhere I turned came another handshake or hug or word of thanks. Praise flowed. I was deeply touched. After speeches and tributes, they gave me a citation and lauded Gail's many contributions to the university. What mattered more than any official recognition, however, was the warmth and laughter that filled the room. This group had become an extended family. Its pride and commitment to the university had deepened over the years, as had its affection for each other.

Later that week, the chief administrators, the faculty senate, the staff council, and others held a massive reception on campus to recognize my tenth anniversary. After they gave me numerous citations and mementos, they asked me to speak. I recounted a story Leonard Bernstein had told about his early career. After thunderous applause and a standing ovation, Bernstein returned for another bow. A small boy in the front row turned to his father and said, "Why is that guy taking all the bows, when the people behind him did all the work?"

That's how I felt. I was privileged to serve as president, but like a conductor, I knew full well that the men and women in the orchestra do the real work. As president, I simply had the privilege to preside, to conduct.

Roughly fifteen hundred people attended the reception. Students, faculty members, grounds people, maintenance workers, alums, staff members, cooks, and even retired faculty all stood in a long, winding line to greet Gail and me, and to say how proud they were of the university.

I never had felt more appreciated than I did that week. It underscored my faith in the university as a committed and caring community. I felt exhilarated about the decade ahead. We had laid a solid foundation for growth and achievement, and I had plans—or more aptly put, a vision and aspiration—for the university for the 1990s.

We were like mountain climbers roped together for the long and difficult climb to the summit. Along the way, we had stumbled and become discouraged at times, but we had hung together, pulled together, climbed together. As a team effort, a helping hand always held fast. We felt we could reach any peak. That night, January 19th, we stood together and rejoiced.

My ebullient mood quickly ended with news that Gail needed surgery. While still waiting for my echocardiogram, we found that she needed a hysterectomy. Her doctor said her condition probably was not cancerous; however, they would not know definitively until after the operation. I felt a ghastly sense of anxiety. Although I was nervous about my own potential heart problem, the thought of anything happening to Gail filled me with dread. I compounded my anxiety by researching uterine cancer and hysterectomies in my medical dictionary and encyclopedia. After twenty-five years of marriage, we were linked so inextricably that I couldn't tell where one of us ended and the other began.

In addition to the hum of activities at the university, I kept myself distracted from my own worries with work on the city's budget commission. We met in Wards all across the city to explain the city's financial problems to the public and to listen to citizens' groups and local advocates. As a cochair of an AIDS coalition, I was involved in distributing funds to community-based efforts to provide AIDS education and support services. My schedule went beyond full.

On the morning of January 30, I finally took the tests at Georgetown University Hospital. I had both an echocardiogram and a nuclear cardiogram. With radioactive dye injected into my bloodstream, I was hooked up to various machines and told to pedal a bicyclelike device while lying on my back. Gail watched the patterns on the screen as I started pedaling and puffing. Like magic, because of the dye, I could see an image of my own heart pumping as I pedaled.

Suddenly the doctor said, "Stop. Everything looks great!" Greatly relieved, I asked him about the earlier test. He explained that sometimes anomalous results arise. The cardiologist encouraged me to exercise more and reduce the stress in my life. Otherwise, he said, my heart looked excellent.

That night I took my protégé in the Mentor Program to a dinner of the Economic Club of Washington. The Mentor Program matches inner-city teenagers with adult professionals who become friends and offer guidance. Gail, too, was a mentor. Her protégé was Rolanda; mine, Eric.

In the two years that we had been friends, Eric and I had become exceptionally close. Never having had a son and perhaps because of the silent relationship I had with my father, I especially enjoyed listening and talking to Eric man-to-man. He was a motivated, talented, hard-working young man who lived with his mother, grandmother, and little brother in a neighborhood increasingly plagued by drugs and violence. Eric and I talked frequently and got together for informal activities, but this black tie dinner was his first formal event. I had given him a tux of mine that no longer fit me. We had it tailored for him, and he looked splendid. Although he was the youngest person at the dinner by at least fifteen years, he chatted with corporate heads and bank presidents with ease and aplomb. I was deeply proud of him. This was a good end to an uplifting day.

That day contrasted sharply with an event I attended the next week. Childhelp USA, a California-based organization, invited me to an information meeting and fundraiser.

Childhelp is the largest national nonprofit organization combating child abuse and neglect. A year earlier, Gail and I had hosted a function for Childhelp at our home. Although I already knew about the group, that evening was unlike any I'd spent before.

The two women who founded the organization spoke starkly and passionately about the awful lives of the children they help. Their devastating descriptions of children who had been burned with irons and others imprisoned and tortured in their own homes shocked the staid Washington audience.

Their words pierced my heart. I had heard and read about abuse over the years, but that evening a part of me felt stunned and oddly awakened. I became uncharacteristically emotional. Tears coursed down my cheeks as I absorbed the pain of the reports. When the women finished their presentation, they asked who would help. My hand was the first one up. I spoke with both women at length and pledged to do whatever I could to assist.

We talked about what it would take to make America wake up to the epidemic of abuse. How did the nation become so complacent, so oblivious to the terrible reality that millions of our children are abused every year? Child abuse stands as our nation's darkest shadow, its most omnipresent evil. Yet, as a society, we refrain from admitting its prevalence or confronting it.

Speaking in an animated and extended way about the issue of abuse helped me focus my feelings. I felt fine until I left to go home. Due to the tight parking, I'd come in the university car. Andrew, the driver, said to me as I got in the car, "How was it?"

I remember saying, "Andrew, there's a lot of pain in this world. More children are confused and hurt than anyone knows."

I slumped in the seat in silence, trying to hide my face. I was profoundly shaken and distraught. My emotions would have made more sense to me if I had connected them to my own abuse, but I didn't. I did not think about my mother or the middle bedroom. Rather, I felt like I'd been struck by a hit-and-run driver who now had vanished. I'd had a powerful encounter with something.

When I got home, I did what I always do to regain control. I went to the bathroom and splashed cold water on my face. I called Gail, who was in California. She asked about the evening. I said it went well and that I continued to be impressed by Childhelp. I told her I found the evening jolting. I didn't elaborate or hint at my distress. Given that I myself didn't understand what had happened, I couldn't tell her. Subconsciously, I think my sentries went onto full alert, warding away questions that might probe too deeply. After talking with her, I turned off the lights and sat alone in the quiet, darkened room. Minutes rolled by. I didn't know if I would implode or explode, but something tumultuous was happening inside me.

Even though I had been cleared by the cardiologist, I still didn't feel right. The year began so ominously, I felt like I heard a metronome ticking, louder and louder. By mid-February, I started to have headaches, which was rare for me, especially as these were migraines. Literally and physically, I felt that I could detonate. Anxiety about Gail's upcoming surgery caused all this, I thought. As long as I had an explanation, I pushed on.

On February 21, I drove Gail to the Columbia Hospital for Women, where she checked in for surgery the next morning. With almost no sleep, I was at her bedside when they came to wheel her away at seven-thirty A.M. We kissed and I said, "I'll be here." I wanted to sound strong and reassuring. I watched the gurney go through swinging doors and then disappear. Alone in her room, I sat and said a quiet prayer. I paced the hallway, but the monotony made me more tense. So I went outside and walked for blocks in the bitter, snapping cold to find a florist that sold Rubrim lilies, Gail's favorite flower.

The surgery lasted several hours. Afterward, her doctors told me it had gone well. She had no cancer. Although Gail was groggy when I saw her, she understood that everything was fine and smiled sleepily through the cloud of anesthesia.

After she fell asleep, I grabbed something from a snack machine and headed back to the university. The annual reception for its founding occurred that day, and I was to preside. By the time I returned to the hospital, Gail's room was filled with flowers. She came home in six days, and theoretically, I should have relaxed. My worst fears were over. But the tension I thought would end drummed even harder inside me. I knew no rational reason why I felt as I did, which frightened me even more.

Logically, this should have been the time to seek help—to talk to my doctor or find a therapist, but that wasn't my way. I believed in my own will. I was as obsessive about my routine as marathon runners are about their pace. I couldn't have slowed if I had wanted to. Besides, I didn't want to.

Late at night I would pace in the bedroom and say to Gail, "My head feels like it's going to burst. There's something wrong, seriously wrong. I don't know what it is, but I feel like I'm going to blow apart."

She looked deeply worried. "Richard, you can't keep going like this. You're under too much pressure. You know it and I know it. Please see a doctor. I almost don't recognize you anymore."

I always agreed with her and promised to slow down. It never happened. Gail and I relied on each other during difficult times. When life got hard, we became more supportive and comforting to each other. When we had been through stressful times before, eventually the pressure abated and life settled again. I think we both felt that time would take care of this, too.

Both of us accepted anxiety and stress as part of my job. Our approach to life always has been optimistic. Ironically, that may have led me to miss the early warning signs of the impending disaster.

Even though I felt intense pressure on the inside, I worked as efficiently as always. Many people noticed that I looked extremely tired. I would have been concerned if my work had suffered, but it continued apace.

In late February, I gave a speech on leadership to a group of several hundred students from across the country. I told them that we needed leadership now more than ever, and cited chilling statistics about America's social crises, some drawn from the Children's Defense Fund. Every eight seconds of the school day, a child drops out. Every thirteen seconds, a child is abused and neglected. Every twenty-six seconds, a child runs away from home. People are aware of the epidemic of teen pregnancy but not the scope: Every day in the United States, thirty to fifty teenage girls give birth to their *third* child. On and on the social problems go. After talking about drugs and violence, I turned to leadership styles.

I told them of the sage observation of Lao-tzu in the sixth century B.C.: "At the end of his days, people will say of a good leader, we did this ourselves." And I closed with the stirring words of Teddy Roosevelt:

"It's not the critic who counts. . . . It's not the man who points out how the strong man stumbled. . . . Credit belongs to the man who really was in the arena, his face marred by dust, sweat, and blood, who strives valiantly, who errs to come short and short again, because there is no effort without error and shortcoming. It is the man who actually strives to do the deeds, who knows the great enthusiasm and knows the great devotion, who spends himself on a worthy cause, who, at best, knows in the end, the triumph of great achievement. And who, at worst, if he fails, at least fails while daring greatly, so that his place shall never be with those cold and cruel souls who know neither victory nor defeat."

The students were rapt. AU students in the audience asked if I would give a similar talk to student leaders on our campus. I did, and thus were born Berendzen's Ten Suggestions for New Student Leaders.

I began by reminding them that the student government and the university existed long before they arrived and would remain long after they left. I said to get their facts straight. And I told them not to project their perspectives on anyone else; in short, don't make life a Rorschach test. Never assume you know someone else's motives. I told them not to say things behind people's backs or through the anonymity of print that they wouldn't dare say to their face, and never to assume moral superiority. Take the long view, I told them: Don't opt for the quick fix. I recommended they place benefit to the university family ahead of themselves. I concluded by urging them to remember during their most trying times the saying from Marcus Aurelius, "This, too, shall pass."

The coming days were consumed with recruitment trips and alumni meetings across the country. I talked at high schools, met with deans and faculty at AU, gave speeches, and became even more active with the city's budget commission. In March, commission members and I went to Baltimore to study its municipal finances, and we discussed budgetary issues with officials from Dallas.

By mid-March, my usual hectic schedule went off-scale. My usual one-hundred-hour workweek moved up to one hundred and twenty. Never before had I felt so exhausted, so drained physically, emotionally, totally. My headaches became worse than ever, with a dull omnipresence that would, without warning, transform into jolts that shot from my forehead through my eyes. My temples throbbed so badly that I'd lose concentration.

On March 28, at my annual meeting with the faculty, the head of the faculty senate read a citation commending me on my ten years as president, and the faculty gave an emotional standing ovation. Afterward, many professors came up to congratulate me individually. There I stood surrounded by the faculty, savoring the success of the university and the praise and thanks from my colleagues. As much as I enjoyed the moment, I knew I had to leave. I thought I would be ill. I stepped into the men's room and returned, but it didn't help. My insides felt like a rumbling caldron, and I was so bone-weary that I wanted to sit rather than stand at any reception. I wanted out of the crowd, to be alone. So I slipped out, out from a reception at which the defining part of the university was extolling my achievements. I just didn't care. Something was profoundly wrong.

Slowly, like a man dragging himself, I walked up the hill to the president's office building. As I collapsed in my chair, I wondered if I should call Gail, lie down, or go to a doctor. Instead, I did what had become intermixed into my frenetic pace, something not on my agenda: I placed another phone call related to child abuse.

After my father's death in 1987 up to 1990, I had placed at most a handful of such calls, usually spaced many months apart. Starting in January of 1990, however, I began to call more frequently. During the next three months, I called perhaps ten to fifteen people, all of them strangers who had placed ads in newspapers to provide child care. No single event sparked this, although I now realize several were catalysts.

I placed the calls from my study in the president's office building. Originally built as the home of the university president decades ago, this "office building" is, in fact, a replica of a Cape Cod captain's house. As president I occupied the first floor; the provost occupied the second. My formal office and conference room used to be the living room. Joan was in the former kitchen, and my study, now a private inner office, used to be the dining room. The bookshelf-lined study is a quiet, private place—ideal for contemplation. The blinds were closed, the door shut. I placed the calls in that darkened room.

Some afternoons, I'd ask Joan, or Roberta, my other assistant, to hold my calls so I could think. I'd slump in my chair, with my head spinning and my temples throbbing. I'd close my eyes and hold my head. I'd start to write a letter or prepare a speech. Then my mind would wander and something inside me would say, "Why don't you call?" I'd reach for the classified section of the newspaper. Once the compulsion took over, I didn't think, "Should I or shouldn't I?" No inner voice said, "Stop, this is wrong. You know you shouldn't do this." Rationality, logic, and reason had nothing to do with those moments. Only some visceral impulse counted, or even seemed to exist. Obviously, I was out of bounds on compulsion's court. What I did was wrong. Any objective, dispassionate observer would know that, just as I thoroughly do now. But at the time, I was neither objective nor dispassionate. I was confused, driven, and sick.

Elsewhere in the building, I could hear the provost's staff laughing and the phones ringing in Joan's office. Outside the window, I could hear birds singing—just as the mockingbirds used to do outside the middle bedroom. But my full intent focused on the calls.

I found a number in the paper, called, waited for someone to answer, had a brief chat, and then insinuated something about children and sexuality. I might mention that in our home the children bathed with my wife and me, or that we all slept in the same bed. I'd wait for a response. The other party would express no interest or would say they didn't do such things in their home. So I'd say we didn't do it much ourselves. We'd just done it a few times. I then quickly ended the conversation.

I never planned the calls. I didn't think, "Tomorrow at three I'll make another call." The impulse to call seemed to arise out of nowhere. In retrospect, I realize that the calls almost always came in the afternoon and often when I felt melancholy. I had rarely felt despondent before, but in 1990 I began to fall into momentary bouts of gloominess. I made many of the calls then.

Most of the calls lasted less than ten minutes. When I hung up, I would sit at my desk thinking, "Why in the world did I do that?" I felt confused and ashamed. "What was that conversation about?" It had nothing to do with my life. I found it all repulsive. Still, I had made the call. Why? I could find no answer. Then I would suddenly remember the meeting I was about to chair. I would glance at my watch and think, "My God! It's in four minutes!"

When I left the office, that was it. I shut the door and shut the call out of my mind, banished it from my consciousness. It was over. Ride a bike. Pound nails. Play baseball. It was over. I had learned, long ago, how to walk away from something once I closed the door. "That was then; this is now."

In March, I called a particular ad. This time, the woman did not end the conversation when I hinted at parents and children being sexually involved. Instead, she spoke at length and encouraged me to call back, which I did. Unbeknownst to me, the police attached a taping device to her phone so my calls could be recorded and subsequently traced.

When I called back, I made up stories about bizarre sexual activities that my wife and I routinely did with the children in my fictitious family. Despite the obvious wrongness of this, I pretended to relish it, I was so intent on finding answers. All that I felt in my soul and had known with my youthful body abhorred child abuse. Yet something in me made me go on.

What interested me were not my comments but the woman's answers to my questions. For the first time, I had called someone who was willing to talk in detail about child abuse. As she later told *The Washington Post*, "I answered his questions in a way I knew he wanted them answered, so that he'd be satisfied, so that he would think he'd found his true love in this world and he would call back. And he did. He fell for it, hook, line, and sinker."

Indeed I did fall for it. I called back with increasing frequency, and we began to talk at length. I did not know that she was answering my questions in ways she thought I wanted them answered so that I'd call back and my calls could be traced. So I described activities in my fabricated home, and asked about activities in hers. I said our children slept with us in the nude, and asked if hers did too. I said my wife had sex with our son, and asked if she did with hers. I asked if she enjoyed it, if she ever wondered how the boy felt, if she cared. I asked why she did it. I described how we punished our children, and asked how she did it in her home. I asked if she controlled her children through sex and intimidation. And I asked what her husband knew about all this.

Over the next two weeks, the discussions became increasingly grotesque. We talked about incest, domination of children, and many forms of child sexual abuse. The conversations spiraled down from one sordid subject to another. They plummeted into Hades. I've heard of people who become so transfixed by a fire that they stick their arm into it. Such actions lie outside of logic; caution and reason have nothing to do with them. During a conversation, I felt numb, not aroused or excited. I was repelled and intrigued at the same time. As the conversations continued, I fell further and further into the flames.

The prosecutor, who studied the tapes, said that these were not average obscene phone calls. They did not include the usual litany of obscene words. That simply wasn't my interest. I was interested in finding information. I was groping. I was lost. The prosecutor told *The*

Washington Post, "I don't want to dignify the calls by saying they were sort of cerebral, but they *were* sort of cerebral. They were probing."

While I made a call, I mentally left my book-lined study. I abandoned the presidency. I forsook my wife and daughters. I turned away from all that I had studied. I put aside restraint and caution. I forgot to defend the university, my family, or myself. I focused all my being on that conversation. What might I learn? What happened in other families and why?

My rational, analytical world played no role here. This came from elsewhere in my mind, from recesses I didn't know I had. My feelings came so fast and from so many directions, they merged into a single blur of fascination, disgust, and more confusion. Not knowing the answers had led to confusion, but the prospect of finding the answers frightened and confused me even more.

On a conscious level at least, I didn't think about the abuse I'd experienced as a child. Memories of that didn't intrude into my day-to-day life, and they didn't when I called. I never connected the calls to what had happened in my own childhood. I had no idea why I was doing what I did. When a call ended, I sat in disbelief. My whole body ached, my hands shook, my vision blurred. I knew everything about the calls was profoundly wrong, yet I had made them. Why? What was happening?

By April, thoughts about these calls, unlike any in the past, began to creep into my normal day. While shaving, I'd think of them and shudder. Had we truly discussed a parent's control, sexual domination, and humiliation of a child? Had I truly said that I did such things in my home, to provoke a response? The thought of all this sickened me—both the calls and the acts themselves. Why did I make such calls? And why would adults do such things to children?

As much as I found the calls repulsive, the compulsion to call again grew even stronger. Part of my life had spun out of control. I was too ashamed and baffled to tell anyone about it. How would I begin? Ninety-nine percent of me was the man the world saw: university president, husband, father. But that other one percent was a bomb about to explode, destroying everything I stood for and had worked to achieve.

Four

CRISIS

O n April 7, 1991, the explosion came.

It was a Saturday morning. I got a haircut, stopped by the office, ran a few errands, and was home by twelve-thirty to have lunch with Gail. She said Ed Carr, the chairman of the board of trustees, had called and asked me to call him back. That was unusual.

He was new to the job, so I thought maybe he had a different approach. He lived in Virginia, but the number he left was in Washington. He answered.

"Hi, Ed, I'm returning your call."

His voice was somber and flat.

"Dick, I'm at one the trustee's offices downtown. A small group of us would like to talk to you at once. It's a serious matter."

"I just walked in. I've been out doing errands, but I'll put on a suit. . . ."

"No, that doesn't matter. We'd like to talk to you at once."

"Okay. I'll be right down."

When I hung up, I told Gail what Carr had said. Although he had called the issue "serious," he didn't say what it was. Gail and I spent a minute or two trying to guess. Maybe Carr was ill, or perhaps a financial or legal problem had arisen about the university. Or maybe it was good news. Maybe we had received a large donation I didn't know about.

As I backed out of the driveway, I thought not. Carr had sounded too sober for this to be good news. I drove to the law office downtown. It was a modern building, empty on the weekend. The guard was expecting me and sent me upstairs.

Ed Carr, three other trustees, and Tony Morella, general counsel for the university, were waiting. I shook hands with them and they wanly smiled. The presence of the general counsel made this meeting even more unusual. In every way, this meeting was unique.

Ed began.

"Dick, we asked to meet with you because a serious matter has come to our attention. Tony will tell you about it."

Tony said that a couple of days before, a detective from the Fairfax County Police Department had contacted him because they had traced a call to the university, which AU subsequently traced to a particular line. The police did not know yet whose line it was. Other people could have used the line, but the police had a tape recording of the party talking.

Tony went on to say that the detective played a portion of the tape for him. He said no one had yet identified the voice or the line to the police. But he added that he and the trustees knew that the line went to the private phone in the president's study.

All ten eyes riveted on me. At the words "police," "traced," and "call," my heart simply fell out of my body, my soul with it. I remained silent for a few seconds.

Then I said, "I'm deeply humiliated. I'm ashamed. I'm saddened. I've thought of you as my friends. I hope you still are and I hope you will remain my friends.

"I, I . . ." The words seemed stalled, hurdles I couldn't get over by sheer will. I took a deep breath. "I want to apologize to everyone." Silence made a terrible trench between us.

"It is my voice on the tape. I'm deeply sorry that I made the calls.

87

I'm sorry for the university. I'm sorry for my family. I'm sorry for it all."

My head was spinning. I felt cold inside. Colder than dead, colder than forgotten. The room was silent. I stammered, "I don't know what to do. I want to do what's right."

The five men looked at me, expressionless. I kept talking, in part because the silence was so unnerving and unbearable.

"I have three concerns. First, I want to protect my family. I'm concerned for Gail and our daughters. Second, I want to protect AU. I want to do what's right for the university. I have dedicated most of my professional life to AU. I love it and have protected it, and I don't want it hurt. And last, as a far lower priority, somehow I would like to survive all this. But my first priorities are, in close order, my family and the university. I'll do whatever is best. How would it be if I took a leave for a while?"

In the sixteen years I had been at AU, I had taken virtually no vacations, and my leave time had accumulated into more than a year, which I had forfeited. Certainly I needed a break. The room remained quiet.

"I want to say to you and make this very clear—irrespective of what was said on that phone—the truth is that I have never engaged in any improper activities involving children and I have no desire to do so whatsoever. For reasons I don't understand, I was seeking information about the subject. I can't explain it, and I know it sounds odd. But I was data gathering. Nothing more. I simply was data gathering. I wanted information. I have no idea why. If I knew, I'd tell you."

The silence was still deafening. So I kept talking. "Would a leave be the right thing to do? Could I leave and then come back, perhaps in six months or a year or two?"

They looked at me, glanced at each other, and one of them replied, "Absolutely not. That won't do."

I said, "Well, I'll do whatever is right. You guys haven't said the word, but if you want me to resign, I'll do it now on the spot. No one has to demand it. I'll do whatever is best. At this stage, I'm frankly dazed by all this. So please help me. I want to do the right thing. Would that be to resign?"

One of the trustees said, "Okay, let's put that into effect."

I interjected, "Well, wait a minute. I mean, is resigning the thing to do?"

"Yes."

"Well, then, I'll do it. But could we take twenty seconds and consider any other option like a leave or a break of some sort?"

"No."

I took another deep breath, as my head spun. "All right then, let's proceed." I paused momentarily, then added, "Look, we're getting into serious issues here. I'm enough of an administrator to know that I shouldn't make serious legal decisions without my own legal counsel. I know that. I'll give my resignation. I promise that. But I would like to consult my lawyer."

They agreed. I didn't have his home number, so I needed to call Gail to get it. Besides, I simply had to let her know what was happening.

I stepped into a private office, paused for a moment, and then called my wife—that loving, rational, and trusting person. She answered at once. "Bunny," I began with my usual pet name for her, "if I ever needed you, I need you now. I'm here with four trustees and Tony. I've made some phone calls, which the police are investigating. And I've resigned the presidency."

"What?" she gasped. "Are you okay?"

I told her I was and that somehow we'd come through this. We'd have to be strong. Then, with a breaking voice, I whispered, "I love you, Bunny. And I'm so very sorry. Forgive me."

We didn't have time then for personal talk, despite its importance. So we turned to business. I needed Richard Marks's home number. She gave me the number, told me she loved me, and would be waiting for me when I got home. For the next few hours, she waited and paced; paced and waited.

Richard Marks was at home when I called.

"Richard, I have a startling thing to tell you. It's difficult, I'm embarrassed, but I have to explain. I'm downtown now with four trustees and Tony Morella. I've just resigned the presidency. I've made some inappropriate phone calls, which I never should have made. I told the trustees I wanted to do what was right, so I resigned on the spot. But I'm really in a daze, I'm lost."

Marks said firmly, "Richard, say nothing more to them! Leave! If you can't leave, stop until I can get there." I said I wanted to cooperate fully. I put him on hold and went back to the trustees and told them I had spoken to Gail and that Marks was on the line. They put him on a speaker phone. He said that I should leave the meeting because it was inappropriate for me to continue discussions without legal representation. He said he would join them. Carr said no, this must be settled at once. Marks pleaded, saying he would be there within an hour. He wanted to stop at his office to get my AU file, but the group insisted on instant action with no legal delays. I told Marks that I appreciated his counsel but that I intended to cooperate fully. Finally, we all agreed that the meeting would disband, and that Marks and I would complete my letter of resignation and deliver it to Carr's home by eleven A.M. Sunday morning.

A longtime trustee said to me, "Richard, I don't understand about the calls, but you should consider getting some therapy."

"Well, I'll do that if it's the right thing to do. I don't know," I replied. "Obviously, something is wrong. I need to find out what. To tell the truth, though, I don't put much stock in those folks. I don't know if a therapist can help. I know I was just data gathering."

He silently stared back.

"I was profoundly curious. I don't know why. It wasn't seductive at all, nothing like that. I didn't intend to harass or seduce or offend anyone."

The other trustees stared at me. I looked at them.

"I want to cooperate. I promise I will. I won't make things difficult for the university or the authorities. If you talk to the Fairfax police, please tell them that. I'm willing, in fact, to go there this afternoon, or take a lie detector test.

"You've got to understand that I've never harmed a child, and never would. I find the whole matter *absolutely* repulsive. Truth is, I'm confused. But I was data gathering, that's it!"

Their faces were expressionless. To bridge the cumbersome silence, I apologized again and said I hoped we could remain friends.

A trustee said, "You'll pull through, Richard. You're a good man. You'll make it." Another one said I was burned out from hard work and that maybe at last I would get some rest. Tony squeezed my shoulder and said, "I'm still your friend."

Somewhere in the midst of this, we agreed that I would give exhaustion as my reason for resigning. We all agreed that the real reason for my departure would remain totally confidential. To ensure that nothing leaked, they said they would not disclose the full story to anyone, including the other trustees or the administration. Carr said he would issue a press release. I asked if I could give him a draft, because I could give a few terse facts about my administration and state why I was resigning. Reluctantly, he agreed, but said I should get it to him by the next day.

One of the trustees said I should begin to disengage immediately. It was April 7; the academic year still had more than a month to go. I asked how to do that. Normally, a resignation would be effective at the end of the academic year. I reminded them that I still had extensive commitments and obligations. They said I should stop all my administrative work at once, and that I should get off campus as soon as possible and remain away.

Just like that?

Just like that.

"But how am I going to do that? I'm really lost here. I've given you my resignation. You'll have the letter tomorrow. But I'd like the opportunity to talk to the university officers and tell them directly that I'm resigning. It's going to come as a thunderous surprise to them, the faculty, the staff, the students. I think if I said something, it might minimize the shock to the campus. And it would look more natural."

Who would believe that I would walk away from my job a month before commencement? The meeting ended with these issues unresolved. Carr made one point clear: Marks was to have my signed resignation to him by eleven A.M. the next day.

As the Saturday afternoon wore on, a trustee said he had to leave. He shook my hand warmly, as did another one who then also left. Finally, at about three-thirty, I shook hands with the remaining three men and left myself. I crossed the street to the parking garage and went to where I thought I'd left my car. I couldn't find it. I searched every level, fearing it had been stolen. After forty-five minutes of frantic hunting, I realized I was in the wrong garage and went to the one next door.

By the time I found the car, I was in a panic to get home and raced through traffic, desperate beyond all measure. I had to see Gail. All

91

she had known for the last three hours was that I had resigned the presidency because of something I'd done.

I careened into the driveway and walked in through the kitchen door. We held each other and didn't say anything for a long, long time. Finally I said, "I'm so sorry. I don't know why, I don't understand. I never wanted to hurt anybody, the university, you, or anybody." We sat at the kitchen table, and I told her about the meeting. I said I had made some phone calls that had been traced to my office. I said the calls were wrong and inappropriate, that they shouldn't have happened, but that they had nothing to do with our marriage. Nothing. I said I had been seeking information, but I didn't know why. I explained about the police investigation and said I was to meet with Richard Marks and some other attorneys that evening to draft my letter of resignation and to discuss how to cooperate with the police.

Gail listened. She didn't probe or push. For both of us, all of this was simultaneously too real and yet unreal. We had just celebrated my tenth year as president; now we were talking about my letter of resignation and what would happen after it was released.

I told Gail we had agreed at the meeting that this would be handled with utmost privacy. She and I needed to think how to respond when people heard that I had resigned. Would they believe the excuse of exhaustion? Maybe, but where would I say I'm going next? Why would I resign without another job in line? Would this story hold up? We didn't know, but we had no choice. We trusted that as long as this was handled discreetly, it might work. After a few days, the press would lose interest. After the initial shock, the campus would adjust, and we could go on with our lives.

For a few moments, we speculated about what I might do next professionally. There was no point on dwelling on that then, though. First I had to prepare the resignation letter and deal with the police.

That evening I met with Richard Marks and other attorneys at his office. He was annoyed that he had not been able to give me full counsel before I resigned. He said that if I wished to resign, fine. That was my prerogative. But details about my contractual relationship with AU should have been worked out, as he'd tried to explain on the speaker phone. If my resignation was to be graceful for AU and for me, creating a story people wouldn't believe wasn't the way to do it.

There was no longer time for debate or discussion. I had pledged my cooperation to the trustees, and that Ed Carr would have my resignation letter the next morning.

As we completed the letter in Marks's office, he shoved his chair back from his desk and looked at me. Only the two of us remained in the suite, and only the lights in his office were on. "Look, Richard, it's just the two of us," he began. "Tell me about this—why, why did you make these calls? What were you trying to do?"

"I don't know. I'm not sure."

I looked at him blankly. I was puzzled by the question, and no answer made sense.

"I was data gathering. I was curious. That's all there is to it. I know it sounds strange, but it's the truth. I was curious."

Marks has known me for years, and he's not a man who's easily impressed. He looked at me incredulously and shook his head. "You were curious? You had these conversations because you were *curious*? I don't get it. Richard, I've known you a long time, but . . ."

I looked at him directly, then looked away and said I didn't understand it either.

We worked until midnight. We completed the letter of resignation, and Marks also drafted a paragraph or two for Carr, which spoke not about me personally but about progress at AU during my presidency about which we all were proud. It seemed logical that if I were leaving due to exhaustion, the board would acknowledge accomplishments during my term.

Marks took both papers to Carr on Sunday morning. He called me immediately afterward. He said Carr had accepted my letter of resignation, but had deleted from the draft press release all comments except the text of my letter itself. Immediately, I realized this release would raise more questions than it would answer. I told Gail that without any of the traditional comments about my service, people might wonder about the explanation, especially given the timing of the resignation. I hoped this omission wouldn't flag attention. Carr would release my letter of resignation on Monday.

I had barely slept Saturday night and was clenched with anxiety about Monday. In the Kafkaesque world in which I now found myself, I had a long-standing obligation for Sunday night. Gail and I were to attend a black-tie dinner in honor of major donors to the university.

Held in an expansive house in an exclusive neighborhood in McLean, Virginia, this event was important for the university. Normally, we looked forward to it, for these benefactors helped to make AU's progress possible. That night, however, I would thank our key contributors only hours after I had resigned as president and a day before they would learn of the resignation. I would ask for their continued support to help make the university's future bright just as my own now appeared so obscure.

Nonetheless, the evening went on. Gail and I greeted everyone. I made a few remarks and then thanked the donors individually. I talked optimistically about AU's future. How bittersweet and surreal! The show was closing after a long run, but only I knew this was the last performance.

After the dinner, I went back to my office and called Tony Morella. "Tony, that was a hell of a meeting yesterday."

"Yeah, I know." After a moment of quiet he continued. "I thought about you in church this morning. I prayed for you at mass. Don't do it."

"Do what?"

"Don't consider suicide."

I told him the thought hadn't crossed my mind. I explained that I called because even though I'd resigned, I was still a tenured professor at AU and proud to be one. After my life got straightened out, I told Tony I wanted at least to consider the possibility of coming back to teach. This had been overlooked in the tailspin the day before.

Tony replied, "They thought about it." He didn't elaborate. I thanked him for his prayers and we ended the conversation.

As I hung up, Gail called me at the office and said that Ed Carr apparently had told the top administrators that I'd resigned, because they were calling our house after having talked to him.

"Really?" I didn't think anyone would know until the next morning, and I had planned to tell my closest colleagues myself. Apparently Ed decided otherwise. I talked to Don Triezenberg, the vice president of development, and to Milt Greenberg, the provost, both of whom found the news baffling. Don's first words to me were "Can I help?" I asked why he asked that, and he replied, "I don't know, Richard. Something doesn't sound right. If you need help, I'm here. This just doesn't add up and the resignation letter doesn't sound like the man I've worked for since 1974." Milt, too, sounded puzzled. He knew my every nuance; we'd worked together closely for a decade. I tried to sound wholehearted. It had been a great ten years, I explained, but I was exhausted and the time had come to move on. Both men had been friends and advisors all these years. They knew I'd conditioned myself to ignore exhaustion. Even so, I didn't go beyond that explanation. I couldn't.

When I realized word was out on Sunday, I called my assistant, Joan Leach, who had worked with me for ten years. She screamed: "No! No! Oh God, what will happen to the university?" Then she sobbed uncontrollably. She and Roberta Goldstein had been a real team, and loyal and devoted to me. I deeply respected these women and owed them a lot, starting with an explanation that I just couldn't give.

When I finally got home, Gail was waiting up for me. She hugged me and said, "Please get medical help. I've said that for months. Now please do it. Immediately!" I agreed, this time sincerely intending to do it. At first we wondered if I could just see a local psychiatrist for an hour or two. But who? Neither of us knew any psychiatrists, and we weren't about to ask friends for referrals. Then we wondered if I should check myself into a major hospital for a thorough exam. But where? The Mayo Clinic in Minnesota, the McLean Hospital in Massachusetts, the Menninger Clinic in Kansas? No, they were too far away.

We talked about Georgetown and George Washington University hospitals locally or The Johns Hopkins Hospital in nearby Baltimore.

But how could I go to any hospital? My calendar was full, including a long-scheduled speech in California on Wednesday. We'd think about it over night and talk more on Monday. At that late hour, we went to bed truly exhausted.

Issues remained, nonetheless. What should we tell Debbie and Natasha? Finally, we decided to tell them just what was in the press release. It seemed unfair. They deserved more, but we didn't know what to say.

Word of my resignation began to spread across campus on Monday. The office was inundated with calls. Credible or not, the exhaustion story seemed to be accepted, at least by those who called. And several dozen of them did, with kind words about my presidency and concern for my health. In addition, with the long-awaited Hubble Space Telescope about to be launched, interview requests started coming in. For an astronomer, the Hubble launch was like waving farewell to Columbus. This new voyage of exploration had the potential to look back through time to the origin of time.

At noon on Monday, I did a live interview with CNN about Hubble. Later, a producer from *Nightline* on ABC News called and invited me to be the sole guest about Hubble that night. I agreed. In between, I fielded calls about my resignation from bewildered faculty members, administrators, and staff. I asked Joan to cancel my forthcoming administrative meetings, in accord with the trustees' directive on Saturday.

That afternoon, I was to meet with my attorneys, who now included a respected trial lawyer, Gerry Treanor, who would represent me with the Fairfax police. Before I met with them, Gail and I again discussed my going to a hospital. Would I go for an afternoon? A day? We knew nothing about treatment. Could I go daily or as an outpatient?

As I drove downtown to the meeting, I decided to make my health and my family my first priority; in fact, for now my sole priority. Despite my long distrust of therapy, I decided that at least I should give it a try. Clearly, something aberrant had led me to make the calls. I had to find out what and cure it once and for all. Maybe psychiatrists could help. Anyway, I knew I needed help from someone.

I asked the lawyers for advice about medical experts. Treanor said Johns Hopkins had a sexual disorders clinic. "But I don't have a sexual disorder." Someone replied, "Well, maybe you don't or maybe you do. We're not equipped to say. But Hopkins has a nationally known sexual disorders clinic. It might be the place to start."

Located in Baltimore, Hopkins was not only perhaps the nation's most highly acclaimed hospital but also convenient. Besides, it was out of Washington, so I might have some privacy. Treanor called a Dr. Malin at Hopkins, who said I should see him the following day at nine A.M. He urged me to pack a suitcase and spend the night before in Baltimore so we could meet the next morning. I told him I was supposed to go to California on Wednesday. Malin paused, then asked if I would go if I'd had a heart attack?

"Of course not, but I didn't have a heart attack." He was quiet momentarily and then replied, "I thought you just told me that you have given your medical treatment highest priority." Yes, I had, but what was I getting myself into? I told Malin that I desperately wanted to get well, that I would do anything to understand my behavior. I'd place myself fully in their hands. I'd take any tests or do anything they said. Just would they please help me? He assured me that they would try. I assured him that I'd be there at nine A.M. the next day.

Then I canceled the rest of my life. I called Joan and told her I'd be away from the office for a while, although I didn't say where I'd be. I asked her to tell the students that I would be unable to moderate their debate that night for Washington's mayoral candidates, and to cancel my California speech. Gail called *Nightline* and told the producer I couldn't do the show. She apologized profusely. *Nightline* was furious. With only hours until airtime, they had no guest. I regretted missing that interview, for it would delve into quintessential cosmology.

Next, I canceled a meeting with the mayor and an interview on the Business Channel. I called off a meeting with deans. Everything in my professional life came to a halt.

I called Gail and asked her to pack a small suitcase for me. Neither of us knew what I should take. What would I need in a hospital for a day or two? She met me at the lawyers' office.

As we left the city in rush hour traffic, I realized I was driving away from my formerly secure world and heading into the unknown. Instead of talking to millions of *Nightline* viewers about the Hubble mission, I was launched on my own exploration, hurtling into a void that appeared dark, barren, and cold. I had no idea where it would lead and no idea when I would return. All I could think of was how many people I had disappointed.

On our way to Baltimore, I kept apologizing. "I was data gathering. I don't know why. I'm so sorry. It was wrong. And I'm so sorry. I'm sorry for intruding into anyone's life, for hurting you, AU, anyone."

Whenever we drive, Gail never reads the maps right. But that day, she steered me well.

"Richard, maybe the doctors can help you. Try to relax. Let yourself go and let them help you. Please."

As we checked into the Marriott Hotel in downtown Baltimore, a man said, "Hi, Dr. Berendzen! Good to see you." We chatted briefly. He turned out to be an alumnus. Was privacy impossible? Once in our room, we were too anxious to sleep. Late into the night, we watched the movie *Glory* on TV. Exhausted by the sadness of the film and our own lives, we finally fell asleep.

Five

TREATMENT

T he world-renowned Johns Hopkins Hospital is in East Baltimore, one of the grimmest parts of town. Even though it is only a couple of miles from the Marriott, it took us an hour to find it. On trips, I never get lost. That day, I couldn't find my way. Gail said maybe I just didn't want to go. Eventually, we found the hospital.

We entered through the oldest building, which dates from the last century. It contains a towering atrium with dark wooden beams in the center of which stands a mammoth marble statue of Jesus. It stopped us in our tracks, it was so large, impressive, and unexpected. We continued on our way through the labyrinth of hallways to Malin's office. "I don't know if this place lives up to its illustrious reputation," I remarked to Gail, "but it sure is huge."

With a beard, ruddy face, and flyaway hair, Dr. Malin looked like a psychiatrist from central casting. His gentleness instantly put me at ease. I followed him into his office while Gail waited outside.

"So, Dr. Berendzen, tell me what happened."

I explained that calls I had made from the president's office had been traced back to me.

"Your lawyer told me about the calls. Why don't you tell me, too?"

"Well, I'm very embarrassed about this. They centered on child sexual abuse."

"I see. And why do you suppose that was?"

"I don't know, Dr. Malin. That's why I'm here."

"Have you had any interest in child sexuality?"

"Well, I seemed to have sought information about it, but I have no interest in doing it or seeing it. I find it utterly repugnant."

Malin was soft-spoken.

"Have you ever seen child pornography?"

"No. Never."

"Would you like to?"

"No."

"Do you think it would be erotic?"

"No. It would be disgusting."

"All right. Well, let's get some information about you. Where were you born? Where did you grow up?"

We went through a routine biographical sketch of my life, with details about my education, marriage, family, and job. Then, without changing expression or tone of voice, he casually asked, "Tell me about your first sexual experience."

Silence. I didn't say a word. Neither did he.

The question filled the silence.

Suddenly I burst into tears. I sobbed uncontrollably for the first time in my memory. At a sexual disorders clinic, such a question makes sense. I should have anticipated it, but I hadn't paused to consider what they would ask or do. My concern had been in too many other places. My tears were as unexpected as they were uncontrollable. I couldn't stop crying. Saying nothing, Malin passed me a box of tissues.

I stammered, "I'm sorry, I'm so out of control."

"Leave your emotions alone. Let your feelings come naturally. Stop trying to control them."

I took a deep breath and blew my nose.

"Now," said Dr. Malin, "could we continue? Tell me about your first sexual experience."

I dissolved again. I cried and shook and coughed. Finally I regained enough composure to say, "Why do I have to talk about that?"

"Well," he said, "why do you think we would ask such a question at this clinic?"

"I don't know. It has nothing to do with anything. I'm concerned about me right now, not back then."

Malin told me again to stop trying to be in control. He might as well have told me not to blink at a sudden flash of light.

After more choking, my sobs finally quieted. The room was silent. I took a deep breath and then ended forty-three years of silence with these words: "When I was eight years old . . ."

I told Dr. Malin about the Sunday afternoon with my parents. He asked about my next experience, which sent me into a spasm of gagging. My involuntary reactions amazed and somewhat frightened me. I had lost all control. Haltingly, I started to tell him about the middle bedroom, but I found that only tears, not words, would come out. I used up a box of Kleenex. Dr. Malin listened and waited. Silence didn't bother him.

Why was he putting me through this? It made no sense. I was extremely uncomfortable and embarrassed talking about the most private part of my life.

Malin asked, "Don't you think those experiences could have had a profound effect on you?"

"Sure they did when I was a kid," I replied. "But that was a long time ago."

When we finished talking, he said he wanted me to meet with Dr. Fred Berlin, the clinic director.

Gail was still waiting for me in the corridor. She sat by an end table with dog-eared medical journals on it across from a crooked painting—no easy-listening music or back issues of *People* magazine here. Gail asked Dr. Malin's secretary about the treatment program. She told Gail it was a sexual disorders clinic and gave her a brochure. Gail only heard the words "sexual disorders." As she read the brochure, she heard a piercing wail from Malin's office. My primal cry was unlike any she'd ever heard. Later, she said it felt like her surgical scars were ripping apart. She didn't know why I cried out or that I felt that I would split apart. While she waited, she wrote in her journal:

When we entered the hospital complex there was a huge statue of Jesus with the words: "Enter here all you who labor and are in pain and I will give you rest.' Richard needs rest, both for his body and soul. He is so humiliated, so crushed by all of this and so confused. He has worked at an inhuman pace for all the years I've known him and as he's gotten older and more burdened with responsibilities, he has taken everything on with more energy. He has used himself up. He is in a very black place right now, but I hope that by being here he will be forced to think of inner repair. It is hard to let go of everything that was his life.

Last night he did not go to the mayoral debate on campus and he canceled out on a wonderful opportunity to discuss a subject he loves on *Nightline*. Today he is not going to a meeting with the mayor about the Berendzen Commission. Knowing that he has let all these people down hit him hard last night.

We spent the night downtown, another dark time for us. I think with each passing moment he will be more and more able to detach himself from the *before* and begin to focus on the *now* of his situation.

Last night as we ate dinner at the Marriott, I thought of giving the AU caterer some suggestions. Then I caught myself. I won't meet with the caterer anymore. I won't plan AU events again. This cutoff of our intense before can not be erased immediately or easily. For me it is difficult. For Richard, it is his lifeline. He is a fighter, and together we will make it. I know we will, but the days ahead are frightening for us both.

My heart is breaking for him. This man of great pride and power and privacy is being subjected to the most dreadful of humiliations, having to open up to any number of people about his problems. I am so upset and there is nowhere to go with my feelings. I don't know what his problems are. I just know he is deeply troubled. I heard him scream in pain with Dr. Malin. It was a cry I will never forget. When he came out, I looked to his face for an answer and found none.

By the time I came out of Malin's office, all the blood had left Gail's face. I hated being the cause of her distress and hated being unable to say anything to comfort her. But I had just been emotionally dismembered and couldn't find any words worth saying.

Dr. Berlin's office was as cluttered as Malin's was neat. Nearly every book on his crowded shelf dealt with child abuse. His black hair seemed headed in several different directions, and his energy and intensity were as immediate as Dr. Malin's were subdued. He was a big man with a big grin and shook my hand forcefully.

We sat down. Berlin is a man who cuts to the chase.

"Tell me about this, tell me about the calls." I thought I had just been through this with Dr. Malin. I felt like saying, "Can't you talk to your colleague?" Instead, I explained as much as I could about the calls. He said I could be admitted to their program, but that he had to make several things clear.

"As Dr. Malin pointed out, you are a patient here, not a scientist or a university president."

"Yes, I beg you to help me understand myself."

"That's fine. All we ask is truthfulness and cooperation." He assured me that all patients were treated confidentially. Then he said, "Tell me about your first sexual experience."

My eyes welled. I said, "Dr. Berlin, Dr. Malin just asked me about that and I explained it to him. Why don't we just leave it at that?"

"We will ask you many questions and do so a number of times."

"But I've already answered that. Why be redundant?"

"Would you stop trying to be in control? You are the patient. We are the doctors. Let us decide what is appropriate."

"Well, I don't know, there are some things . . ."

He leaned forward and rumbled out: "No, we are the doctors. You may be Dr. Berendzen on your campus, but we are the doctors here. Now, tell me about your first sexual experience."

I told him I couldn't see the point of going back forty years; I wanted to understand what had happened in the last four weeks. Berlin was gentle, but much tougher than Malin. He didn't have to repeat the question. It waited in his eyes, which focused directly on me. He seemed to be studying everything about me—my words, my gestures, my breathing. I wondered, who is this man? Why does he smile, wait, and then say, "All right, let's try it again."

For the next hour, I repeated the story, crying and sobbing as I had with Dr. Malin. I was ambushed by feelings that seemed to jump out of nowhere. I didn't think I had a tear left, yet out they gushed, as if from hidden springs. My eyes were stinging, and my throat dry. Once more, Gail could hear me sobbing.

At some point, Berlin said, "That's enough for now. Why don't you and your wife have lunch. Come back and fill out the admission forms in the business office. Then we'll take you up to Meyer 5."

What a relief to have that questioning over! I had never before met people like Malin and Berlin. Thank goodness I was finished with them. Once I was admitted, I thought I could begin to heal in a peaceful setting under supervision of some doctors upstairs. I didn't know how the Sexual Disorders Clinic worked or about the extensive resources of Johns Hopkins. What lay ahead of me, I could never have imagined.

Lunch over, paperwork completed, we followed Berlin to the fifth floor of the Meyer building, "Meyer 5," as it was known throughout the hospital. I learned that Meyer 5, a mixed ward, had in-patients from the clinic as well as other patients. When we got off the elevator, we arrived in a small vestibule. Berlin rang a bell, and the nurse on the other side of the door looked up, smiled, and buzzed us in. Gail and I looked at each other. "My God, it's a locked ward!" I thought to myself.

Later I learned it was kept locked to keep elderly or confused patients from wandering off, not to incarcerate the rest of us. But I didn't know that when I walked through the doorway the first time. In forty-eight hours I had gone from being university president to psychiatric patient in a locked ward. Most of the patients looked ordinary, like people in a shopping mall. A few stared blankly at the wall, and one or two had running monologues with themselves.

My room was small, with a single built-in bunk and a chair. There was a small counter and a few dresser drawers for storage. It resembled a dorm room. Patients in adjacent rooms shared a bathroom in the hall. I unpacked under the watchful gaze of a supervisor who told me to relinquish all sharp objects. They took my razor blades and anything with a point.

I couldn't believe it. Here I am locked in a ward with no sharp objects. Would basket weaving be next? I glanced at the mirror. It seemed out of focus until I realized it was a reflective surface instead of glass. Glass might break. Surely, I thought, I could put up with anything for a few days or maybe a week, even this.

Saying good-bye to Gail hurt. I was alone and scared. News of my resignation would be in the papers the next morning. Would the exhaustion story hold? I was anxious. However, the university had promised me confidentiality. With that protection, I thought that when I left Hopkins I could get on with my life. I paced the corridors of Meyer 5 to get my bearings. It wasn't an unpleasant place. Neat, antiseptic, and sparse, it felt like an orderly but Spartan office building or a new dorm.

Gail drove home alone. Throughout the trying day, she had put up a brave front, remaining her usual citadel of strength. That evening she told everyone who called that everything was fine. Later that night, as I learned months later, the preceding four days of fear and pain finally overwhelmed her. She went into our bedroom to put away clothes she had taken out but not packed for Baltimore. A pair of my pants had fallen off the doorknob. When she stopped to pick them up, she fell to her knees in tears and cried herself to sleep on the floor. She woke in the morning still clutching my trousers. And Sparky, Natasha's aging childhood dog, who was never allowed upstairs, was curled up beside her.

I went to bed that first night at ten P.M. The staff said they would get me up again at six A.M. I offered to set my alarm, but they said that was unnecessary. They would wake me. Despite my illness as a child, I'd never before stayed overnight in a hospital. I put on pajamas and got into bed at least four hours before my normal bedtime. How would I ever adjust to this life? I read through "quiet time" and was still wide awake when someone said "lights out" at eleven. Shortly, a nurse came in. She told me nurses would check me at least once an hour during the night. "When we come in at three or four in the morning," the nurse said, "we don't want to awaken you. If you are awake, please say so. We need a record of your sleeping pattern." She said good night and shut the door.

So much for privacy, so much for sleep. If they were going to get me at six, I had to get to sleep. But I was wide awake. My pillow felt like plywood, my bed was exactly my length. So I either bumped my head or dangled my feet.

Except for my wife, the attorneys, and the Hopkins people, no one on earth even knew where I was. I felt like an alien. It was the loneliest night of my life.

I thought of Gail, driving back alone to the big empty house. What had I done to my wife? My institution? What if my daughters found out, or our friends? My humiliation and shame weighed me down like cement. I could bear the feelings only because I felt confident that the real story of my resignation would remain private. After a few days of treatment, a week at the most, I'd be home. The police aspect, which was all new to me, still loomed large. I had no idea what it would bring, but I hoped it could be resolved quickly and quietly. If so, maybe Gail and I could take a long-overdue vacation and figure out where we go from here.

It all seemed frightening, yet possibly we could pull through battered but not beaten. Then I heard it. The scream. It made my bones shiver and my breath stop. "Let me out, let me out!" a voice cried. "This goddamn place is locked and they won't let me out! I'm perfectly sane and I should be out!"

These desperate, anguished screams echoed ones I'd heard when I visited my mother in the mental institution. Where was I—in her cell or my room? Was this the nightly ritual on Meyer 5—cries from an East Baltimore hell? I put the small pillow over my face to blot out the sound and felt like I would smother. The next morning, I learned that the screaming patient, who was not in the Sexual Disorders Clinic, had been moved to another floor. On that first night though, those stiletto screams made sleep almost impossible. Finally, I dozed off near dawn, to be awakened at six A.M. by someone wanting to draw blood.

I showered and had breakfast. On the way back to my room, a nurse said, "You're on this morning with the doctors. They would like you in the music room in ten minutes." The music room? It had an aura of nineteenth-century gentility. Since I didn't know the hospital routine yet, I assumed this would be a meeting to explain my treatment protocol.

I ambled into the music room, not expecting a cello and a harp, but completely unprepared for the blizzard of white lab jackets seated in a semicircle. One wooden chair stood empty in the center of the room. At least twenty people silently looked at me. Besides Berlin, I recognized Jo, the head nurse I had met yesterday, and Pam, a clinical social worker. Everyone else was a stranger. They shut the door. Someone motioned me to the empty chair.

What the hell is this? I soon learned that my weeping sessions the day before simply had been an admissions interview. Now the real work began. This was the meltdown.

Someone asked me the routine questions: my name, where I lived, what I did. Then I was asked if I had made some calls.

"Yes, I shamefully admit that I did."

"How would you characterize the calls?"

"They were wrong, inappropriate. I shouldn't have made them."

"Then why did you?"

"I don't know. That's why I'm here."

"What did you talk about?"

"Childhood sexual abuse."

"Why did you make the calls?"

"I was looking for information. I was searching for something."

"What were you searching for?"

"Something about why this happens."

"What happens."

"Sexual abuse of children."

"Why do you think a university president, a PhD, and a man your age would have such an interest?"

"I don't know. That baffles me."

Then from the back of the room came the soft but rumbly voice of Fred Berlin, who was nibbling on ice chips in a cup. In a steady and firm tone he said, "You are eight years old. Tell me about your mother and father."

I thought I would die, literally. I had told him something in private, something so horrid that I never wanted it revealed to another person. In all my life, I had told only two people—Malin and Berlin. Now he blurts this out!

"I don't want to talk about that," I protested.

"That's not what I asked. You had sex with them, didn't you?"

"Well, not exactly, I mean, sort of."

"Don't tell us about 'not exactly.' What were your feelings? Did you enjoy it?"

"I don't know."

"Were you scared?"

And so it went. The tears returned and I gagged again. He wouldn't let up. More questions; more tears. Finally, he finished. Thank God! Now, let me out of here. Then a woman spoke.

"Why did you join them?"

"I don't know. I walked in the house and heard noises. And some-one said 'Come here.' "

"Who said that?"

"Why is that relevant? I don't care to get into that."

Every time I put up a defense, they bashed it down. It was relent-less. I cried. They sat and stared. Someone said, "Could we continue please?"

"What happened at age eleven?" This time Berlin's voice boomed from the rear of the room.

"Why do I have to tell all of you? What are you trying to do? I don't understand where this is going."

"Please, let us do the questioning. We are trying to help you. What did you feel when you walked into that bedroom?"

Berlin would not stop. He was like a semi-automatic weapon, firing question after question.

"At age eleven, what did you do?"

It was incessant.

"Did you take off your clothes?"

"You got into bed?"

"What did you do?"

"How did you feel then? How do you feel about it now?"

"I don't know. I don't think I feel one way or another."

"You don't *feel* anything? Do you really *believe* those words?"

"Well, no, but I mean I'm just telling you about it. I'm not feeling anything."

"Not feeling anything! Is that why you've used up a box of Klee-nex?"

"I don't know, it's hard. You're a group of strangers. I'd never talked about this at all before yesterday. I thought I was here to understand something about the phone calls I made."

"Fine. Let's get on with it. Now, you are eleven years old . . ."

Back we went, over and over what seemed like every nuance of every second.

How did you feel? What did you feel? Tell us about the feelings that went through your mind? What did you feel afterward?

"Lost and confused."

"Why did you feel confused?"

"Well, I was a kid and I didn't know what was going on."

"Why didn't you tell someone?"

"Who would I tell?"

"Didn't you talk to your dad?"

"Please, I don't think I can talk about this anymore."

"Why don't you want to talk about it?"

"It's private. It's not why I'm here."

"Richard, we want to help you, and to do that, we need to talk about many things. Now, do you remember talking to yourself at the time? What did you say?"

"I'd say I don't know why this is happening."

"You can remember that?"

"Now I can, this sort of made it come to the fore."

"Is your father still living?"

"No, he died."

"When did he die?"

"June 1, 1987."

"How did he die?"

My voice got strangled in whispers.

"Talk to us about that, Richard. Tell us what you felt."

I told them the facts of his death, that I had been at the university when the call came, and that Gail and I had left at once for Dallas. I talked until I got to the point of going into the middle bedroom again. I had to stop. I couldn't talk any more. I knew I would vomit if I continued.

The room was silent. Everyone stared at me. I was chilled, numbed. My innermost self felt splayed and displayed before strangers. I knew they were trained professionals, but that didn't matter. They were strangers. People I had never seen before had invaded every corner, every fissure of my soul, like a conquering army. I couldn't take any more. I said so.

"I'm sorry, but I think I'm going to be ill if I talk anymore. I can't, really, I can't. . . ."

Berlin jumped in. "Okay, well, thank you, that's enough for now.

Why don't you walk around a bit, go back to your room, do whatever you want to do. Lunch will come soon. We have a full schedule for you, and we'll talk to you more a little later on."

I walked out of that room feeling like my legs were feathers, my heart, a stone. Room 505, which had initially seemed so Spartan and unfriendly, now looked like a refuge against a battering storm. I sat on the edge of the bed, my head in my hands.

What the hell was happening? That day, Wednesday, word of my resignation would be in *The Washington Post*. What about the police? Gerry Treanor, my new lawyer, told me over the phone that they wanted to search our house and talk to Debbie, Natasha, and Gail. Oh, God! Clearly, the girls would know about the calls. What shame I had brought on my innocent daughters. And on Gail. It hurt to imagine her anguish. AU had been her career, too. Worse, it hurt me to think that she had no one to share all this with. Over the years, we had comforted and consoled each other in times of pain. Now I was the cause of it. Would Debbie and Natasha worry or wonder why they couldn't see me? And what about me—would anything be left after Hopkins finished? I had come to the hospital for help. I never expected what I'd found so far.

My life had exploded before my eyes like the Challenger spacecraft. Everything I had ever been or known was scattered into small pieces over an ocean of shame. I knew I could not go through another session like the one that morning.

I stood in line in the hallway and waited my turn for the pay phone. I called Gail. She said she was okay and would come to see me later in the afternoon. I said the morning had been unusual. I did not elaborate. She had more than enough to cope with. Also, I was still protecting my secret. The doctors, and now the staff, knew about my childhood abuse, but I would never tell anyone else. They were medical professionals; they'd keep it confidential. Although I couldn't see the therapeutic reason for going over and over something that had happened forty years before, I would trust their judgment. However, nothing could make me tell my wife or daughters or anyone else.

I asked Gail to bring some pictures of our family and my pillow—as silly as it seemed, this was something in my life I could still fix. I wanted to make my quarters more like home. Of course, I intended to be there no more than three or four days. A few hours later, when I saw Berlin in the hall, I asked him how long he thought I should stay.

"A week. Count on at least a week, although it could go to two."

"Two weeks! Dr. Berlin, I couldn't possibly stay two weeks. You don't understand how much I've got to do."

"Right now you have to deal with yourself first. You said you would take this seriously."

"Yes, but . . ."

"Then I hope you'll stay the length of time we recommend."

When Gail arrived, I told her I might be there longer than we'd planned. I said I was sorry. She asked me about the morning. I said it was hard, not because they were mean, but because they were unrelenting. It was an incredible experience, but I said I didn't want to go into details.

We made small talk, which after the intensity of the morning, came as a blessing. Did you bring this, do you need that? I pinned up the photos Gail had brought, and I also tacked up a copy of "If," the poem by Rudyard Kipling that my father gave me on my twenty-first birthday. Even though the poem is hackneyed, it meant a lot to me. I carry a folded copy of it in my wallet. Aside from its wisdom, it was one of the few things my father ever gave me.

After the press ran the story about my resignation, Gail said the phone rang incessantly. She told everyone that I was exhausted and the time had come to make a change. She said I was fine but needed rest. If anyone asked why I didn't wait until after commencement, about six weeks away, she said, "Well, Richard just decided this was best." Although Gail didn't bring it up, I knew how much she hates to lie, even if it's to protect someone she loves.

After she left for Washington, a nurse told me it was time for "group." Time for dinner, time for a break, okay. But "group"? My blank reaction prompted an explanation. Apparently, some of the doctors and all of the patients got together every day to talk. I hadn't mingled much with the other patients, because I wanted to keep my anonymity. I didn't want anyone to recognize me or connect me with the university.

So it was back to the music room, with its small broken electric organ. I found a chair in a corner. Berlin came in along with about eight patients, a student nurse, and a woman from occupational therapy. They asked us to introduce ourselves.

Someone might say, "My name is Alan and I have a sexually related problem." Berlin would probe. "Just tell us what it is."

"Well, the police have said I might have sexually abused young girls."

Berlin's baritone voice filled the room. "Well, did you? We've talked about it before and you've seemed evasive."

Alan shrugged and looked at the floor.

"We'll come back to you."

"My name is Bob and I'm here because of theft."

"Why did you steal?"

"I needed money to pay prostitutes."

When I heard that, I thought Bob must have a compulsive desire for sex. He was bright, handsome, and his smile hinted that a good laugh was close behind. Berlin followed up.

"Why did you pay prostitutes? You wanted sex?"

"No, that wasn't it. I didn't have sex with them."

"What did you want them to do then?"

"I wanted them to abuse me."

"How would they abuse you?"

"All kinds of ways. Physically, verbally. There was extreme pain."

"You felt you had to do this?"

"Yes, I really did."

"What specifically did you have them do?"

"It had to do with fire."

"Go on."

"I paid them to burn my back."

"How did they do it?"

"With a candle or cigarette lighter."

"And what did they do while that was happening?"

"Chew gum, watch TV, smoke."

Unimaginable. I looked at him and tried to comprehend what he said. He looked so ordinary that his story became even more shocking. Soft spoken, gentle. Yet he paid prostitutes to burn him! Why?

When my turn came, I said, "My name is Richard, and I am here because I made some inappropriate phone calls."

Berlin said, "You said these calls were inappropriate. What was the subject matter?"

"Child sexual abuse."

"Is it true you talked with a woman?"

"Yes."

His dark eyes canvassed the room. "Any of you have anything to say?"

"Yeah, a few years ago I got into trouble for making obscene phone calls." The patient described how he had tried to seduce women over the phone. And he had had erotic fantasies that sexually aroused him. He looked at me and said, "So, was that your thing?"

"No, not at all." Just the thought made me feel vile.

"Did you feel relieved or stimulated afterwards?"

"No. I felt peace for an instant, and then revolted by the content of the call. Then I pushed it out of my mind completely and went back to work." The room was quiet.

Dr. Berlin interrupted the stillness. "Richard, this morning you met with some of us and I think it would be useful to discuss that here. Can you tell us what happened with you sexually as a child?"

"Oh, my God!" I said, "Wait a minute! I talked to Dr. Malin yesterday and to you and then this morning with all those people in white lab coats, but this is going too far."

"Fine. Now what was the role of your mother and father in it?"

A patient interjected, "I was sexually abused by a parent, too." He talked about feeling ashamed and degraded. I hated hearing him talk, but felt that as long as he did, I wouldn't have to. He had been abused by his father and brothers and uncles.

Bob, who paid prostitutes to hold flames against his skin, talked emotionally about his family. He told how, as a child, his father had degraded him physically and verbally. Berlin asked him how he'd felt at the time. Through tears, Bob replied, "Like trash. Like worthless trash."

"Like filthy, worthless trash that should be destroyed?" Berlin asked.

"Yes," Bob answered.

Berlin came back to me. "Richard, tell us what happened with your mother." He kept coming back to the word feelings. "Now how did that make you feel?"

113

"I felt ashamed."

"Did you ever enjoy it?"

Silence. Then I said, "There might have been a moment or two."

"So why do you suppose you enjoyed it?"

"I don't know."

"Do you feel that your body betrayed you?"

"Maybe I betrayed me."

"How do you feel about it now?"

"Ashamed."

"Why do you suppose it started?"

"I don't know."

"Why did it stop?"

"No idea. It just ended."

"Why?"

"I don't know."

"Did it ever bother you?"

"Yes, for a time, but I stopped thinking about it."

"Did it ever come back in your mind?"

"Yes. There was an incident at my father's funeral."

"Why don't you tell us about that."

"But Dr. Berlin!" I was trying not to let my exasperation show too much. "I've gone through that already, and I had a really hard time saying it."

"Okay, well, why don't you just try."

I started the story all over again. As hard as I tried to control my feelings, I failed. The crying and choking returned, as if I were telling it for the first time. I felt so embarrassed. I wasn't sitting in a room with trained professionals in white lab coats. I was with guys in jeans and T-shirts, many in their twenties and thirties. Mostly, guys who punched a time clock for a paycheck.

I was burning with embarrassment. Berlin kept asking me about my feelings. "How did you feel then about what happened to you?"

I said I had felt confused, hurt, and mystified. I wondered if I were the only boy who had ever had this happen. I felt alone.

"Alone?" Berlin replied. "You felt alone? You just heard a man talk about being abused. Maybe you had no one to talk to at the time, but you were far from alone in your experiences or your feelings. Do you think you are the only person that things like this ever happened to?" He and the group questioned and probed. I thought they'd never stop. Finally, my turn ended.

I later learned that was how group worked. Each man introduced himself, and then the group questioned him for at least thirty or forty minutes. (Women go to the Sexual Disorders Clinic for treatment, too, but when I was there the patients were all men.) I learned quickly that the patients could be as tough—if not tougher—than the doctors. They didn't waste time on jargon.

"Bullshit!" I remember a patient shouting to another patient. "You're telling me you were alone with that pretty young girl and didn't get turned on? You expect me to believe that you never did anything to her? Come on."

Board meetings and faculty meetings can be contentious, but not like this. It was all new to me. After a group session, the patients would have dinner and then in the evening they'd play checkers or work on jigsaw puzzles. To me, puzzles always seemed like a waste of time. Nonetheless, I worked on a few at Hopkins. Despite the gut-wrenching honesty of the sessions, once they ended, everyone became friendly and supportive.

One night I played chess with a man who had abused young boys. There we sat playing this ancient game of concentration and planning: I, a former university president, and he, a rough-hewn unemployed laborer. He wiped me out in eight moves! It reminded me of the Ingmar Bergman movie in which the protagonist plays chess with Death. It turned out that this patient had been an amateur chess champion. Another patient was incredibly funny and could do parodies of everyone on the staff. His talent rivaled a David Letterman or Billy Crystal. The police had sent him to Hopkins because of his sexual disorder, which I learned came from intense abuse when he was a child.

Patients shared bathrooms. The next morning, as I went to shower, I glimpsed Bob, the man who paid prostitutes to burn him. He was toweling off. His back looked like the rugged, cratered surface of the Moon. It was covered with thick, uneven, and grotesque scars. Despite the shock of those scars, I knew they were minor compared with his inner scars. In the next few days, Bob's back became a strong metaphor to me about the truly devastating effects of childhood abuse.

After breakfast at about eight, doctors would make rounds. Then we would be called one by one into the music room for a private session, which might last for twenty to forty minutes. Sometimes people watched soap operas or game shows while waiting their turn. Michael Landon seemed to be on the screen morning or night. Meanwhile, I stood in line to use the pay phone in the hallway.

By day two, Gail found that some people weren't buying the exhaustion story about my resignation. This didn't bother me initially, because the rumors said I was moving to a higher post. Some reporter apparently contacted MIT, which was looking for a new president, to see if I had been tapped for that job. *The Washington Times* ran an item that said I might be appointed secretary of education. I was flattered and relieved that the rumors were so positive, with no hint of scandal.

Everything felt upside down. Here I was listening to a child abuser be given the third degree in a group session while rumors chased around Washington that I might be picked for a cabinet appointment. Unbelievable! Meanwhile, I maintained my anonymity with the patients. The clinic used no last names with patients, and although they would pull every detail out in group about your illness or your childhood, they avoided any discussion that would expose the patient's current life. (Patients' names used here are fictitious.)

I called Gerry Treanor to see about the status of the police investigation. He said he had told them who I was and where I was, and that I intended to cooperate fully. I asked Gerry to tell them that I had never abused a child and never would. He said he had. Nevertheless, they had to investigate everything. They made it clear to Gerry that they were doing so.

One afternoon a detective went through our house with Gail. Gail said afterward that he was sensitive and courteous, given the circumstances. Still, he went room to room, from basement to attic, opening closets and drawers. Gail handled this with her characteristic aplomb. While her husband searched for himself in a psychiatric ward at Johns Hopkins, she escorted a detective who searched for evidence of child sexual abuse or child pornography. This woman, hailed as one of Washington's most respected and genteel hostesses, now was showing her home to a stranger investigating for perversions. It made my soul ache.

For the next few days at the clinic, Berlin bore in on me like an oil driller exploring a deep, subterranean lake. The individual sessions in the music room were the worst. Mine lasted an hour. Although never rude or cruel, Berlin was unrelenting, and also uncanny in his ability to pound and drill on the most sensitive issues.

Over meals, Berlin was the chief topic among the patients. "How did he treat you today?" Just as students often respect the toughest professor, the patients unanimously respected Berlin. They all knew he brooked no double-talk and would go for the nerve. Yet they also knew he gave his all to help them. And I knew he was helping me, too. But, Lord, what a painful process.

One day, after my morning session with another snowbank of white lab jackets, a doctor who frequently attended these meetings introduced himself: Paul McHugh, chairman of the Department of Psychiatry and Behavioral Sciences. He was chief of psychiatry at Hopkins. He had questioned me before I knew who he was. After we were introduced, he assured me that I would be treated like everyone else in the program, but he also wanted me to know that he had taken a personal interest in my case because it was one of the very few in which a professionally prominent man publicly had to confront the effects of childhood abuse.

McHugh, like so many of the others, asked me about anger. Was I angry at my mother? "No," I said. Each time, though, I felt I'd given the wrong answer. The silence that followed was heavy with disbelief. "Surely, you must feel some anger."

"At this age? After all these years?" I tried to find a way to put my feelings into words. "My mother had so many psychiatric problems that it doesn't make sense to be angry with her. Now, in addition, she's old and confused. I can feel disappointed or hurt, but not really angry."

"But Richard, at the time, weren't you ever angry?"

"At the time? Yes, I was angry, I was intensely angry. I don't know how to describe the anger I felt. It was an absolute, hating, detesting fury." I explained to the doctors that as a boy I was angry; as a teenager, confused; and as an adult, disappointed.

The questioning and probing was not confined to the scheduled sessions in the music room. Several times a day, a nurse or social worker would approach me in the hall and say, "Let's talk."

For the next hour, the two of us would go over the same information again. When did the abuse begin? How did I feel? How had I coped with it? Each interrogator would have a different slant. As a child, was I angry at my father? Why did my mother abuse me? Why did she stop? How had I dealt with my memories? Why did I make the calls? Why did I risk so much? Why did I feel so driven to make them? What did I feel when I did?

Sometimes the approach baffled me, and I did not understand the repetition. I asked Berlin to explain. He said, "Well, first, stop trying to be the doctor. You've always operated on a cognitive level. We want you to respond on an affective realm and begin to deal with your feelings."

I told him I wasn't sure what he was talking about. "That's part of your problem," he replied. "When was the last time you had a frank conversation with a man?" I had to think awhile about that. I had male friends when I was growing up, but I couldn't remember having a personal conversation with a man in years that wasn't somehow work-related.

Berlin looked at me. "You're always trying to maintain control. You need to release, let loose. Remember what I told you when you arrived. You're not a university president here, you're a patient. Don't try to figure out what we're trying to do. Stop intellectualizing. Just let go."

I had been at Hopkins for about five days when the doctors asked me if I had ever heard of Post Traumatic Stress Disorder.

"Vietnam vets have that."

"Do you think it's a disease they catch?" Berlin asked.

"They're the only ones I know that have the problem," I replied.

"You don't think anything like that could have happened to you then, do you?"

"I wasn't in Vietnam," I explained, amazed that Berlin had found yet another line of irrelevant questioning to pursue. What had this got to do with the calls, which, after all, were why I was at Hopkins?

"No, you weren't in Vietnam, but you were in the middle bedroom." Berlin explained that sexual abuse could lead to PTSD if it was never resolved. This time, I let my exasperation show.

"You guys have these broad, generic theories to categorize people. Maybe they apply in some cases, but this one doesn't apply to me."

"Then can you tell us why you made those calls?" Berlin asked.

"No, I can't. That's why I'm here."

"Then can you tell us what's wrong with the possibility that this is a case of Post Traumatic Stress Disorder?"

"But, Dr. Berlin, you're never going to convince me that something from so long ago could come back, bother me now, and cause me to do what I did."

"So you assume that once you have something under your control, you can control it forever?"

"Precisely."

"You speak so authoritatively. Will you please define PTSD for us? Tell us exactly what it is and how it works?

I felt like an undergraduate in an oral exam. "Frankly, I'm not sure. I've heard the term before, of course. But I guess I don't know that much about it."

Berlin grinned. "Don't worry. You soon will."

At last, it was Friday night. Weekends were supposed to be more restful around Meyer 5. I asked if I could go home and was told no. However, I could get a pass and spend a few hours on the weekend away from the hospital with Gail.

As it turned out, that first Friday night the patients had a party. One of them organized it. We sat in the music room and drank sodas and munched chips. The week before, I had been in a tux dining with prominent donors. Now I was drinking Diet Coke and eating Doritos with child molesters and other psychiatric patients, while my wife was home telling people I'd resigned because of exhaustion and was away resting. Because I'd been scheduled to speak in California, many people thought I was still there. Instead, I had a view of the rooftops of gritty East Baltimore from a "music room" with some sturdy chairs, a warped Ping-Pong table, and a broken organ. I felt lonely, ashamed, and scared.

Even so, there was comic relief. Each afternoon, the patients held their own meeting with a staff member sitting in. They discussed common concerns. Who left the teapot on? Would a patient who could get a pass bring back a pizza? Different patients chaired the meeting. One day they asked me to do so. Later, a delegation came to see me. The spokesman was a manic depressive who wasn't part of the clinic. "We've talked it over and would like to ask if you'd serve as president of the patients? All you'll have to do is run our meetings." "Sure," I said, as I quietly smiled at the irony.

A few evenings later, a patient in the clinic challenged me to a Ping-Pong game. Bored beyond belief and desperately wanting to think about anything beyond myself, I agreed. The last time I'd played was in grad school, when I'd made the mistake of taking on a young student from China who crushed me 21 to 0. I resolved to do better against the patient. To my amazement, the score turned out 21 to 0 in my favor. My slams to the sides of the table seemed especially effective. My momentary pride in my newly found skill dissolved, however, when I learned that he had severe tunnel vision.

Gail came the next afternoon. On this my first outing, we went to the splendid Watkins Gallery. It seemed a million light years from Meyer 5. Even though I had been at Hopkins only a few days, it felt strange to be back in the mainstream of people and traffic. This past week had been unlike any I had ever experienced in my fifty-one years. After the gallery, we wandered through Little Italy and had an early dinner at a restaurant near the harbor. Gail asked about my treatment. I just said it was rough, but provided few details. I didn't want her ever to know about my mother.

Actually, on that first Saturday I felt a modicum of relief. I thought that I had told everyone I would ever have to tell. It had been grueling to go over and over the memories at the clinic. Now with that behind me, I felt calmer. We had such a lovely afternoon; I wanted to hold on to it.

Instead, I went back to the empty music room and started to tinker with the organ, determined to fix the damn thing. By the time a nurse told me it was "lights out," the organ worked.

Gail returned the next afternoon, and we went out for Chinese food and saw the sequel to *The Gods Must Be Crazy*. The audience laughed throughout this eccentric and goofy film, but I couldn't. My eyes kept welling up with tears. "What's wrong with me? My humor is gone. I can't smile or laugh."

"Give it time, Richard," Gail said with a worried look. I hugged her when we said good-bye. "Happy Birthday, Bunny. This sure was one helluva way to spend it."

Gail had brought me a few books and a Bible, as well as a stack of letters. Even the simplest notes were heartening. "Sorry to hear you are resigning. Sure wish you well. . . ." I spent the rest of the evening working on a jigsaw puzzle with two other patients. It was of blue skies and blue water, one big blue blur. The pieces all seemed the same size and shape. I turned them around and around to find a fit. The pieces were there, but I just couldn't put the puzzle together. It was maddening.

The physical tests at Hopkins were as thorough and comprehensive as my therapy sessions. One day it was a CAT scan of my brain; the next, a complete neurological exam; then a battery of psychological tests.

Suddenly I was launched into space-age medicine and having a three-dimensional photograph made of my brain. Then I was wired up to have my central nervous system scanned. The psychological tests were more sophisticated than I had imagined. Some of the tests were timed, while others were more probing and analytical, designed, I learned later, to search for antisocial or psychopathic tendencies.

Never before had I received such medical attention. I felt vulnerable but also fascinated. Every few days they hit me with some other medical test, a routine seemingly with no end. After about a week, Berlin said they wanted to give me a sodium Amytal interview. "Fine," I said. "I've had plenty of interviews before."

"No, no. This isn't like anything you've done," he replied. Sodium Amytal is commonly known as truth serum, he explained, and it is administered intravenously.

Over dinner, an experienced patient told me, "You'll feel like you're a little drunk." That explanation helped me not at all. I never drink, because I don't like the taste and because to me the buzz many people crave symbolizes loss of control. I agreed to the sodium Amytal interview. I was ready to try anything. The drug, they told me, would make me so relaxed that I might remember things my conscious mind had blocked.

So at three the following afternoon, a nurse put a needle in the back of my hand and a clear liquid started dripping into my bloodstream. The room was dark, with the drapes closed. In a few minutes I began to feel drowsy, then intense sleepiness moved in quietly like a dense fog, as I lay comfortably on my bed. Three doctors, including Berlin and Malin, a nurse, and a medical secretary who took notes watched intently.

Berlin's voice seemed to beam in from space. "Richard, close your eyes and relax. Totally relax. Do you hear me? . . . Okay, I want you to count back slowly from one hundred."

I remember beginning. I felt wonderfully relaxed. "One hundred . . . ninety-nine . . . ninety-eight . . ." The numbers came in an even and predictable rhythm. Then I got to "sixty-one . . . sixty . . ." and I could not remember what came next. After a long pause, I said "fifty-nine . . . fifty-eight?" I wasn't sure anymore.

"That's enough." Berlin was ready to begin.

I know this because I've listened to a recording of the session. Without the tape, I wouldn't have recalled much of anything. At the time, I just wanted to fall asleep. I felt lethargic and resented the questioning, which kept me from the deep sleep I so desired.

Berlin began. "You are eleven years old. Tell me how you felt after being with your mother in the middle bedroom?"

My sleepy voice replied. "I was confused. Why was she doing this to me, what did she want?" When I started nodding off, Berlin would rouse me.

"Were you mad at your mother? Tell me as much as you can remember."

"Yes, I was very mad at her. I hated her. I loathed her. I hated, hated, hated her. But sometimes I loved her. She was there when I needed her. She took care of me when I was sick."

"Tell me some more about how you felt about your mother. Did you feel guilty being with her?"

"Yes. I . . . I . . . I . . . never understood why she did those things to me. I never wanted my friends to find out."

And on it went, with my voice becoming thicker and thicker as I slipped farther into a sleepy fog. Then he asked about the phone calls.

"Tell me about the first call. Why did you make it?" He probed me about how the McMartin case had attracted my attention.

Then he asked, "How did you feel when you talked to someone?"

"Curious."

"Did you feel aroused?"

"No."

"Was it an exciting event?"

"No. It wasn't like that."

"What was it like?"

"I wanted information."

"But you were a scholar, a university president. Why didn't you do research? Read books? Find a specialist to talk to?"

By now my voice sounded like a recording at the wrong speed. "I did a little reading. But I wanted to talk to someone who might give me real insights."

"But you could have found that in a book."

"I didn't want a lot of jargon. I didn't want academic bullshit!"

On the questions went. "Why do you suppose you made the calls in the afternoon?" "What time of day did your mother call you to the middle bedroom?" And he probed deeply about my feelings about my mother, then and now; about my attitudes about child abuse generally; and more about the calls. Finally, I drifted off.

When a nurse woke me, I felt like I was in a deep stupor. She said it was time for the out-patient group. Still too dazed to walk alone, a nurse helped me to the elevator.

About thirty men attended the group, many of whom had been in-patients before and now came back for regular follow-up sessions. They ranged in age from twenty to seventy. Some looked like they worked in corporate suites; others in factories. I was still so groggy that I chose a corner chair and hunched against the wall, hoping for obscurity and a nap.

A woman therapist led the session. Attendance at regular weekly out-patient meetings is required for everyone in the Sexual Disorders Clinic. It helps to reinforce behavioral change and keep individuals accountable to their toughest peers, other patients just like themselves.

With my eyes closed, I was slipping into tranquil sleep when Berlin's voice crashed like a thunderclap.

"Richard, you're five years old. It is Christmas Eve and your mother slaps you so hard you spin around and slam against the wall. In fact, you have rheumatic fever at the time and are quite sick. It is a special occasion for you even to be out of bed. How did you feel?"

All eyes locked on me. But I couldn't form any words.

"Richard, come on, you're awake now."

"How did you know that?" I stammered out.

"Never mind that. How did you feel? Do you remember the incident?"

"It's coming back."

"Tell us about it."

"It was a special night because we were setting up the Christmas tree with my dad. I was five or six years old. My mother was arranging everything. She decided we would sing Christmas carols. I said, 'I don't know any Christmas carols and I don't like to sing!'

"She told me, 'You *will* sing a Christmas carol! Sing, now!'

"I couldn't sing because I didn't know the words. Kids used to learn them in school, but I wasn't in school. She screamed, 'Sing "Silent Night"! I want you to sing. Sing it, goddamnit!'

" 'But I don't know it. I can't sing it.' "

I had started to cry, and did so again when I recalled it that evening at Hopkins. The entire group of patients and doctors waited until I regained composure. Then I went on.

" 'At good homes, on Christmas Eve they sing Christmas carols, damnit, that's what we are going to do here!'

"Her hand came out of nowhere like a giant's fist. My head snapped back, and I reeled across the room, smashed into the wall, and slumped to the floor. I was too scared to stand up. She raged over me. 'Get back into bed. Get out of here!' "

Like a gust of air on dying embers, telling the story made it burst into flames inside me. For a few moments, I felt scared and tense all over again. To a group of strangers, I had told something I had not even remembered until Berlin reminded me. It had sprung forth completely formed, a smothered memory unleashed by a clear fluid leaked into my veins. Clearly, he'd learned about it through the interview, although I couldn't remember any of that.

"You're very tired, Richard," Berlin said gently. "If you want to go upstairs now, that's fine."

I fell into my bed as if it were a grave. This was one of the few nights at Hopkins when I had a deep sleep.

Berlin and the other doctors met with me the following day to listen to the tape. They described it as a classic sodium Amytal interview.

What I said under the drug corroborated what I had told them previously. They used it to help me understand Post Traumatic Stress Disorder.

Still, I had a hard time accepting the premise of PTSD—that unresolved trauma can surface with full emotional impact decades later. To reexperience trauma can be as devastating the second time as the first. This cut against everything I believed. I had survived and achieved on my own, through determined self-control. This self-control was integral to my being. Now the psychiatrists told me that something from forty years earlier could override my restraints. I balked at the notion that traumatic memories could affect behavior.

"I'm a man who always has been under control," I tried to explain. "I've known what I was doing with my life. You like to fit people into your neat theories. This time it doesn't work."

"What makes you different from everyone else? Why should you be impervious to trauma? If you had such great self-control," Berlin asked, "how come you made the phone calls?"

"I don't know."

Berlin talked about combat soldiers, rape victims, and survivors of hurricanes and plane crashes. Traumatic memories, he stressed, cannot be willed away. They can be resolved only if they are dealt with. If left alone, they are like a fault line in a person's life. One day, for obvious reasons or not, stress that has built up along that fault line suddenly can erupt. In the ensuing earthquake, a life can be reduced to rubble.

To understand how PTSD could relate to me, I first had to realize how severe my childhood trauma had been. Clearly, breaking the silence and talking about my past had overwhelmed me emotionally. When I dissolved with Malin and Berlin during the admission interviews, I realized I was traversing sensitive ground; the subsequent sessions reinforced that fact. But I had not equated what happened between my mother and me to the experience of a marine in Vietnam or on Normandy beach seeing his buddies blown apart. Nor did I equate abuse to rape.

My emotional stability had depended upon denial. I had to minimize the experience to survive it. It had happened; it was past. That was then; this is now. My mother was sick, but she wanted the best for me and tried hard to provide it. I believed my parents really loved me. What child doesn't?

My trauma happened incrementally. It wasn't like a car accident or plane crash. That wasn't my car, smothered beneath a collapsed freeway. I never walked away from a flaming wreckage in a field. Such calamities I would have recognized as real trauma worthy of attention.

My focus had been on the intellectual aspect of my abuse. Why did it happen? What did it mean? Could I predict when it might happen again? Was this supposedly good for me? Why did it stop when it did?

The doctors and staff at Hopkins made me excavate old feelings, chipping and chiseling out my past like a lost city buried beneath forty years of repression. I was annoyed to find how much was there. At first I remembered nothing about how anguished I had felt. Then a fleeting image would unlock a scene and frame a memory. After that, I dealt with the pain and hideousness of what had happened. Before I could understand myself, I had to confront those feelings. Nothing I have ever done has been harder.

But why do it, especially given the pain involved? I cooperated with the doctors, answered all their questions, and let myself be grilled in group sessions by strangers. I needed help, so I put my trust in the program. Even so, for days I could not understand why I needed to remember my feelings from forty years earlier. Eventually, I started to appreciate that if you don't experience the pain in your life, you'll never fully appreciate the joy. By denying one, you deny the other. To survive my childhood, I had stopped feeling a lot of things. I didn't feel a range of emotions. I lived almost exclusively in my mind. That adaptive behavior had to be unlearned.

This awareness came to me gradually, on the installment plan. During my first weeks, I could not see where Berlin and company were headed. I thought I was wasting my time and doing so with intense pain. For someone who once figured out how many minutes he'd live, to waste time was sacrilegious.

Yet I also realized how much I was learning—about myself, about therapy, and about an array of physicians and patients. As I listened to the sodium Amytal interview, I began to comprehend that I had lived two lives: the one I remembered and the one I forgot. When the memory of trying to sing "Silent Night" came into focus, I started to connect with my past as I never had before. Horror, fear, humiliation, and shame were no longer just facts; they were feelings.

Over the years I had achieved a certain arrogance. I had worked hard, been successful, and felt I could handle any problem in my life. At the hospital I began to learn that, like everyone else, I was vulnerable. Men don't like to think of themselves as vulnerable. We solder our achievements into a shield. Then, armor in place, we are ready to take on the world. Wrong. I had a false sense of security.

A day or two after the truth serum interview, I was to take a polygraph test. An experienced polygrapher unconnected with the hospital, who worked with police departments and the FBI, would give the lie detector exam. The results would go to my doctors, my attorneys, and the police.

Dr. Malin drove me to my appointment with the polygrapher. We almost didn't make it. When we got to the hospital garage, we found that his car had a flat. That delayed us nearly two hours. We made it to the beltway in time for bumper-to-bumper rush hour traffic all the way. By the time we arrived, it was five P.M., and we were several hours late. I was so tense I thought I couldn't say my name without looking like a liar.

Malin and the polygrapher met privately for forty-five minutes, which gave me more time to worry. Gerry Treanor and the polygrapher talked by phone. They picked questions the police might want to ask.

As nervous as I was, the scientist in me found the experience fascinating. I sat in a chair facing a wall and was hooked up to the polygraph machine—so called because it takes many graphs at once. Bands encircled my chest to measure my breathing. Other wires would monitor my heart rate, blood pressure, and galvanic skin response. The machine itself, about the size of a suitcase, sat on a desk.

Polygraphs are based on fear. Nature designs our bodies to protect us. If you're walking late at night and hear a frightening sound, your body will react physically. Adrenaline will pump into your bloodstream to give you speed and agility; your eyes will dilate to aid your vision. This happens automatically. In fact, you can't stop such reflexes. And that is the key to a polygraph test.

When a threatening question is asked, your body will respond before you can speak. The polygrapher, an old-time Virginian who had seen it all in police work, explained the procedure to me. Then he told me how the questions would work.

"I'm going to ask you some background questions. Then I'm going to probe whether you have ever sexually abused or molested a child, whether you've had a desire to do so, and whether you had sexual relations with your mother."

He told me that the "hot" questions would be phrased so I should answer no. Also, he would ask some slightly ambiguous questions, but I should answer them either yes or no, even if I was unsure. Shades of gray or "on the other hand" didn't work here. Only yes or no.

He said he would give me four separate tests, and that it was useless to try to outsmart them.

A wire looped one of my fingers, others circled my chest, while still others monitored my heart rate and blood pressure. It was like something out of the movies.

"Is your name Richard Berendzen?"

"Yes."

"Were you president of The American University?"

"Yes."

"Before 1985, did you ever lie to an authority?"

What a curious question. What's an authority? A teacher about an assignment, a librarian about an overdue book? Nonetheless, he wanted a quick, clear answer.

On the first test, he told me when a hot question would come. If you know in advance the fourth question will be key, your body will anticipate it physiologically.

"Have you ever molested a child?"

"No."

More general questions led up to the next hot one, about my mother sexually abusing me.

"Did you lie when you said that your mother sexually abused you as a young boy?"

"No."

Then he asked me to pick a number between five and ten. I chose eight. Then he told me to say no to every question about the numbers.

"Did you pick six?"

"No."

"Seven?"

"No."

"Eight?"

"No."

This untrue reply is what children might call a white lie. It seemed inconsequential to me.

On the first test, I was nervous, wondering if my body would betray me. My heart rate was 120. But I remembered the saying Gail quotes: "The truth shall set ye free." I was telling the truth and I had nothing to fear. So I relaxed. The pattern of questions remained similar for the first three tests. On the fourth one, though, I didn't know when a hot question would come. A hot one followed another hot one, then several routine queries, and then more hot ones.

"Richard, have you ever molested a child?"

"No."

"Have you ever wanted to have sex with a child?"

"No."

"Is this year 1990?"

"Yes."

Finally, the polygrapher unstrapped me and went into another room to study the tracings. When he returned, he showed me the tracings and said he found no sign of deception.

"We've been through this now four times, and the results are completely consistent."

It struck me how different the tracing looked when I told the lie about the number eight. Although I wasn't telling the truth, I had no stake in the question. Nonetheless, the graphs had jumped appreciably. Odd to see my body outsmart my mind. On the hot questions, the graphs remained steady. As grueling as this experience was, it gave me one hell of an education.

Back at the hospital, the questioning continued. Later I learned that they were testing various hypotheses and, as with the polygraph, one reason they questioned me over and over about the same material was to detect consistency and patterns in my responses. They also wanted to see my response to a variety of questioners. And so there was Jo, my main nurse; Astria, an older nurse from Europe; Lisa, a young occupational therapist; Pam, a social worker who wore a suit instead of a lab jacket; Bernie, a male nurse with a beard; Dr. Hansen, a Scandinavian physician; and many others who stopped me in the hall.

One afternoon, one of the nurses, Olivia, took a new tack:

"Richard, we've heard that when you were in charge of the university you took risks, but always protected the school. Logically, you should have a similar attitude about yourself. Making phone calls as you did was very risky. Are you a risk taker? Do you do risky things?"

I said I didn't. She asked if I liked to go mountain climbing or sky diving. "No." Did I drive a sports car? "No."

"Why, then, do you think you engaged in such high-risk behavior?"

"I don't know. I didn't sit down and do a cost-benefit analysis. The calls were a compulsion. I never even considered the downside."

An unusually perceptive person, Olivia then asked, "Why didn't you take the safe approach and just call one of the 900 sex lines? You would have had no problem."

"Because I wasn't after sex. I was after information."

In time I got used to the persistent questioning and even became more comfortable talking about myself. Or so I thought until Dr. Berlin fired a missile into my heart. "Richard, have you discussed what you've told us with your wife?"

"No, absolutely not! Nor do I intend to."

"We think you should."

"No! I will not budge on this. She has no need to know. It's like with national security and 'need-to-know' criteria. She has no need to know. This was all decades ago. Leave the tombstones alone. Besides, my mother is still living and we still have to deal with her. It would upset Gail too much."

"Why is that?"

"It might make her uncomfortable. It might change the way she thinks of me. . . ."

"Really, why?"

"She might think there's something wrong with me."

"Do you?"

"No. But Dr. Berlin, I will not do it. There is nothing to be gained. Don't try to push me on this."

"I thought we agreed when you arrived that you would cooperate fully and would let us decide your therapy."

I was getting angry. I rarely get mad, but I felt a flush of real anger. "Look, Dr. Berlin, I think you'll agree that I've been extremely cooperative. You order up a CAT scan and I lie in a cold tube for an hour and a half. You drain every fluid from my body to check this or that, and then you and half of Hopkins' staff beat me apart in these damn therapy sessions. At some point, enough is enough! I will *not* tell Gail a thing."

"Yes, you will. One other thing—we want you to draw a picture."

"Swell! Now, it's art therapy."

"Think about how you felt back then and draw pictures of yourself now and of your mother."

"I suppose you want me to use crayons?"

"Or markers, whatever."

"Listen, Dr. Berlin, I never went to kindergarten. I can't color or stay inside of lines. So skip me on this one."

"Let's not make this a big deal. In your spare time, I'd like you to try it."

I was so relieved the discussion about Gail had ended that I went to find felt-tip pens. My primitive pictures reflected that I hadn't drawn since fourth grade, but I was surprised how involved I became in my pictures.

I drew myself in profile. When I showed the drawing to the staff, they asked why I drew it that way. I explained that, as a novice artist, I could sketch a profile but a full-face view went beyond my talent.

Despite that logic, they asked if it wasn't also true that I had drawn only half of myself? Where was the hidden Richard, the half we couldn't see? Intriguing interpretation.

The drawing of my mother was a jumble of confusing colors. Red, her favorite color, predominated, interspersed with purple, orange, and black. Her picture showed no person, but rather a disarray of light, with explosions of color alongside patches of black. Pictorial gibberish.

"Have you talked to Gail yet?"

"No I haven't and I'm not going to."

"Well, we expect you to. Also, we want you to write a letter to your mother. Of course, we won't mail it. We want you to pretend you're eleven years old, and write what you would have said to her then if you could."

How could such smart doctors come up with such dumb ideas? Since arriving at Hopkins, I had begun to revise my old low opinion of therapists. But this made me wonder if my initial assessment hadn't been on target. So all right, I'd try to humor them. If I cooperated on the small things, like a letter and drawings, maybe they'd ease up on the big issue—my talking to Gail.

Eventually I sat down with a legal pad. It seemed blank beyond belief. I stared at it for quite a while. Over the years I had always prepared my own speeches, and was not used to being at a loss for words. But now I was.

I sat in a plain room in a huge hospital, a grown man, trying to reconnect with a little boy in the middle bedroom long ago. Finally, the words began to come, slowly at first, and then with a speed that surprised me. And so I wrote to my mother:

Why did you do all this? Why the first time and the other times? Did you ever wonder what *I* was feeling? Or thinking? Did you care? What did you want from me? And why did you pick me? Was it because you could dominate me completely? Was this your odd way to express love? Did you think that you had to teach me EVERYTHING. . . .

I'm confused. What you did in your bedroom revolted me, scared me, excited me, disgusted me, and confused me. Do you realize the hell you made?

I'm trying hard to understand you. From the time I was a child, you told me repeatedly that above all else—pride in self, devotion to country, or love of God—a boy must love his mother. Well, I guess I love you. But mostly, I pity you because of your sickness and I loathe you for your shouts and slaps. And most of all for the middle bedroom. . . .

I remember the ghastly sex. It was unemotional, uncaring, exploitive, and wrong. It was as cold and dark as that darkroom. And you left me afterwards just as alone as I'll be someday when you and Dad die. With no brothers or sisters, I'll be the last of our direct family. And I'll be alone—alone just as I was whenever you finished with me and left the room. There I sat, alone, in the middle bedroom—alone with my shame, fear, and confusion. Sometimes I felt that I had died and my corpse was in the bed. Sometimes I wished it were. . . .

Your son, Richard.

While I wrote, my room became dark, as afternoon gave way to evening. I stared out into the empty street and across at another ponderous Hopkins medical building. I felt vulnerable and insignificant as I filled the yellow pages of the legal pad. For years I had believed that temples of science and learning, like the building across the street, could provide nearly all the security and answers I would need. Now I knew there was more to it than that. When all is said, more courage lies in the human heart than in any book.

I finally realized the time had come to talk to Gail. Despite constant pounding from all the staff, I had avoided the issue for days. My marriage was my fortress. I felt I was being forced to tell my wife things that might undermine my most precious relationship. As much as I resisted the idea, somewhere deep inside I knew I could not hide from the most vital person in my life. The next time Berlin asked "When are you going to talk to Gail?," I looked him in the eye and said, "Tomorrow."

That night I barely slept. Fear and apprehension were riptides that carried me farther and farther away from safe shores. I got up early and tried making notes on a pad, but I didn't get far. Earlier in the week, Olivia, who knew I was avoiding talking to Gail, asked if I was afraid she would divorce me. Actually, that thought hadn't entered my mind. I was simply afraid our relationship would change. How could it not? How would Gail feel about me once she knew? Would our intimate relationship stay the same? I think I felt like a rape victim who is afraid her husband will see her as damaged if he knows the truth. Dawn was close when I finally decided I could not write or rehearse a speech for Gail. Whatever came out of my mouth was what I'd say. And I knew I couldn't tell her only part of the story, because Berlin and the others told me they would talk to her afterward, to provide her with support. I appreciated their sensitivity about her, but I also knew I had no way out. They would check what I said. I had to tell the full, blunt story.

Gail arrived that afternoon for what she thought would be a regular visit. We went into my room and I sat on the bed, my back propped against the wall. I asked her to sit on my only chair, directly in front of me.

"I have something I need to talk to you about. The doctors insist that I do. I didn't intend to, and frankly, I don't want to do it. God, I wish I didn't have to, but now I know I must. Undoubtedly, you are wondering what's happening to me and why I'm here."

Gail was quiet. I continued.

"Well, I need to go back in time, all the way to my childhood. I don't have to explain how strange and unpredictable my mother can be. The doctors said I had to tell you in detail about all this. In fact, they offered to be in the room when I did, but I said that wasn't necessary and it wasn't how we did things. I wanted to talk to you in private. They want to help you, if you need them. I said you might talk to them afterward. It was up to you."

By now Gail sensed the tornado on the horizon. In spite of my effort to be calm and reassuring, I was wound like a clock about to break. She'd never before seen me so serious or so nervous. I talked for the next two hours. I started with the incident when I was eight years old and found my parents in bed together, and continued through the episodes in the darkroom and the middle bedroom. I told her about the physical abuse as well—about the yardstick and having to pull down my pants and be beaten until I couldn't breathe.

Even though I had talked and talked about this with my psychiatrists and in group, even though I had probed every crevice in my head and heart, I still could not tell it without crying.

Much of the time I thought the words would never leave my mouth. My lips felt welded together. My eyes were wet, and my throat dry. I talked and cried, cried and talked. I told Gail how I had fallen apart when I went into the middle bedroom to get the suit for my father's burial. I explained how the phone calls started very infrequently and then, in the weeks before my resignation, happened more often. I finally ran out of words. There was nothing left to say, and the room was as silent as a tomb.

A few seconds went by, then a few more. Gail looked at me. She was not crying. Her voice was even and strong.

"I have three things to say. The first is that I love you now more than I ever loved you before. I can't believe you have done so many wonderful things in life with all of that inside you. Second, if your mother were in this room right now, I would kill her. If there were a button to push to eliminate her from the face of this Earth, I would push it without guilt or fear. And third, you were a victim as a child, and now you are a victim again—all this because of that original abuse."

For me, her first words were the only ones I needed to hear. I had never heard Gail speak with rage, but she did now about my mother. This, from a woman who will shoo a moth out a window so she doesn't have to kill it. As a boy, I had never thought of myself as a victim. These were just things that happened to me. I think I felt more like a survivor.

When Gail said she loved me, I felt as if I had just been freed from a crushing boulder. I could actually feel the physical change in my body. I felt indescribable relief. I felt restored.

We held each other and cried. I murmured, "Thank you for being you, for being here, and for being with me. Somehow, and only God knows how, we'll make it through."

Gail's relief may have been even greater than mine. At last it all made sense to her. She could put the phone calls into context. My resignation and hospitalization momentarily broke the circuit of our marriage. Now that Gail knew the truth, however, we reconnected and felt a surge of love, and for me, peace.

For Gail, the most immediate feeling was a rage unlike any she had known before. She later told me that her trip home burned that rage into her memory. She slammed into the house, stalked upstairs, grabbed up the pictures of my parents she had thought might help me grieve, and threw them into the back of a metal cabinet. Then she started to pace. She walked upstairs, around the bedroom, then back downstairs, through the family room and the living room, and around the dining room table. She didn't stop to change clothes, eat, get a drink, or listen to the answering machine. She walked to outdistance her rage. She walked in defiance, as if to prove to a cruel sergeant that she would not give in, would not be defeated, and would not tire of this trek. She didn't cry or call anyone. She walked alone, oblivious to the time from seven at night until two in the morning.

When I saw her the next day, I thought she looked tired and asked her if she slept poorly. No, she said she walked.

"Walked? Where did you walk?"

"In circles around the house."

She didn't realize until she stopped that old Sparky, our dog, had followed her for seven hours. He didn't leave his bed the next day. Gail described her feelings that night as a rolling rage that would engulf her if she stopped, just as surely as a tidal wave would sink a moored ship.

My night brought such blessed relief that I finally slept soundly. The next morning I told the staff that apparently they knew what they were doing after all. My corrosive distrust of therapists had dissolved. Finally, I genuinely appreciated the good the profession could do.

That night, I attended another group session, like the one after the sodium Amytal interview. Of the thirty men there, a few clearly had lower IQs. Clinically, they would be called retarded. Nature may have retarded their minds, but it didn't hold back their spirits. These men moved me deeply. What courage they showed! And what struggles they fought. The program had overwhelmed me and I'd been consumed with my own problems, despite being blessed with a normal mind, a good education, and a loving wife and daughters. Here, with these brave men, I met dignity and determination. Their minds may have been too limited even to see their own valor, but it humbled and inspired me.

For some of the men, the group became the one stable thing in their lives. Donald, who had lived in numerous homes for the retarded, had a sex drive he could not restrain. It had to be controlled. Yet he also desperately wanted companionship. His residence did not permit him to date or have any social interaction with females. So he manipulated people, both male and female, into having sex with him. He was accused of rape and wound up at Hopkins.

The doctors, who could be so tough with me, were gentle with Donald. They tried to teach him values, and the group members— men from vastly different socioeconomic and educational levels— affirmed the doctors: "Donald, you must respect people and not just think of your own desires." The discussion moved from generalities to frank specifics.

Phil, who had served time as a pedophile, said friends had invited him for a weekend visit. He wanted to go, even though the couple had a ten-year-old daughter.

The woman therapist who led the session told Phil that he must not put himself in a high-risk situation. He agreed in principle, but hoped the group would give him permission to go. He was sure he could control himself.

"Cut the crap!" said a man near me. "You're interested in this girl, aren't you? I know where you're coming from."

"I really think I'd be fine with her."

"Do you ever think about her?"

"Yeah, sometimes, a little."

"Have you had erotic thoughts about her?"

"I might have, maybe once or twice in the past."

The group crashed down on Phil. Unanimously, they said he absolutely should not go. When he quietly disagreed, the therapist, who had been silent through all this, said, "Phil, I agree completely with the group. I want it clearly on the record that you are *not* to go. Tell your friends that you are not going. Then call me by noon tomorrow and give me a detailed report about your conversation. Next week, the group will expect you to describe what you did instead of going. Do you understand?"

"Yes, ma'am."

The burly man next to me had a mosaic of tattoos on his forearms and the girth of someone who had downed too many. With missing teeth and a deep raspy laugh, he would pound the table with his hamlike hands when someone said something he liked. He spoke about being abused as a child.

"I was very young the first time my parents had sex with me. They liked to watch. My mother watched me with my father, and my father watched me with my mother. Then they made me do things with my sister so they both could watch. I was so ashamed."

Tears ran down his stubby cheeks. His bass voice cracked. And from his barrel chest came a groan that froze my skin—it was the muffled scream of a small boy echoing through time.

I could have been eavesdropping on a hidden chamber of my own heart. The anguish, revulsion, humiliation, and shame he described could have been me talking about myself. He spoke of the profound and inexplicable confusion that dogged him ever since he was abused. Then an accountant spoke up and said he felt the same way. And a man who worked in a religious order said he did, too. Money, status, and achievement may have separated us in society, but in our world we were men with the same wounds and similar scars. Families can be the deadliest of biological weapons.

For men who have been abused, part of the deep conflict is the enjoyment. Because of our anatomy, it is impossible to disassociate ourselves completely from the abusive sex while it happens. To a boy, with little understanding of anatomy, erection implies at least desire, if not consent. So even if a boy's mind says he doesn't want this to happen, his body sends a different message. Ultimately, that triggers enormous turmoil.

Berlin then joined the session and asked the big man beside me how he felt when he was that little boy. His tears turned into a torrent. "Do you know what it's like to be totally humiliated and feel you're worthless scum, that you're of no value, that your only worth is to play in someone's sick game? There was nowhere to hide."

The woman doctor said to another man, "Ben, your situation was similar. How did you handle it as a boy?"

"I didn't. I didn't say anything. My brothers and sisters were forced to do it, too. I couldn't tell the school. I didn't think they'd believe me. Besides, the other kids would have found out. Do you know how cruel kids can be with each other?"

Berlin asked him how long he had suppressed the memory.

"For quite a while. It would come back, but after a while it would go away. Now it makes me sick when I think about it."

"Well," Berlin responded, "we'll have to work on that. You need to learn how to deal with the memories constructively."

"Carl, have you ever abused anyone?"

"Yes."

"What did you do?"

"Kind of what was done to me."

"Why did you do that?"

"I don't know."

"Are you doing it now?"

"No."

"What made you stop?"

"The police and this program. You put me on Depo-Provera, and I come here all the time and talk."

"Are you ever going to abuse anyone again?"

"No. I'm pretty sure I have it under control now. And you're on my case all the time."

Conversation continued like this for the next two hours. Each man, it seemed, had a shocking, terrible story to tell. All the men who had been abused were over age twenty-five and one was at least seventy. I don't think I fully understood the choke hold on life that early trauma can have until I heard that gentle old man talk about his abuse as a child. His memories were razor-sharp and sounded hours rather than decades old. I asked Berlin later if many of his patients had been abused themselves as children, and he said between 50 to 80 percent of them had been. He pointed out that most people who have been abused never abuse anyone else; statistically, less than a third do, and those are the ones who wind up in programs like Hopkins.

But there are too few such programs. Most offenders are locked up but never treated. Once released, many of them abuse again. No way exists to "cure" sex offenders, but with proper therapy, medication, and support, they can curb their impulses and stop hurting people.

Unfortunately, help exists for only a small fraction of the people who need it, with almost no programs available for female abusers. California, with fifteen thousand jailed sex offenders, has just one experimental program, which treats forty-six of them. Studies show that treatment can work. Although it is not an exact science, treatment does sharply reduce recidivism.

Many things touched me that night, including the candor and honesty with which the men spoke and how much they wanted to change. Many of them came from childhoods far more tortured and brutal than mine. Yet they still had hope. As humiliated and ashamed as I felt, as scared and uncertain as I was about the future, my life could have been dramatically worse. I went the way of most survivors and never physically abused anyone. But what if I had gone the other way? Oh, God! I said a quiet prayer of gratitude that night.

I realized that—while I loathed the crimes and sins these men had committed—as I listened to them I responded to their humanness. To most people—indeed to me only ten days earlier—these men were the truly unforgivable, the unlovable who deserved whatever they got. Now, having heard their stories and seen their pain, I found I could hate the sin yet still love the sinner. It sounds biblical, but this came from no sermon. It is simply what I learned. What an education this was!

They were learning to rely on each other. They might disappoint themselves, but they couldn't let down their group. "Your friend Bob asked you to go to that porno movie with him last week. The group decided you shouldn't go. Tell us what happened."

"I told Bob that my group said I couldn't go."

To an outsider, it sounds childish, but that's part of the point; it is. These men had to learn the rules of behavior that their own disturbed and violent upbringings had never taught. In effect, the group functioned as a caring but strict parent who wants to know where you're going, with whom, and what time you'll be back.

My talking to Gail was a pivotal point in my treatment. It removed my last mask. I felt relieved and more optimistic than I had since my resignation. Since Gail now knew everything, I also had an ally. Even though she had never left, I felt my best friend now was truly with me. For me, the group sessions now became more therapeutic than interrogative.

Each day I checked in at my office with either Joan or Roberta from the pay phone in the hall. When I called on the morning of April 19, Joan said Ed Carr was chairing the president's weekly cabinet meeting. The meeting was routine, Carr's presence was not. Joan said they had been behind closed doors for several hours.

I assumed they were discussing the transition. I asked Joan to tell Carr that I was on the phone and see if I could say hello. I just wanted to keep in touch. A few seconds went by and then minutes lapsed. Other people on the floor who wanted to use the phone shot impatient glances my way.

Joan came back on the line. "I asked him, but he said he would not talk to you."

"What?"

"He refuses to take your call. I don't know what else to say. Carr looks like death itself."

Completely baffled, that afternoon I called Don Myers, the university's vice president for finance. He didn't sound like himself. Guarded and terse, my old colleague had no smile in his voice. He seemed exceedingly nervous. We talked only briefly.

Then I called Milt Greenberg. We, too, had another cautious, inconsequential chat. Now I sensed that something strange was in the air. Later that afternoon, I called Don Triezenberg, the vice president for development, who also was in charge of university relations and admissions. His secretary put me on hold. I waited fifteen minutes. Scowling patients who wanted the phone muttered to themselves.

When the secretary came back on the line, she said he was still on another call. Would I hold? Another fifteen minutes elapsed. I'd never waited this long for anyone. Don and I had worked together for sixteen years. When I had arrived at the university, he was an assistant to the dean. He had impressed me immediately. Don had a doctorate in physics and was a few years younger than I. He became my protégé, and over the years, his rise paralleled mine. He became my closest colleague, and we developed deep mutual admiration.

When Don finally came on the line, his voice was lifeless. He said nothing about the long delay.

"I'm editing a letter at the request of Ed Carr. He asked me to look it over. It's his letter."

I asked him what it said. "I'm not at liberty to divulge that yet," Don replied.

"What? I don't understand."

"It's Ed's letter. After I show it to him, perhaps I can share it with you."

He said he would see Carr in a few minutes, and I said I'd call back.

Now my adrenaline flowed. I called Joan again. "Something strange seems to be going on," I began.

"I know. The vibes here are weird. Carr looks incredibly tense. They're going to meet again in your office later this afternoon."

I was supposed to go to a group therapy session, but I begged off without an explanation. I waited an hour before I called back. I felt cold and clammy. My stomach tumbled, as Triezenberg finally took my call.

He sounded starchly matter-of-fact. "Ed Carr has prepared a letter, potentially to go to the press. It's finished and he said I could read it to you over the phone. I'll drop off a copy for you. You still live at the president's house, don't you?"

"That's right," I replied. "What's the letter?"

It was addressed "To the American University Community." With an emotionless voice Don read:

"The last two weeks have been a difficult time in the life of our university. Each of us has been trying to come to terms with the implications of the sudden resignation of the president of The American University, Dr. Richard Berendzen. Now, it is important that we as a university move forward. I ask each of you to join me as I rededicate myself to the continued progress of The American University."

I stopped breathing.

"On April 6, 1990, I first became aware of the allegation of improper behavior by Dr. Berendzen. I want to emphasize that these allegations concerned personal actions of Dr. Berendzen and were in no way related to his role as president of the university. No one else in the university community was in any way involved in the alleged improprieties."

My heart raced, or maybe it stopped.

"Despite the private nature of Dr. Berendzen's problems, it was concluded that his resignation would be in the best interest of the university so that the university did not become involved in their resolution. I deeply regret the necessity of this action, and my thoughts have been with Dr. Berendzen and his family during this difficult time. . . ."

The letter went on to say that my resignation would be effective at the end of the academic year and that I would not be returning to campus. It talked about the transition, the future, and Carr's hope that when the university celebrated its centennial, each member would be "even prouder" to be a part of The American University family.

"Don, what's happening?"

"Well, we've had inquiries from the media. People are still curious about why you left. This letter won't go out unless the press is about to come out with a story."

"Don," I said, feeling caught in eddies of panic, "Don't you understand? That letter will be the hot button that launches World War III, if not for the university, then for me. Why do this? It sounds like you are all trying to distance yourselves from me. I'm very concerned."

"Rest assured that I have the letter. It won't go out unless the media is on the verge of doing something."

"Well, at least it's in your responsible hands, but I don't like this. I plead with you not to blow us all apart."

The conversation ended. Don had said he would drop a copy of the letter at the house later that day. It was Thursday. I called Richard Marks who said he'd call Carr.

Friday morning the pay phone rang. A patient came down to my room and said it was for me. Impossible. Almost no one knew I was there. When I got to the phone, I found Joan on the line. Gail had given her the number because Joan said she had to speak to me urgently. All she knew, however, was that I was somewhere in Maryland.

"A trustee just called me. He has talked with Ed Carr who told him about a letter. The trustee said he thinks the letter will go to the press today at eleven A.M."

My heart pounded so hard my entire left side ached. I said I'd check into it and thanked her for calling.

I rushed to find Berlin and told him everything. He took me into a private room and urged me to calm down. His strength, which could feel intimidating when he questioned me, felt reassuring in my panic. My former battering ram became my fortress.

"Dr. Berlin, you've got to understand that if this letter comes out today with talk of alleged improprieties, my world will explode. I must resign at once from the Budget Commission and every other board, committee, or group I belong to. I can't do that from a pay phone. If there's an empty office, could I call from it?"

I was hyper, with every neuron in my body on overdrive.

"Richard, slow down. Don't start taking on the burdens of the world. You are here to take care of yourself. Stop thinking you must resign from everything all at once. We don't even know for a fact that the letter has been released. Calm down. It's almost time for group."

I did go to the morning session, which helped me to focus. It actually proved therapeutic to talk this through with the other patients. We were a strange bunch. Never could anyone have convinced me that a child molester could have said anything helpful to me, but I was wrong.

Despite the hideousness of their deeds and the awfulness of their own lives, or maybe because of it, these men genuinely responded to my pain and heard the anguish in my voice. I still didn't divulge my identity, but they saw my fright that something about me might appear in the press.

"Hang in there," one of them said. "An article about me appeared in the paper, and it really hurt."

These men, who had been strangers to me only days before, and who had led such troubled lives, genuinely seemed to care about me. Paradoxically, my key university colleagues, who had worked closely with me for more than ten years, expressed no concern. It was as if I had fallen off the planet. The roar of silence felt hostile.

I talked to Gail that afternoon, Friday. I kept checking in with my lawyers. They hadn't been able to pin down anything on the letter. That weekend, prospective freshmen would visit campus with their parents. It seemed unimaginable to me that Carr would release the letter then, but I didn't know what might be imminent in the press.

Gail found a copy of the letter under our door Saturday morning and took it to Richard Marks. Marks and I talked on Saturday. He said that although parts of the letter troubled him, he didn't see what could be done at this point.

Marks suggested that maybe a few key trustees might like to meet with the doctors on Sunday, the following day, and have an update on my situation. After all, no trustee even knew where I was, much less how I was doing. At that stage, the doctors couldn't give a conclusive report. They could, however, give a progress report. I approached Berlin, who was working that Saturday, with the idea. He said a meeting could be arranged for Sunday afternoon, if the trustees were willing.

Early Sunday morning, Marks spoke to Tony Morella, the university's general counsel. He divulged to Tony where I was and suggested that a few trustees might like to meet with my doctors. Marks also asked about the letter. Specifically, why the reference to "alleged improprieties"? How did this square with the pledge of privacy the trustees had given me?

Morella promised to get back to Marks later that day about both the meeting and the letter. Gail came over that afternoon, and we went to a shabby park near the hospital and sat under a tree. The day was as beautiful as my mood was forlorn. The big sturdy tree I leaned against felt comforting, like the large oaks in our yard that had given me such solace. With my head in Gail's lap, I slept for two hours.

When I got back to Meyer 5, I called Marks. The news stunned me. Tony reported that the executive committee of the Board had held a special meeting that afternoon officially to accept my resignation. They would not meet with my doctors. There was nothing to discuss about the letter because it already had been sent. People would receive it on Monday.

I felt like I had taken a cannon round in my chest. "Once the letter arrives, all hell will break loose."

"I'm sorry, Richard," Marks replied.

"Don't they even wonder what happened to me?"

"I guess not."

"But I've worked with some of them for sixteen years!"

"Richard, I don't know what to say. I'm sorry."

"Look, I resigned in writing many days ago. That's history. Don't they care about me as a person?"

Marks replied, "Richard, that's not their focus right now."

I'd been cut off. Abandoned. All bets were off, but we didn't know why. It seemed the trustees wanted to distance themselves and the university from me, thereby minimizing the impact of any press that might appear about me. As an administrator, I fully understood the need for the institution to be cautious. But, damnit, what about me as a human being? And why were they afraid even to find out my condition?

By Monday morning, I felt like a condemned man whose final appeal had been denied. The letter would arrive today. Then the Washington press corps—perhaps the toughest and most penetrating in the nation—would be on the scent. They'd have the story soon. Or if they already had it but were hesitant to run it without corroboration, Carr's letter would provide it. The story would be out within hours. My reputation would be ruined, my career over. The thought of attending group that morning seemed absurd. I told Berlin that, but he insisted that I go. "I don't want you just sitting alone," he said. "Now more than ever you need human interaction and comradeship. There will be plenty of opportunity later for private introspection." So I went. Never in the past would I have admitted fear to another man, let alone panic. Now I did.

I had not slept the night before and barely could bring myself to eat. The doctors offered me more medication, but I refused. I took only a small dose because I didn't want to be groggy the next day. Berlin tried to steady me, to no avail. I felt paralyzed by dread. When you feel as if you are about to die, knowing someone will attend your funeral doesn't matter much.

My sleep was nightmarish. I would doze off, then awake in twenty minutes with a jolt. The clinic had a "lights out" rule: Except to go to the restroom, no one could walk the halls or go to the TV room. Nurses were on call if you needed help; otherwise, you were to remain in your room. I counted the minutes until I could call Gail from my cellular phone. It's reception was poor, but we couldn't use the pay phone until eight A.M. I knew our newspaper would be on the doorstep earlier than that. Gail answered immediately.

"It's here and it's on page one, above the fold. The headline says: 'AU President's Resignation Clouded, Letter Points to Allegations of Improper Behavior.' "

I couldn't speak. Gail continued.

" 'American University president Richard E. Berendzen, whose abrupt departure this month baffled students and faculty, resigned in the best interest of the university after allegations of improper behavior, according to a letter released yesterday by university officials.

" 'The letter, dated Friday and signed by Board of Trustees chairman Edward R. Carr, did not specify the nature of the allegations, but alluded to their private nature and said they concerned personal actions. University officials refused to elaborate.' "

The article continued at some length, saying my whereabouts were unknown. I could not be reached for comment. It gave a summary of my career at the university, and said I resigned "from exhaustion." It added that the university decided to shift gears because of suspicion at AU and in the media about the real reason for my departure. Rumors were so rampant, the article explained, that the trustees decided to write the letter.

The red flag was up. The story would spill out soon. When Berlin arrived on the floor, I told him what had happened. This husky man, who had bashed down my every defense, squeezed my arm, looked me squarely in the eye, and said, "Richard, you're a good man. You're a good father and a loving husband. You've lived with pain and yet you've survived. And you'll survive this, too. We'll be here to help you." Most of Tuesday, the staff tried to hold me together.

That afternoon I made another trip to my special, quiet place of repose. Several days earlier I had asked if the hospital had a chapel. I made my way through a maze of corridors, to find the chapel tucked behind a children's zoo of stuffed animals. It became my refuge. That Tuesday, like many times before, I sat there alone and thought and meditated and prayed.

Gail had been besieged by reporters at home when I first resigned. Although the majority were sensitive and responsible, a few were not. People popped up on our lawn at odd hours. Gail rigged sheets over the kitchen windows after people peeked around the blinds. We knew the story in the *Post* would unleash relentless press inquiries. So we decided that Gail would fly to Boston at once to meet with Natasha, who was approaching her freshman year final exams. We worried that reporters would get to Natasha before Gail did. Our fear was well founded. As it turned out, someone who had an early edition of the *Post* called Natasha at her dorm at midnight and asked about her father's "alleged improprieties." Natasha didn't know what that meant. So he gave her examples—things like stealing the university's money, or drug abuse. She was shocked. The reporter went on, "Look, I can save your father. But you have got to tell me everything." Natasha hung up. A woman also called, who started the conversation by saying, "I really like your father and want to have his side of things. So tell me all you know." To Gail and me, vultures were preying on our daughter.

Gail and Natasha went to a coffee shop near her dorm. Gail told her that I truly was tired, although not exhausted. There was more to the story, though. Terrible things had happened to me as a boy. I had been abused, which had led me to make phone calls I shouldn't have made. I was getting help and everything would be okay. Natasha, who had listened intently throughout this difficult conversation, seemed relieved.

Gail then met with her mother, and for the first time unburdened her sorrow. Her mother was compassionate and supportive. Gail, who inherited much of her integrity from her mother, had her strength renewed.

Afterward, Gail flew back to Washington to talk to Debbie, who came by our house. She told Debbie what she had told Natasha. Debbie's immediate response was, "Is that it? I had visions of him having tubes up his nose and being hooked up to machines. I've been terrified." She'd imagined scenarios far worse than what had actually happened.

I called home and spoke briefly to Gail. Then Deb came on the line. I was nervous. All I could get out was "Hi, big girl. How are you?"

"Dad, I love you, I'm with you. I'm so glad you're okay. Gail told me everything. Don't doubt my love for a minute. If your body were hurting, people would send you flowers, but if your mind is hurting, they throw bricks."

I couldn't talk. For a minute or more, I stood mute—in gratitude and pride—there at a pay phone on Meyer 5.

Next I called Natasha. "Hi, Tasha. Mommy told me she met with you. Are you all right?"

"Yes. She explained everything. My friends are calling and coming to my room to say they support me."

"I'm glad of that," I tried to console her. "I'm truly sorry for all this, Natasha. Please know that I love you dearly. This may get rugged for a while. But we'll pull through it. The doctors are taking good care of me. I'll be okay. So don't worry. Do you think you'll be all right?"

"Yeah, I'm fine," she replied. "Actually my friends and I don't quite understand why this is such a big deal. But anyway, I'm okay, although I hope those stupid reporters go away."

"They may not for a time, Natasha. I hope no one will bother you too much. Try to be strong. I know this may be hard going."

After I had talked with both girls, I felt relieved. They sounded fine. As a parent, you think you know your children. Then sometimes they come through so resoundingly that you see them with new depth.

Soon, though, I sank into depression. I knew things would get worse. The story of "alleged improprieties" was like bait thrown off a fishing boat to draw sharks. You feel their presence before they strike. That night felt like churning dark water.

Sometime around one A.M. Wednesday, I dozed off, only to wake up at three-fifteen A.M. Three hours and counting until I could call Gail and ask her to read me that day's *Post*.

Florine Adora Harrison,
my mother

My mother and I,
when I was three
years old

CHICAGO·1933

Earl Berendzen at
the Chicago World's
Fair, on one of his
few trips out of
Oklahoma until his
marriage

My father
helping me keep
my balance

My mother and I in
Portland, Oregon,
during World War II

My father
and I around the
same time

My fourth birthday

My tenth birthday,
on the front porch of our
home in Dallas

My annual Christmas ritual: Awaken, put on a suit, pose with (but do not touch) the unwrapped gifts on display, change into play clothes, and then play with the gifts—all of which came marked from my mother, not from Santa Claus or my father.

A snapshot
taken by my mother

Piano practice beneath the
photo gallery

My mother and I when I was
ten years old

The house where I grew up as it appeared in 1991. The trees
planted in the past are now fully grown and the screen door is torn
to let in the neighborhood cats.

The fort I made for
my high school Latin
class. My father
came up with a way
to keep the blocks
from crumbling.

Catching a fly
at age ten

At age eleven, with a different view of the world

I paced in my small quarters, four steps turn, four steps back. Around and around I went. Someone checked in every hour. I refused more medication. The agitation I felt was overpowering. Never had I experienced anything like this. When I first heard the words "Come here" and when I entered my father's room to get his burial suit were monumental moments in my life, but they caught me unaware and unprepared. Now I had hours of anticipation. Each hour was like a log thrown onto a burning pyre. The flames grew hotter and hotter.

The minutes crawled after six. I was a prisoner of the clock. Six-twelve . . . six-thirteen . . . six-fourteen. Then I punched in the familiar numbers. Gail knew it was me.

"It's on page one again. I hate to have to read this to you."

"Go ahead."

"Are you sure you're ready?"

"Well, if the world knows, so should I."

" 'Obscene Phone Calls Are Traced to AU President.' "

"Oh, God!" Sweat poured off my head. My pulse raced. My veins felt like they'd burst.

Gail's voice was quiet but steady.

" 'Richard E. Berendzen abruptly resigned this month as president of American University while Fairfax County police were investigating obscene phone calls that led directly—and unexpectedly—to the president's private phone, informed sources said yesterday.' "

I gagged and threw up on the floor. I couldn't speak, so, after a pause, Gail kept on reading.

" 'The investigation began several weeks ago, when Fairfax police received several complaints, some of them from people employed in daycare or babysitting-related jobs, about dirty calls, according to an informed source.

" 'The source said that the caller in question, in telephone conversations with the adult women daycare providers, made inappropriate or sexually oriented comments about children under their care.

" 'Berendzen has not been charged with any crime.' "

"Gail, wait a minute. I've got two daughters, a wife, students, the university, and on page one of *The Washington Post* it says I've made sexually oriented comments about children? Oh, God! My God . . ."

She asked me if I wanted her to go on. I didn't but I did. I gagged so much that Gail stopped. "Richard, are you all right? Should I continue? Should you call a nurse?"

"No. Go on. I've got to know what everyone else knows." I had to hear even though it was like sticking my hand in acid. I wanted to pull it out, but part of me wanted to leave it in. I slumped to the floor, the cellular phone in my hand.

When Gail finished the article, she softly said, "Richard, I love you." Her voice quivered. She sounded on the verge of tears. "I know this is so hard, but I love you."

"But what about Debbie and Natasha? What will they think of their dad?"

"They'll love you. Don't worry. They'll be okay."

"And what about our friends?"

"If they're our friends, they're our friends. If they're not, they're not. You are the one I care about."

"Bunny, I love you. But I've got to hang up. I want to call Gerry Treanor."

I didn't tell her how sick I felt. I feared I might be having a heart attack. After splashing cold water on my face, I sat for a moment with my head to my knees. I tried to regain some composure.

Reaching for the cellular phone, I called Gerry.

"Not good," I said.

"Not good," he replied. "I'm really sorry, Richard."

"What do you think is going to happen?"

He said he didn't know, but he would talk to the prosecutor. I should let him worry about the legal matters, and I should take care of myself.

I hung up, because I could barely breathe. My glasses were fogged with perspiration. My head was pouring like a fountain. My wet clothes stuck to my clammy body. "Oh, Lord," I thought. "I *am* having a heart attack."

I wobbled from my room to the night desk. The nurse jumped to her feet.

"My God, what's going on here? What happened to you?" She had me lie down, and took my pulse and blood pressure. She felt my brow and put smelling salts under my nose.

"I was talking to my wife, and she read me this article about obscene phone calls, and it's on page one of *The Washington Post.*"

150

"Wait a minute. You said you were talking to your wife?" The nurse thought I was delusional.

"Where is your wife?"

"In Washington."

"Not in your room?"

"No, not in my room." They had patients who talked to the walls. The nurse gave me a quizzical look.

"I talked to her on my phone."

"What phone?"

Then I knew I had blundered. I showed her my cellular phone. She said this was against the rules.

"But I've got to have it! You don't understand. Dr. Berlin will let me keep it, I'm sure." The phone was my lifeline. I couldn't get through this crisis if I had to wait until eight A.M. to use the pay phone.

She said she was going to get me some juice. She came back in ten minutes with both the juice and Dr. Berlin, who was followed by an entourage.

He asked me about the newspaper article and how I felt. I said I thought I would die. He told me I had to relinquish the phone. "It's against the rules. This is a hospital. We don't make up these rules arbitrarily. I'm a doctor and you are here to get well. My role is to mend you physically and psychologically. I'm not going to argue with you. You will *not* keep that phone."

"But Dr. Berlin . . ."

"Look at yourself. Look what you have done to yourself in the last hour because of the phone. You tell me, is that good medicine?"

I was given some medication and a shot. Someone left the room with the phone. A nurse sat on my chair. Berlin left and returned in an hour.

He had read the *Post*. He was firm but kind.

"Richard, our role is to get you well and we will see you through this. If patients have a heart attack, we're with them. If they have a stroke, we're with them. I have to tell you that the press has descended on this hospital. Somehow, they figured out that you are here. They know about the clinic and are asking if you're in it."

Paul McHugh, the chief of psychiatry, arrived. Both he and Berlin feared that a reporter would slip in, like Bob Woodward did when

CIA chief William Casey was on his deathbed. Even though the ward was locked, they worried that someone could pose as a visitor. Obviously, that could be bad therapeutically, not only for me but also for the other patients.

The doctors said I would be moved from Room 505 to Room 519 down the hall. My windows should be covered because someone with a camera lens the size of a small telescope had been spotted outside the building. I glanced out the window, and sure enough, there was a man with a lens two feet long scanning the building.

McHugh and Berlin said to keep my drapes pulled. They also posted a guard on the ward twenty-four hours a day, just to be safe.

Dr. McHugh said, "Richard, I know this must be hell for you. We're going to see you through. I want you to know that the full resources of this hospital are available to help you. We'd do no less for any patient with the trauma you're now experiencing.

"As you know, I've sat in on many of your sessions. I'm going to continue to do that. In addition, I'll be dropping by from time to time."

Dr. Berlin chimed in. "We've treated you just like any other patient. None of that will change, but I also know what pain you're in now. So all of us are going to check on you frequently."

McHugh interrupted. "Yes, and let me ask you right now: How's your mood? I'll be direct about it. Are you feeling suicidal?"

I assured him that I wasn't. "That's good," he said with a smile. Then, more serious, he went on. "But this could change. If it does, let us know at once. Many people on the staff will be asking you about this. That's just because we care."

"In that regard," Berlin added, "we want to be here for Gail, too. You're the patient, not her. But in times of extreme duress, the close family become our patients as well. How's she doing?"

"Probably a lot better than I am. But I'm concerned about her. She never complains, so you never know how she may be hurting. I'd be grateful if you folks would talk to her."

"Of course we will," Berlin said. "In fact, I want to see her when she arrives today. And, if it will help, we're here for your daughters, too."

Their support reassured me. Nonetheless, I knew I was in a protective cocoon while a cyclone raged outside. I had to get a weather report. So I went to the pay phone and called Joan, my assistant.

She said the calls had been nonstop, mostly from the press but also from friends and supporters who were confused and alarmed and concerned. Gail arrived looking beleaguered. She said our home phone had rung incessantly. She hadn't answered it but could hear the calls coming in on the machine. Again, although most were reporters, many were faculty members, students, and trustees, who said they had seen the story and wanted me to know they believed in me and were sorry because I must be going through hell.

I tried to go on with the clinic routine, hoping the structure might help me get a grasp again. It didn't. I felt too helpless and besieged. Dr. McHugh came back and sat down.

"How are you doing?"

"I don't know."

"Look, I'll ask you again. Are you thinking of suicide?"

"No," I said, "But I'm feeling awfully down."

"I'm not trying to plant ideas, but you're an intelligent man who's in a crisis. We have a responsibility to you and we wouldn't be good doctors if we didn't ask you often how you felt and what you thought about the future."

I told him I didn't know what a future meant anymore.

McHugh said that even though Berlin was my attending physician, he wanted me to have his home number and told me to call if I ever needed him.

A couple of hours later, I talked with Gerry Treanor again. He said many reporters had called. They were asking him if I would be charged the next day and if the police would remove me from Hopkins. I was dumbstruck. Treanor said he had talked to the police, and they seemed to have no intention of removing me from Hopkins. Every assurance felt fragile.

Then Gerry Treanor, Richard Marks, and I conferred by phone. Since my resignation, I had remained silent and out of sight. I had taken the therapy program seriously and tried to minimize outside distractions, which in the last few days had proved impossible. With the disclosure in today's press, the time had come for me to issue a public apology. Certainly I felt I owed one to many people, but I couldn't make it earlier because the details hadn't yet become public. Now that they had, I asked Gerry and Richard to help me write an apology. As we talked, they wrote. With a patient urging me to let him have the phone, I listened as they read it back. I okayed it, and Gerry said he'd release it to the press.

I expressed remorse about the effect my resignation had had on AU and the Washington community. "I cannot begin to convey my embarrassment, or my torment," it stated. I described my therapy at Hopkins as "intense, difficult, and mentally painful." It was helping me, I said. And I added that, "I am determined, with medical help, to regain my health. It is difficult to see beyond that now."

I'd heard that rumors, speculations, and allegations abounded in the press and in the public about the calls. I intended neither to confirm nor deny those views, even though many of them were wrong. Rather, I wanted to say that I was embarrassed and that I apologized. And I wanted that conveyed at once.

The day proved harrowing. The television in the TV room flashed my face on the screen, and the patients recognized me. The doctors, the nurses, the patients all offered their support. My internal assault became so furious, though, that little else mattered. Everything that defined me had died; now I felt like I was dying. I couldn't eat. I couldn't sleep. The sleeping pill did nothing. As I tossed on my bed, nurses checked on me regularly. At about two A.M., I left my room and chatted briefly with the guard. I said I was sorry he was stuck there. "Hey, man, it's a job. You just take care of yourself." How odd, I thought, that this guard unintentionally gave me a strong message. In the past, I had taken care of my job. Now, my job was to take care of myself.

Finally I went to Liz, a night nurse, and said nothing was working. The sleeping pill did nothing. I was too tense to read. Aside from needing sleep, I had to turn off my mind. Did she have any suggestions?

"Have you tried guided imagery?" I hadn't but would try anything. She told me to go back to my room and lie down.

"Close your eyes. Concentrate on your breathing." She spoke softly. "Focus yourself. Breathe in, breathe out. That's good. Nice, long, deep breaths."

I went to MIT in physics for this? It sounded like a throwback to the 1960s. But I was desperate. So I tried to listen.

"Imagine that you are walking toward a huge mountain. You're carrying a load of problems. When you get to the base of the mountain, you set them down. Now you start to climb the mountain. It's a hard climb, but when you get to the top it's sunny. The air is clear, the breeze is fresh, and the skies are the most beautiful blue you've ever seen. The world looks beautiful. . . ."

It was the damnedest thing! The next thing I knew, it was morning, four-thirty in the morning. I had slept solidly for two and a half hours. Still, I felt sick when I woke up. The nurse examined me, but found nothing wrong. At eight, I called Gail. My public apology was covered on page one. Other than that, nothing in the paper. Later I talked to Gerry Treanor. The police told him that they didn't plan to interrupt my therapy by filing charges.

That good news didn't bring me much relief. When I got back to my room, I closed the door and turned off the lights. I sat on my bed with my knees pulled to my chest. I was depressed. That I knew. This depression was unlike anything I'd ever felt before. The anguish and horror of the past few days had turned into a toxic black cloud that eclipsed my whole being.

The hideous part of the publicity arose not so much from the shame of the phone calls, bad as that was, but from the question everyone had to be asking: "Is Berendzen a child molester?" As I passed the TV room, I caught a couple of phrases from a local newscast.

I wanted to hide, but where could I go? "Are you okay?" Olivia, a nurse, asked. "Do you want to talk?"

Usually the staff talked to me in the hallway away from patients. This time, I asked if we could talk in a private office. With the door shut, I said, "Olivia, I'm truly scared. Some awful darkness is coming over me. I can't describe it. It terrifies me."

"You've been through a lot. You wouldn't be human if you didn't hurt now. If a train had hit you, you'd sure be hurting. Psychologically, a train has hit you. Why don't you lie down in your room. I'll call Dr. Berlin."

As I lay in my bed, suicide drifted in and out of my mind like smoke. If I signed out to go to the cafeteria, could I take the elevator to the top floor and jump off? I remembered what Berlin and McHugh had said. I knew I should tell them what was going through my mind, but I was afraid that if they knew, they would move me to another unit. Could they lock me up?

The next few days became a blur, as I slid into clinical depression. No horror, no hell can equal it. Beyond any physical pain I'd ever known, this agony permeated all of me. I wanted only to stay in my room with the lights off, drapes drawn, and door shut. I wanted to close in on myself, just as a dying star becomes a black hole.

After a supernova explosion, a star may lose its internal equilibrium. If so, it will begin to contract upon itself. Ultimately, even light cannot escape its awesome inward pull. It blinks out of sight and continues its mad collapse until a once massive and luminous star shines no more and literally disappears from the cosmos. So it was with my depression. I'd entered the black hole of the human spirit.

With such a star, once something enters this warping of space and time, nothing can save it. It is doomed to fall ever farther into the hole, until crushed to oblivion. Is that the inevitable fate of a person caught in severe depression?

And what should I to do with my recurring thought of suicide?

The alternative to suicide is the will to live. That requires a purpose. Part of the purpose comes from friends and associates wanting you to live. Besides my other torment, I wondered why the university had never inquired about me. Since I was so upset, I may have read too much into the silence, but I took it as total abandonment. I knew I'd brought shock and shame to the university. For that, I was profoundly sorry, just as I was that my calls had intruded into anyone's life. Whatever the explanation, the university's official silence cut me deeply.

Inquiries came about other patients in the clinic; the men mentioned them in group. One man had been sent to Hopkins by his company, another by his church. In both cases, the employers called to see how they were doing. The university had been my extended family, and I concluded that no official of the institution cared.

Ironically, students offered instant support. They dropped off messages of encouragement at the house and left them on the answering machine. "Hang in there, Dr. B. We're behind you. We know you'll make it. . . ." I heard from faculty, alumni, and individual trustees. Florence, our housekeeper, and other cleaning women at AU held a special prayer service for me. She, too, was badgered by reporters who wanted to know my whereabouts. They couldn't confirm that I was at Hopkins. Gail had instructed her to tell the truth. The truth was, she didn't know.

"Aren't you doing his laundry?" a reporter asked at the front door. Seeing Florence's exasperation, the husky Mediterranean plumber who was fixing a leak walked to the door with his monkey wrench, and asked, "Do you have an appointment?" Obviously, the reporter didn't. The plumber said, "He's a good man. He asks about my family. Stop bothering them. Get out of here!" He did.

Gail would recount these stories to me. I'd smile, but I couldn't keep it for more than a second or two. The image kept coming to my mind of a wounded Eskimo left on the ice floe by his tribe. Two weeks ago he may have been their leader; now he would hold the tribe back. So they leave him. They move ever farther from him as he waits to die.

The only life I could envision for Gail and me was in a fishing village in Alaska or Norway or New Zealand. The doctors told me I would survive my ordeal. They said I still had much to offer. My education and achievements remained, and my family still loved me. Still, to me in my state of depression, fear, and self-pity, their words rang hollow.

The staff gave me pamphlets and books to read, trying to encourage me. Some of the material seemed corny in its simplicity. A month earlier, I would have ridiculed it, but not now.

One article, entitled "So You Think You're a Failure?" described a man who, after his fiancée died, was defeated for the legislature, had a nervous breakdown, lost another position, then, after finally winning election, was defeated again for the senate, missed out on a chance at the vice presidency, and then lost another race for the senate. Finally, in 1860, Abraham Lincoln became president. As I read this, I felt like a little boy again, reading about the one hundred most influential people of all time.

They also gave me a booklet on depressive illnesses. I checked off every symptom: loss of appetite, feeling irritable, trouble coping, lack of interest in personal appearance, poor sleep, inability to concentrate, nausea, headaches, feeling hopeless, self-blame, uncontrollable crying, apathy. If it had been a lottery ticket, I would have won with a clean sweep.

Of course they tried antidepressants. However, the side effects almost rivaled the depression itself. My mouth became completely dry, I had stomach problems and felt woozy and light-headed if I stood up quickly. The only relief the medicine brought was that I worried about the side effects rather than the depression.

At about eleven P.M. one evening, as I sat morosely in my room, someone knocked on my door. It was Dr. Berlin. "Goodness. Why are you here so late, Dr. Berlin? I saw you at eight this morning. Don't you ever go home?"

He grinned and said, "I'll get there. First I wanted to see how you're doing. Your sleep reports still aren't good. I gather you have a hard time getting to sleep and staying asleep. In depression, nights can be especially tough. So I wanted to stop by."

I thanked him, and we stood talking for almost an hour. Since the press stories broke, he and the entire staff had shown real compassion and support for us. Jo, one of the nurses, repeatedly offered to talk with Gail, and Berlin offered to do likewise with Natasha and Deborah. Earlier, as part of their investigation to determine if I had ever expressed pedophilic interests, he had talked with both daughters, as had a police detective. Apparently both men handled the conversations with real sensitivity; neither daughter minded the sessions. All of this added to my embarrassment and anxiety, nonetheless.

Throughout this ordeal, the Hopkins staff aided my family and me in every way. Their initial probing and pounding on me had hurt while it helped. When my crisis broke in the press, they rallied to support my family and me. Perhaps most important, they provided us with high quality medical attention and humane personal attention. In my darkest hour, they essentially saved my mind, if not my life.

They also took on difficult tasks. Dr. Berlin and a female doctor had tried to talk to my mother. Now senile, she didn't understand about my resignation and got confused even about where I'd worked. Reporters tried talking to her, too. Later I learned that she was oblivious to it all.

The next day we got a new patient on the floor. He was admitted because he allegedly had had sex with his adolescent daughter. He was a small, ordinary man, someone you wouldn't notice in the supermarket. I became uncharacteristically angry with him. He didn't think what he had done was a big deal, although he neither admitted nor denied anything.

I took him aside at lunch. "Look," I said, "although I don't have medical training, I want to talk to you. I don't know for sure what you did to that girl. But think of the effect you may have had on her in later life. Don't you give a goddamn?"

"I didn't mean to hurt her."

In the program I had met others who had molested children, but something about this man's utter indifference set me off. I ripped into him.

"I hate to think what Berlin will do with you, but I'll tell you what I think. I think you have caused more hell than you will ever know. If therapy or Depo-Provera helps you, I hope you get it. If it's insight that makes you stop, I hope you get that. I hope this clinic can help you. But if you're unwilling or unable to see the evil you've done and stop it forever, I frankly hope you go to prison for a long time."

He sat mute. I was bigger, older, and more verbal than he. This was not an even match. He murmured something about being sorry.

While listening to abusers at the Sexual Disorders Clinic, I learned about the intense egotism of some of them. I asked one man who had abused young boys why he did it. He told me because the boys enjoyed it. I asked how he knew that. He said, "They say so, and they tell me they want it."

As we talked, it became clear to me that he was the one who enjoyed the sexual encounters and projected similar feelings onto his victims. I asked him if he ever worried about long-term consequences of his actions. He shrugged and said no. He said sometimes he saw boys the day after their encounter and they seemed fine. Had he ever thought what they might be like twenty-four years later, instead of twenty-four hours? Obviously, he hadn't.

Another new arrival appeared on the floor that afternoon, this one a general psychiatric patient. Wearing a flowing priest's robe, she told anyone who would listen or no one at all that she was the daughter of Hitler. She took over the pay phone and repeatedly tried to call the mayor of Baltimore and the president. Although we had time limits for using the pay phone, she would shout into the receiver for hours. Then I discovered that she put in no coins. She was severely manic, and reminded me of my mother at her worst.

In an odd way, the man I had confronted over lunch reminded me more of my mother than she did. His lack of concern about his actions, his amoral attitude, and his ego were what upset me. How could he do things so utterly devastating without any feeling? My mother's craziness didn't perplex me. Mania is an electrical thunderstorm in the brain, with bolts flashing at random. I was more troubled by the calculating, manipulative woman who would say from the middle bedroom, "Come here." Like my mother, this man expressed not an inkling of remorse. When my mother was obviously sick, I didn't expect her to have a conscience; when she seemed sane, I couldn't understand why she was devoid of one.

Rage briefly cut through my depression, which then closed over me as a trap door seals in darkness. There was no escape. I felt frustrated that something existed inside me that I couldn't see and wouldn't show on a CAT scan or X ray. There wasn't a pill to cure it or a shot to ameliorate its effects. It was with me wherever I went; talking in group didn't help, and speaking privately with my doctors still left me in the same place—depressed and scared by my utter absence of a will to live. My insides felt rotted. My Spartan room was lonely beyond belief. I cared about no one and no one cared about me. My one small bouquet of flowers from Gail testified to that. Did I feel sorry for myself? You bet. My misery was exacerbated by the inescapable fact that I had brought this on myself. It was all my fault.

Natasha called Gail from Boston and said she wanted to see me. This came the same day I had the furious encounter with the new patient over lunch. Gail assured her that I was fine, but she kept saying, "I don't understand. I don't get what's going on." She decided to take the midnight train from Boston on Friday night. After catching up on sleep Saturday, she and Gail came to see me Sunday morning.

Nervous and excited, excited and nervous, my feelings were locked in a tug-of-war when I thought about finally seeing Natasha. I waited in the lobby of the Meyer building. I did not want Gail to take her to my floor. The woman who thought she was Hitler's daughter was gone, but you never knew who might turn up. Even though there was no comparison, at some level I wanted to protect Natasha from the agony I felt when I went to visit my mother at the mental institution.

On this Sunday morning, the lounge was empty. I got there an hour early. When they arrived, my nervousness vanished as I rushed to give Natasha a hug. I was overjoyed to see her, and she seemed relieved to see me. "Hi, Tasha," I said. With a shy smile and a hug back, she simply replied, "Hi." That was enough, for I know Natasha. She'd left school in the middle of her freshman year final exams to travel all night to see me. She wanted to see for herself that I was okay and to understand what had happened. I was proud of her courage and reassured by her obvious concern for her dad. Despite the press, despite the accusations, despite the confusion, despite it all—she was there.

Gail left us alone, and Natasha and I sat and talked. Without burdening her with details, I told her about my childhood trauma, my father's death, and the phone calls. She really wanted to know why I was at Hopkins and what they were doing to me. I described the sodium Amytal interview, the lie detector tests, and the CAT scan. I did not tell her about the intense therapy sessions. With keen interest, she asked questions and we talked at length.

The extraordinary aspect of her visit was that it helped me realize how much I meant to her. We had a good relationship before, but my crisis galvanized her love and made it three-dimensional. It was no longer a passive fact, but a reservoir of feeling from which I could draw strength. Or maybe pain and humiliation had opened my heart and enabled me to receive love in a way I never had before.

Gail joined us for lunch in the cafeteria, and the three of us laughed and kidded. I wanted to hold on to the peace of the afternoon, but I couldn't. I watched them leave. For only a few hours, I could be AWOL from my depression.

This is a frustrating aspect of the illness. You can neither control nor escape it. No one can tell you how long it will last or what makes it end. Once it settles over you, it's like smog. The wind may move it, sometimes the Sun pops through, but then, without sound or warning, the depression closes back again.

The totality of my circumstance overwhelmed me. Everything I had been, I wasn't any longer. I used to think I had value as a teacher, educator, astronomer, and administrator. Now that was over. When life had no value, it felt hopeless, and hopelessness is kindling for suicide. I hadn't picked a day or a time, but suicide still haunted me.

The metaphor that kept coming back was of free-fall. I could see myself falling, falling, falling to the center of the Earth. I thought I had found hell. But would the fall ever end? I kept waiting to hit bottom. How far down could I fall? Each time I thought I was there, I found another level lower. If I could just hit bottom, I might be able to begin the long climb out of the hole.

"Please, God, let me hit bottom," became my silent prayer. After the series of newspaper stories in the Washington papers, there were items in the news magazines and then op-ed pieces. It was like running an unending gauntlet. I never felt safe.

I wouldn't have survived without the persistent support and understanding of the Hopkins staff. A nurse named Bernie got me talking about films one day. It turned out that we were both fans of *It's a Wonderful Life*. We talked at length about the film, and Bernie used it to nudge me into a discussion about suicide. He reminded me of George Bailey's suicidal thoughts.

I dismissed this. "Yeah, that's a movie, this is life. Frank Capra could make up a fairy tale with a happy ending, but I don't have a guardian angel." Bernie kept after me, "What did they say at the end? Tell me what they said at the end of the movie."

At first I couldn't remember. Then I did. The line is, "No man is a failure who has friends." That sentence became my lifeline. I felt like the ultimate failure; I had failed my profession and university, I had failed my family and myself. Gradually, I realized I still had friends and legions of well-wishers, many of them strangers, including ministers, priests, and rabbis I'd never met.

Gail played our answering machine to me over the phone every day. In a time of crisis, people's nobility comes to the fore. Gail's friends rallied around both of us. Natasha's young friends and their parents asked how they could help. The AU faculty senate sent a letter expressing compassion and sympathy. Acquaintances I barely knew telephoned to wish me well. Business leaders in Washington expressed their concern and support. I heard from my childhood friends, school classmates, and long-lost cousins and second cousins. An extended array of my friends came to our side. Gail's brother said he supported us fully, and asked how he could help. Seth, Deb's six-foot, three-inch boyfriend said if anyone tried to harass Gail at home, to let him know. He had become part of our family and wanted to protect it. A friend called from Europe. "We read about you in the *International Herald Tribune,* and we want you to know that we love you. You're part of our family. Whatever the problem is, we just want you to know we're here."

George Bailey was saved by his friends, I was saved by mine. As much as it saddens me to say this, I don't think my family alone could have pulled me through without the Hopkins staff and all these well-wishers. Even though my family is the center of my being, my sense of failure was so great that without outside intervention I could not have survived. I only could think of how many people I had let down. I felt colossal guilt.

Why hadn't the weight of my responsibility checked my behavior? After all, I was the quintessential organized and self-disciplined professional devoted to his job. Why, then, didn't I stop myself? Why did I make the first call? Didn't I know the risks?

I did, yet I didn't. At one level, I knew, but that wasn't the level that counted. My compulsion to call overrode everything else. My behavior was arational, not irrational.

As April came to a close, Gail began to urge that I come home. She thought I had achieved about all the benefit I was likely to get from the hospital, and that I might be less depressed at home. In addition, she wanted us to start thinking about the future. I hadn't told her how truly depressed I'd become. When she came to visit, I tried hard to look less despondent. Nor had I told her how I thought of suicide. I never considered it seriously, but it kept lingering in my mind. She remained resolutely optimistic, insisting that we could pull through and make a new, meaningful life for ourselves.

One Sunday afternoon, I let myself believe her soothing words. To avoid the reporters who still came to the hospital, we hid in a corner of the cafeteria. We whiled away the time by casually talking and flipping through magazines. Gail said, "The worst is over. Things will quiet down now, and we can start climbing the ladder out of this pit." Just then I came across my picture and a story about the calls in a national magazine. I blew up at Gail.

"You and your damned optimism! You're always fanatically searching for the glimmer of life, of hope. Did you ever consider for one damn moment that it might be ultimately, genuinely gone? I'm falling and I can't hit bottom. And you keep telling me I am going to climb some ladder and get out. You claim it'll take work, but we'll do it together. Gail, there is *no* ladder! There is *no* bottom and there is *no* hope! I'm telling you, there is *no hope*."

I didn't understand it then and wouldn't for many more months, but ultimately the difference between depression and nondepression, the difference between giving up and going on, is hope. Love is not enough. You have to have hope. I knew my family loved me. Still I had no hope. Gail had hope, my doctors and daughters had hope, but I did not.

I glared at Gail and shouted, "Just go home! You're doing no good here. All of your homilies sound dandy, but they mean nothing. This isn't some Frank Capra movie. I'm telling you, there is *no* hope. Listen to me! There is *no* hope. Just leave me and get out of here."

Gail looked destroyed. I couldn't have hurt her more if I had hit her. Color drained from her face. The air seemed to leave the room. In the remaining vacuum, the stillness was emptier than in interstellar space. She looked at me one more time and then walked away. I sat alone in the cafeteria, hoping she might come back and knowing I'd hate it if she did.

Ten minutes went by, then twenty. Gail was gone. Later I learned she took the elevator back upstairs twice, but couldn't bring herself to get off and find me. So she drove home.

I went back to Meyer 5, where I paced the music room in a big figure eight. Once that became monotonous, I went back downstairs to the chapel. It was empty. I knelt to pray, sure I knew the prayer to pray. "Make it all go away. Stop the torment. Take away the pain." That would do it.

But spontaneously, I changed the prayer. It happened in a flash. Instead of pleading to hit bottom, instead of begging for stability and a chance to rebuild, instead of trying to get something from God, instead of asking God to meet my needs, I simply prayed, "Thy will be done."

Just let go. "Thy will be done." Maybe I already had hit bottom. Maybe there was no bottom. I didn't know. Whatever the case, I realized I had neither the insight nor the ability to control these matters. So I stopped trying and placed it all in higher hands. I didn't know the liberation of this prayer until I prayed it.

"Thy will be done," not mine. I don't know where the words came from. I had known the Lord's Prayer since childhood, but it wasn't in my mind. Although I don't know why those words came to me then, I do know what happened next. I felt a rush of tranquillity. Having relinquished control, I felt more centered and stable than I had since the crisis began, or perhaps since my life began. Releasing control differed from giving up; I didn't give up, I let go. Okay, here I am. Show me what to do. It's your move.

People say that God speaks to us in mysterious ways. I believe this happened in my life. After I found genuine humility and simply prayed "Thy will be done," I rose and sat near the front of the chapel. As I had done so many times before, I gazed at the curved tile wall, which proclaimed the opening verses of the Twenty-third Psalm. "The Lord is my Shepherd . . ." These reassuring words have comforted countless people.

This time as I reread them I noticed something extraordinary, something simple yet profound, something obvious yet obscure, something I had looked at a hundred times before yet had not seen until now. The tile mason had set apart the first words of the third verse. They linked to the rest but stood apart. They were special: "And he restoreth my soul." Before, I had looked; at that moment, I saw. And I knew. Moments earlier, another simple sentence had touched me: "Thy will be done." Like bursts of light and hope, for me they became an epiphany.

Inexplicably, I began to cherish my life. I told myself not to focus on what I had lost—my job, my identity—but on what I still had. Berlin had advocated this tack with me for days without success. Now I caught the breeze and was able to run with it. Yes, indeed, I had my education, my family, and my friends. I was outrageously healthy. I didn't have cancer or heart disease or AIDS. Certainly I had immense problems, but they were finite and solvable. I had a future whenever I was ready to claim it.

After I left the chapel, I called Gail to apologize. She wasn't there. I began to worry. Had she been in an accident? Had I driven her away? When I finally reached her an hour later, I told her how sorry I was. Of course there was hope. There always is hope, I said. We both cried.

Now I realize that my angry outburst at Gail actually began to transform my pain. I had avoided anger most of my life. It had seemed a destructive, wasted emotion, one that replaced reason with rage. What did it accomplish? Anger only meant loss of self-control. Now I see it also has the power to transform, the ability to liberate. I had prayed to hit bottom. When I finally lost control and shouted at Gail, "There is no hope!," I began the journey toward finding it.

A Catholic priest came into the program shortly before I left Hopkins. Now that I had been there three and a half weeks, I began to sense who was telling the truth. I thought the priest wasn't.

Had he molested adolescent girls? He gave evasive answers. Berlin bristled. "Do you expect us to believe this? Come on." I knew Berlin wouldn't let up until he got the truth.

The priest, who was soft-spoken and well-educated, responded in generalities. "Well, occasionally, a thought might pass through my mind. They probably float in and out of every man's mind. That's part of the human condition. That's part of our human frailty. I just thought about it. I don't think I did anything." His eyes pinched, his lips quivered. But he remained unwavering.

Later, at lunch, I said to him, "Look, I leave tomorrow and I'll never see you again. I want to give you some advice. Be honest. Don't sit there like a brick. If you don't let these people help you, you'll miss the chance of your life. Open up. They'll find you out anyway. Let them make you well or at least better."

Even as I said these words, I realized his dilemma. If he remained mute, he'd miss the opportunity for help. If he spoke up, he might go to prison for years. If he was guilty, certainly he should go to prison, but once released, might he abuse again? How, as a society, can we break this horrid cycle?

This priest constituted, I thought, a stunning example of the challenge facing professionals in the child abuse field. Few abusers are ever caught. When they are, their young victims make tragic and often unreliable witnesses. Many of the perpetrators go free, only to abuse again. Those who are convicted are brutalized in prison by inmates, and then released. Their recidivism rate is appallingly high. Programs like the one at Hopkins help to reduce recidivism, thereby healing the perpetrator and protecting the public. These programs are not perfect, however, and some of their former patients abuse again. Those cases attract wide, negative publicity. Too few talented, young health care professionals see such work as a desirable and laudatory career, and too little cooperation exists between such medical pro-grams and the law enforcement community. And the nation continues to pretend that there are no problems or solutions, even while the problems grow and the solutions, albeit partial and imperfect, exist.

On May 4, I checked out of Johns Hopkins. I had a final physical, my blood was drawn for the last time, labeled, and left in a vial. With it I left much of the pain and confusion of my past, and I took with me new insights and strengths.

I learned more in my three and a half weeks at Hopkins than I had in any other period of my life. The tuition had been far higher, too! This was an education unlike any other. Before, I had understood Newton and Einstein and the forces that hold the universe together. Now I understood one man, Richard Berendzen, and the forces that held him together.

How could I say good-bye to the people who helped make this possible? The staff and patients alike had seen me through the most painful period of my life. They had watched me disintegrate into tears and had seen me grasping and groping, trying to hang on to anything to survive.

In a way, we patients had been like a platoon that gets split off from the main division and survives, alone, for weeks in the jungle. We had to rely on each other. We had, and that changed some of us irrevocably. Oddly I found in this motley group a common humanity. Although we came from across the nation and from diverse back-grounds and socioeconomic levels, we relied on each other and found—to my amazement—that what united us exceeded what di-vided us. This had something to do with basic human connectedness, what a theologian might call a meeting of souls, even tormented ones. And it had something to do with men under duress learning how to share with and support each other. Those aren't bad lessons to learn. Like so many men of my background, I had judged people too much by their résumés and not enough by their hearts.

Then there was the staff. Experienced professionals, they had seen it all before. Even so, they seemed to take a personal interest in each of us. They were the first people to know everything about my child-hood and about the calls. They helped me understand it all, and, although they never excused the calls, they enabled me to compre-hend them, to see them in full context.

They taught me something else quite profound: how to trust. Over the years, Gail, my daughters, and numerous friends had taught me the same thing without knowing it. The Hopkins staff drove the message home. One of the horrible lingering legacies for a male victim of childhood sexual abuse often is a diminished ability to trust. Without trust, you cannot rely on those around you; you must keep things to yourself and do the task yourself. The Hopkins staff, along with my family and friends, taught me that trust is resilient. If it has been brutally betrayed before, it won't necessarily be again. I learned to lower my defenses and accept other people's trustworthiness. That, too, became an enriching new connectedness for me.

As I departed, I realized that at the hospital, like back at the university, the high-level professionals got most of the attention and praise. Yet staff at all levels had contributed in their own unique ways. The receptionist had told me over and over, "We think the best of you and, believe me, you're going to be all right." On my bad days she could read my face, and would say, "Now, why don't you talk to me for a moment. You look like you need a friend." She was a receptionist, not a physician. As I checked out, she came from behind her desk, tears brimming in her eyes, and we hugged. So it went with every nurse, social worker, orderly, cook, and cleaning person.

Gail met me at my room, where they returned objects to me that they had confiscated when I checked in—scissors, razor, shirt pin— flotsam from my previous life. I began to feel like a real person again, an ordinary person.

Six

IN LIMBO

W e left in a downpour. Even with an umbrella, the cold and blowing rain drenched us before we reached the car. I glanced at my watch and realized the trustees were in the middle of their spring meeting, undoubtedly discussing my resignation.

I wanted to go home and begin my life anew. I wanted to stand beneath the sheltering oak trees in the backyard and sit in the family room and watch the fish in the aquarium. I wanted to sleep in my own bed and watch the morning sunlight play on the wall.

But we weren't headed home. A friend had offered us a cottage in Middleburg, in the Virginia countryside. The police had not yet decided about pressing charges, and reporters still hounded Gail and hung around Hopkins. Since my resignation, I had not talked to reporters or given interviews. Many requests for interviews had arrived, but I decided not to speak to anyone until the legal issues were settled, one way or another. I would not circumvent the process in any way. My lawyers told me to keep out of sight for the time being. Only they and the police would know my whereabouts.

We headed for the Virginia hunt country, being neither hunters nor riders. A drive that should have taken three hours stretched into five because of rain and traffic. Finally, we turned off the main road, and slogged down country lanes, in total darkness, looking for the tree where we were to turn.

Our destination lay at the end of a gravel drive now reduced to mud. The small cottage might have been charming, except that it hadn't been used in months and the heat was off. The cold, dark, dismal night chilled our bones and froze our spirits. Brackish water flowed from rusty taps. When we pulled back the blankets, we discovered that a mother mouse had made a nest there.

After Gail and I had waited weeks to be together, the euphoria of our reunion was tempered by the immensity of what lay ahead. Being romantics and having humor, we usually can make the best of anything. That night, however, hit me hard. I no longer had the familiarity and security of my strange home on Meyer 5. After weeks of torment, I was with my wife again. We had to get accustomed to each other all over. The wretched night hardly helped. Instead of warmth and relief, we found a frigid cabin and undrinkable water. Even worse, I realized why we were there.

"Gail, we're hiding out like criminals!" But then, maybe I soon would be charged as a criminal. "Bunny, it's nuts, but I want to go home."

So we left our hideaway at two A.M. in dense fog. Once in Washington, we drove down Massachusetts Avenue. We passed the gates of the university bathed in a halo of misty white light—the gates I helped design, and the university I helped build. I felt like a man with no country standing at the border of his former homeland.

We were exhausted beyond sensibility when we finally pulled into our driveway on Nebraska Avenue. As I opened the kitchen door, Sparky bounced off the floor, his tail wagging madly. Slowly, I went through every room. Then I went out into the damp night and looked at the trees that had sheltered and shaded us. It was four in the morning, a cloudy, starless night. The trees stood enduring and peaceful. This was a safe place to feel terrible. I mourned the passing of my former life.

After an hour at home, I told Gail I wanted to go back to Virginia. When I was in the woods, I wanted to go home; at home, I wanted to go back to the woods. Thirty-three hundred Nebraska Avenue was our home; it was filled with our memories and belongings. That was the problem. It felt too much like home. I was tormented by the realization of all I'd destroyed.

Each room had a memory—young Natasha's laughter, a student's question, a professor's greeting at our opening day reception. Being in that house was like leafing through a scrapbook meticulously kept for ten years. It overwhelmed me. The cottage had no heat; it also had no memories. How could you get through deep pain in an environment that once brought you unremitting happiness?

When you feel truly defeated, life seems completely over. I needed the detachment of Hopkins or the cabin in the woods until I could gather my strength and courage, if I ever could.

Each ounce of pleasure was followed by a pound of pain. I was happy to be with Gail; then, boom, I realized we had no future and had no home. What would I do? Where would we live? Each question had no answer.

Just before dawn, we went through the house scooping up some staples to take back to the woods: We filled containers with tap water and took towels and fresh clothes. We didn't know if we would stay there for days or weeks. If the police filed charges, I certainly didn't want to be home. No telling who would show up on our doorstep or camp out on our lawn.

By five-thirty A.M., we headed back to Middleburg. Exhausted when we began the trek, we now ran on fumes. Once back at the cabin, despite the morning chill, we both fell dead asleep.

When we woke, I felt sad and lost. I had no home. As difficult and traumatic as my childhood was, I always had a home. Now Gail and I were like a planet without a star, moving without a fixed orbit, floating aimlessly through space.

So now what? Where did I start? Here it was, the proverbial first day of the rest of my life, and I hadn't a clue. When I was president, I carried my daily schedule in my breast pocket. At Hopkins, my day was structured, which helped me feel secure.

I, who had been so professionally obsessed with time, suddenly didn't know what to do with it. Getting a haircut seemed like a reasonable beginning. We drove into Middleburg and parked near a barbershop. Both of us were wary—too wary and too paranoid, as it turned out—about being discovered.

After the haircut, we returned to the cabin and took a long walk along the country roads. At last, we felt some of the beauty surrounding us. The earlier rain made the day seem spangled and bright. Horses and rolling hills and serene homes brought us pleasure, yet they felt transitory, like paintings in a museum, which you admire but don't own. They remain and you leave. We were in a borrowed cottage. We had no home, much less the bucolic serenity of horses and meadows. This was a beautiful, fleeting mirage.

Late that night, I talked with Richard Marks. If charges were filed, they would be misdemeanor counts. He patiently explained what the next legal steps might be.

When I hung up, Gail looked despondent. She missed our house. She wanted to go back. This time, to stay.

Mild, mellow Gail came to where I was sitting, slamming the door behind her. With her fists clenched, she yelled, "I'm mad. I'm so damned mad! Why do we have to hide?" She wanted to go home, and move about in the world as she always had. I knew she was right, although I didn't share her confidence.

After two days in the cabin, we returned home to stay. Debbie came over the next day, on Sunday morning, for us to talk in person for the first time since the crisis. She gave me a big hug and said, "Daddy, I love you." In the past, I thought that she did love me, but I don't think I fully realized how much until that moment.

We talked and talked. I spoke in general terms about my treatment at Hopkins as she asked many questions. Then I filled her in on the legal aspects. I apologized for embarrassing her, and said I was sorry I had brought this on her.

"Daddy," she said, looking directly at me, "I'm proud that Berendzen is my name. Everything is just fine because you're okay. That's what counts. The people I know and care about just look at the whole thing, and say something went wrong. He's a good man and everything will work out. At my job, the people have said, "Hope you're okay. I'm with you.' "

As I had with Natasha, I alluded to the abuse in my childhood but didn't identify my abuser. I think both girls figured it out. Over the years they had seen my mother's mood swings and erratic behavior. They knew she had hovered nearby for years in her studio apartments. She had been a perpetual presence, even if rarely part of our lives.

At Hopkins the doctors had insisted that I tell Gail everything, but they hadn't mentioned my daughters. In retrospect, I know I should have told them everything, too. As a parent, though, I wanted to shield them from the horrors of the world and protect their image of me. I didn't want them to feel sorry for me or pity me. Although it was irrational, I feared losing their respect. I didn't want them to think of their dad as damaged. Neither the doctors nor I thought of me that way, but I feared others might, including my daughters.

Debbie and Natasha saw me as vulnerable for the first time. Ultimately this strengthened our relationships; the honesty of our communication improved, our bonds became even stronger. Initially, however, I was worried that my tarnished reputation would reflect on them. I had embarrassed them. I felt I had let them down. Even though they didn't feel that way about me, no one could have convinced me then.

After Deb's Sunday visit, but not because of it, I went back into deep depression. Depression, as an illness, resembles miles upon miles of black uncharted water. Sometimes the seas are calm; other times, turbulent.

Maddeningly, you look essentially the same. As you look at yourself in the mirror, you wonder why you can't shake out of it. Just get going. Your family looks at you and sees the same person. Well, why can't they help you? They just can't. Then they feel terrible; you feel worse.

Increasingly I learned that the difference between wanting life or death is simple: It's hope. Hope makes it possible to love, and love makes it possible to live. When you lose your faith and wonder and awe about life, you effectively die. Your body might go on for years, but without hope you will be part of the living dead.

I know because I was. I got up on Monday morning, showered and shaved, and then had nowhere to go. I didn't have a routine. In the hospital, my job was to get well. I approached each day as if I were going to work on myself.

At home, I had nothing. I had no work to do; worse, I had no goal.

I had taken almost no sick days since I'd been president. I can't remember spending a weekday lounging at home. I had been part of a community at the university, and part of a community on Meyer 5. When I was at Hopkins, I worried about the future. Now that it was here, I saw it for what it was: dreadful.

So far, no charges had been placed. If they were filed, I didn't know when a court hearing would come. This could take days or even months. So I effectively placed myself under house arrest, with an indeterminate sentence.

With all the blinds closed, I slunk around the cavernous house. Time stood still. Had our clocks stopped? A minute seemed to take an hour; an hour, a day. My life once had been so bright and fast, like a comet passing the Sun. Then, as a comet moves into cold and dark space, it dims and slows almost to a standstill. So had my life.

I resorted to my old reliable coping mechanism: I read. For hours I poured over Marcus Aurelius's *Meditations*. I was drawn to his wisdom and his stoicism. Often people look to the ancient Greeks for insight; in those lost days, I found strength with a Roman. He said, for example, "When pain is unbearable, it destroys us; when it does not, it is bearable." I was determined to bear my pain.

Also, I read the *Britannica*. During the next three weeks, I think I read half of it. I skipped from volume to volume, and offered Gail interesting but unessential information. "Let me tell you about Burma." "What do you think of Pushkin's poetry?" With the encyclopedia I could span all epochs, all people, and all places. Mostly, I could escape my home jail.

I returned to the nineteenth-century writers and philosophers who had enchanted me when I was young: Emerson, Longfellow, Dickens, Keats, Shelley. From this century, Churchill fascinated me, as did Rudyard Kipling.

Even with such giants at my side, depression would rudely return. My faithful literary companions had to wait as I again slid into this inky, ominous, fathomless abyss. Why am I sitting in this living tomb on a joyous spring day? Is it spring? Is there joy? And in a world with so many problems to solve, why am I reading Ben Franklin and Robert Frost?

My loving and constant Gail felt the turbulence of my melancholy. During those forlorn days, my only comrades were Gail, writers from the past, and our dog Sparky. Gail became the target of my frustration.

"Let me tell you about reality. It's not a place of sunshine and birds the way you keep thinking. There is no hope for me. I'm afraid I'll suck you into my awful world. For me, there is no future."

As the depression bored into my soul, I lay in bed until afternoon. Why get up? I had no place to go, except to rejoin Marcus or Wadsworth. I'd lie unshaven, staring at the darkened room. Only hunger would rouse me. Eventually, I would get up, have a bowl of soup, and then stare at the books. Reading them became impossible. My eyes saw words, but my brain didn't see sentences. Worse still, I didn't perceive their ideas. Or, more aptly put, I had only one idea: my all-absorbing doom. I knew I had to break this ego-locked grip. I had to break this hold and find hope. I knew I did. I just couldn't. Not then, not yet.

The worse I got, the more resolute Gail became. She had made a small bird station near our kitchen, with a fountain, sculpture, and flowers. Every day in mid-afternoon, two pewter-colored doves would arrive. Despite my gloom or because of it, she found beauty and inspiration in those two birds. For her, they became far more than birds. They were a couple that watched out for each other and flew freely.

At first, I refused to look at them. Why should I peer out from behind the sheets covering the windows to look at fancy pigeons? We had real problems, and she wanted to look at these birds!

"Oh, Richard, you must see the doves. The male checks the fountain to be sure it's safe before the female lands."

I would yell, "Gail, the world isn't like that! Forget about life being pretty and nice. Damnit, can't you understand? Any day charges may be filed against me, I don't have a job, I don't have a career. Where are we going to live? Where will we be a month from now or a year from now?"

"Richard, we still have each other. We have our health. We're going to be fine."

I realized that I needed help. So I called Berlin and McHugh. They said to come back, I could be readmitted if necessary. No, I did not want to be readmitted, but I did want to talk to them. To get there became an adventure. To travel incognito, I put on a droopy brim hat, pulled the sun visors down in the car, and took a circuitous route to Baltimore. The doctors kept saying, in many ways, "This, too, shall pass." I returned to Hopkins twice a week for several weeks. Once again, I tried antidepressants; once again, the cure was as bad as the illness. After switching medication a few times, I stopped it altogether.

Hopkins represented security to me. Dr. Berlin assured me that it would take time but that I'd recover. He told me about other patients' recoveries. He kept offering me hope, in case the day came when I'd take it. But I wasn't ready yet.

In depression, time has no meaning. It doesn't matter because you don't care. It's like a black hole, in which both space and time are distorted. Time inside such a sinkhole in the cosmos runs at a different rate than outside. And once inside a black hole, you could not get information out. There would be no way to communicate. Depression feels like that. It is a shout with no sound, a scream of silence.

A black hole forms an accretion disk, which sucks nearby matter into it. Similarly, those around you can be pulled into the mire of depression. When an object is caught in such a disk, no force in the cosmos can release it. It is doomed to be crushed in the hole. I feared that would be the case with Gail: Once caught nearby my depression, she would be pulled in, and no one could save her, just as no one could save me. I didn't want her trapped with me in the hole; I didn't want her perilously close to it either.

For moments I would seem to blast from my abyss. One afternoon, while looking for something in a drawer, I came across the photographs Gail had spread around the house after my father's funeral. As I focused on my mother's image, I unleashed a fury that had welled-up from four decades earlier.

The rationalizations I had clung to at Hopkins dissolved in rage. Repeatedly I had told the doctors, "She was sick. I can't get angry at a sick person." That afternoon, I did.

I smashed my mother's picture on the floor and said to it what I had wanted to say to her forty years ago. "Why?" I seethed. "Why did you do what you did? What was the matter with you?" Talking to her broken picture seemed even more real than talking to her.

My anger at my mother spilled into anger at myself. I went into the bathroom to splash cold water on my face, but it didn't help. I shouted at the face in the mirror, "Why didn't you get help? Why didn't you get it after your father died? Why have you done this to yourself, to your family, to AU?" Mixing despair and hopelessness with wrath makes a combustible blend.

But it brought me to life. When I was severely depressed, I didn't feel any emotion. I felt neither love nor hate. With this burst of anger, that changed. I felt a surge of energy.

At last I understood why the doctors had tried to help me tap my anger. I couldn't flee from it until I was free from it. I had layed out acres of rationalizations denying the simple truth that I hated my mother for what she had done to me. My mind had created a wall between me and my rage, a barrier of rationality to keep feelings out. That barrier dissolved in the meltdown of my depression.

I had been home about eight days when AU held its commencement on Sunday, May 13th. Washington springtime blessed the day with a silky breeze and mild temperatures, as blossoms were just beginning to poke from their buds.

For me, graduation day was more than special; it was the culmination and pinnacle of the academic year, a time when families gathered and the university family itself came together. As president, I had led the ceremony, which was always held on Mother's Day.

In this special ceremony, universities return to their medieval past, as professors and students don attire from a bygone yet not forgotten age. Parents and grandparents and brothers and sisters and sometimes graduates' children proudly packed the arena. They, plus the faculty and students, totaled some six thousand people. I always began the ceremony the same way. "Good afternoon. Today is a very special day." After a brief hush and a pause, as everyone anticipated the graduation, I went on. "It's Mother's Day! Will all the mothers please rise and receive our thanks." It brought down the house. The graduates stood, whistled, and cheered. "Hey, Mom! Thanks."

At the time I didn't realize the paradox in my leading a salute to motherhood. The ceremony symbolized study and achievement and family bonding. Pride overflowed the arena—pride of parents in the graduates, pride of professors in their students, and pride of us all in the university. All of us on the staff understood the day's significance, so we tried to give the graduates a dignified yet exuberant send-off.

On May 13th, 1990, I sat alone in the family room of our house, knowing that only a few hundred yards away, thousands of students and parents were gathering for commencement. Many of these students I'd helped recruit. When I had first met them, they had been eager and nervous high school seniors. Many of them that day had to be wondering, "What happened to Berendzen?" All they knew was that I had made phone calls focusing on childhood sexual abuse.

In a meager attempt at distraction, I decided to venture ten steps from the kitchen door to take out the trash. I squinted in the bright sunlight and, for a moment, noticed the flowers and lush shrubbery. As I casually glanced toward the street, I saw a graduate in his resplendent AU regalia—the academic robe I'd helped design—walking to the arena with his family. Their carefree happiness spilled into the space around them. I stood there holding the bag of trash and watched them walk out of sight. When I got back inside, I broke down.

The rest of the day, I sat in the family room, my favorite room in the house, with the blinds drawn. I gazed at the miniature world within our large aquarium. With the door shut and lights off, I just sat. And stared. And remembered. And thought.

Locked out of the ceremony physically, I locked into it mentally, playing it out moment by moment as if watching a video. I heard the thunderous applause as we thanked parents and families for their love and support and then saluted the faculty.

Before we presented the diplomas, I would stop the flow of the ceremony and ask the graduates to go back for a moment and realize that, in our rush through life, every moment can seem like every other. One day can blend into the next, one year into the following. Yet there are special, exceptional times, and this was one of them. I would remind them of when they were in high school, dreaming of college and growing up. When they wondered what the world would be like, and how they would fit in. I would remind them of taking exams, sending in their college application, and being accepted. Did they remember the trepidation of their first day, as they met their dorm mate and professors? Along the way they may have wondered, when does it come together? I would tell them that the rest of their life streams out in front of them now. This is a unique benchmark in their life. They should remember it and savor it.

Then I would return to the script and intone: "By authority of the congress of the United States of America, vested in the board of trustees of The American University, and by that board, delegated to me, I hearby bestow upon you the degrees for which you have been recommended and certified. . . ." As each name was called out, more than a thousand of them, the graduate would bound across the stage, shake my hand, and smile for a commencement photograph.

As I sat in my dark room I could see the smiles and hear the cheers. I was an outcast, and felt then that I deserved to be. It hurt to be so near yet so far from my university family. I still had no idea what the police and courts might do. Whatever it was, it couldn't equal the punishment that day brought.

The next morning I went back to Hopkins and talked to Berlin. I did not feel optimistic about my life or future. His encouragement, like Gail's, sounded sincere but hollow. They just didn't see the hideous bleakness ahead of me that I saw. By now, my anguish from the middle bedroom was resolved. The seemingly insuperable challenge before me was simply to get on with life. I kept my regular appointments with Berlin. I had faith in him, but not in myself.

Late one night, Sparky started barking relentlessly. We checked and heard someone rifling through our garbage cans. Since tabloid reporters had come to the door, we wondered if one of them was snooping. What anyone would have found of interest was beyond us. Nonetheless, we started bundling our trash in large green lawn-bags and taking it on my visits to Hopkins to dump. Just what Baltimore needed: trash from D.C.!

Ironically, my strong defenses, which kept out support from Gail and the doctors, could be breached. What penetrated it were dozens, then hundreds of letters from strangers. While I still hoped the university officials would ask how I was doing, instead the greatest solace was coming from people whom we scarcely knew and others whom we'd never met. They looked beyond the headlines; they wanted to provide comfort and hope.

My childhood had made me acutely self-reliant. Now, when I was at my lowest ebb and capsized in self-loathing, people I had never met, people who had no connection to AU, wrote to say they were thinking of me and praying for my family. I got to see the genuine goodness of people.

I was especially gratified when I heard from alumni, students, and faculty. Parents of graduating students wrote, as did parents of in-coming freshmen. As the days went by and the number of letters and calls grew, the scientist in me began to notice trends. A large per-centage of the mail came from groups that had faced adversity and discrimination: certain minority groups and women. They understood travail and compassion.

I also heard from religious leaders from many faiths. What a re-markable experience that was! They seemed genuinely in touch with the human experience. Their concern and ability to speak straight from the heart touched me.

In the past, when I'd sought inspiration, I had looked to the lives of great leaders and nineteenth century writers. I'd never before realized the exceptional ability of people all around me to provide inspiration and encouragement. Their thoughtfulness and selflessness moved me; their grace inspired me.

Gail got through those dark days by writing in her diary. "I'm scared. Richard is so sad. He gets really down. His suffering over-whelms me, too. What he has been through and what he has to deal with now is sometimes more than I can stand. . . . I need to get on with my life, but there is nothing to get on to. I can't shake this sadness and hopelessness. I can't be strong anymore. I want to do something . . . writing is good. Some of the sadness is now on paper and off my mind. I won't focus on the big threats to us, the uncer-tainties, the anger I feel. I'll make little victories today. I'll do plan-ning at the house for the move, throw stuff out, clear away years of clutter, and clarify my life."

Gerry Treanor said charges probably would be filed, perhaps by the end of May. In discussing options, he said the court could order me to another hospital for another assessment. I didn't think I could go through that. And the thought of going to court filled me with anxiety; the possibility of a trial was paralyzing.

For moments during this period, I was beyond suicide. Suicide requires some planning and some action. I was in a blind, whirling, lost daze. I felt so humiliated. The effects of what I had done to my family and to AU were more than I could bear. Suicide, at that point, would have been redundant.

I shouted at Gail, "I am dead! I died! You are simply seeing a corpse that should be buried. It's a perversity of nature that I'm still standing."

She would look at me and say, "Richard, what you were died, but what really counts about you continues to live. And I need you."

By mid May, charges were filed: two misdemeanor counts of making indecent phone calls. This now became part of the public record, and a court date seemed imminent. Gerry thought the hearing could come as early as the next week.

For good reason, I was still reluctant to go outside. When the press heard about the court hearing, reporters reappeared. Numerous news organizations asked for interviews.

A man tried to look in our closed windows, peered in our garage, and opened the backyard gate. Someone sat all day in a car across the street, and someone else stood for hours behind the front bushes.

Still, Gail insisted that I stop being a recluse. She said I needed fresh air. So sometimes at night I would go out in the yard and walk beneath the trees. Springtime was at its most luxurious. Azaleas, magnolias, rhododendrons, and dogwood bathed the neighborhood in colors and fragrances. For me, this had become the year with no spring. There, in the dark at night, I found it. But I couldn't appreciate it.

A friend offered his condominium in Western Maryland. We decided to go there for a few days. Gail said I should get away, and I half agreed. Besides, I didn't have the energy to argue.

We drove through low and rolling hill country, past Camp David, and found the tiny town, wedged in close to the West Virginia and Pennsylvania borders. Our muffler had gone out. So we found an auto repair shop. As the car rose on the lift, we noticed the bumper sticker: THE AMERICAN UNIVERSITY, NO. 0001. Few people would realize that this was the university president's sticker, but someone might identify the car with AU and me. We wanted total anonymity. With Gail's nail file, we dug the sticker out in strips from the rubber bumper. This last symbol of my presidency we ripped to shreds, bit by bit. Now it seems silly, but in our crisis mentality, it seemed not only logical but prudent.

For a few days we managed to turn down the volume on our anxiety level as we enjoyed the scenery and unassuming life of Western

Maryland. The farm folk and the coal miners came to town to the single movie house for its one showing. We joined them. They were real people, with neither the sophistication nor the phoniness of Washington. They faced tough economic times with apparent calm. The area is known for its beauty. It should be known for its people.

When the court appearance was only a few days away, we returned home. Every mile closer to Washington, my tension rose. Except for a couple of brief outings in remote locales, I had not appeared in public since the stories about the calls had appeared in the press. When the press hit, I was at Hopkins behind a bulwark of security.

Now there was no such security. Part of me felt relieved that I would be able to put this behind me, finally. But what path did I have to walk to get from here to there? My stomach knotted with anxiety. The court date was set for Wednesday, May 23, at eleven A.M.

I knew the charges but had no idea what the judge would do. From the outset I had intended to plead guilty. Gerry Treanor talked to the prosecutor. In exchange for my pleading guilty, he would recommend that I be given two suspended thirty-day sentences and no fine. Although the judge considers the prosecutor's recommendation, it is nonbinding. The judge could impose a different sentence or call for a report from another hospital before passing judgment.

Since my release from Hopkins, my most haunting anguish had been that I couldn't communicate my remorse to the many people whose trust I'd betrayed. They deserved to know the facts, to have an explanation. Initially, I thought about meeting with the press generally. My lawyers and I discussed it and ultimately decided that if I were to agree to any interview, it should be with one journalist.

After I had been home about a week or two from Hopkins, Ted Koppel talked to me about being a guest on *Nightline*. I'd been on that program a number of times, and I respected it. It was serious and nonsensational. I told him I would make no public statement until the court proceeding ended. I agreed to do the show then, but I would not identify my abuser. Otherwise, I had no stipulations; neither did he. *Nightline* would begin with a pre-taped piece as it usually does; then I would answer questions. He thought it might be informative to have one of my doctors on the program.

Meanwhile, at my request, Johns Hopkins wrote a detailed report about my treatment program and their findings. This report went to

Gerry Treanor, who gave it to the prosecutor. Thus the Virginia authorities had complete information from the hospital. They knew about the various tests I'd been given. In fact, they received all of my polygraph tracings. They had this information long before the court hearing.

Hopkins also prepared a slightly edited version of the report. The one for the police gave full details; the edited version did not identify my abuser. To reach people and let them know the truth, I took the unusual and painful step of releasing the edited version, which disclosed my confidential medical records. I felt that the university community and others deserved comprehensive, factual information about me. For weeks, speculation and rumors had been rampant. I thought people should have the facts.

I told Koppel that I would give him the public report, and agreed that I would do a special, extended version of *Nightline* the night of my court appearance. The other guest would be Dr. Paul McHugh, chief psychiatrist at Hopkins. Beyond that, we discussed nothing else about the program. It would be live.

The night before my court appearance, Gail and I accepted a friend's offer to stay at her apartment while she was away. I paced from one end of the apartment to another, saying, "Gail, I don't know how I'm going to get through this. Suppose the judge wants a few weeks to think about the case? I can't hole up any longer, reading Marcus Aurelius. What if the judge doesn't accept the plea bargain? What if the prosecutor changes his mind? And what about the press? Do you suppose they'll be at the court? I'm not sure if they know about the hearing. But, frankly, I'm scared."

Gail tried to be soothing. "Things will work out, Richard. We can get through this. It may be tough, but we're together. I know we can make it."

"You see nothing but birds and flowers," I told her gruffly. "How will it work out? You have absolutely nothing to base that on. Maybe it will, maybe it won't. We can't count on anything."

I walked around the dining-room table nonstop. I felt Gail was being Pollyannaish, convinced that the truth would ultimately set me free. She said I knew who I was, I knew what had happened, and I didn't have anything to hide. Her faith in me was unshakable; mine, nonexistent.

"You defy gravity," I told her. "You're not of this world. Your feet don't touch the ground."

When I woke up the next morning after hardly any sleep, my stomach was pitching and rolling. I felt seasick, standing solidly on the ground. I told Gail that I loved her dearly and apologized for putting her through such hell. I added that it was fine with me if she didn't go to the courthouse. "Of course I'm going!" she snapped back. "We'll be there together."

For the first time in many weeks, I put on a suit and tie. We met Richard Marks outside in his car. As we drove, I wondered what lay ahead. I hoped it would be brief and reasonably private. Would there be any press? We didn't know for sure.

"Good God!" I whispered as we neared the courthouse. A human wall of reporters spread in front of us. Gail took my hand. I squeezed hers back, and we started down the long sidewalk, directly toward them. How would we get through them? Questions pelted me like hail. "How do you feel?" "How do you plan to plead?" "What are your plans for the future?"

Marks took charge and said there would be a statement after the court appearance. One of the reporters asked, "There will be? Great! Thank you." Instantly, the wall parted. Instead of questions, the reporters now nodded at me, and some warmly smiled.

Treanor escorted Gail to a law library, which was reasonably private. I went to the restroom, primarily to be alone. It's odd what you'll think of when you're under duress. I thought back to the story that gave me courage when I was sick as a child. I thought of the little steam engine trying to make it over the mountain. "I think I can, I think I can . . ." It may have been a strange choice for inspiration, but that's what rushed into my mind.

When I rejoined Gail in the library, a reporter was talking to her. She gently asked if Gail had anything to say. Gail said she didn't. The reporter said she understood and left. Her sensitivity at that trying moment meant a lot. Gerry's staff took us into an office, which would be more private than the library. The woman who had the office greeted me warmly and pointed to a picture on the wall. It was of her son shaking my hand as he received his degree at commencement. In a day of pitched emotions, this was one of the finest. An employee of the Fairfax Court, she said she was sorry I had to be there and that she had faith in me. She said her son and other employees did, too. This act of grace gave me a measure of courage.

Reporters and police officers and everyone else with business at the courthouse that day jammed the hallways. At about ten forty-five, Gerry escorted Gail and me into the courtroom. We sat on one of the long, pewlike benches. It reminded me of church. The courtroom was filled to capacity, with people lining the walls. Gail and I held hands as people turned to stare at us.

"Richard Berendzen." When my name was called, Gerry motioned to me to come forward. The room became silent. I gave myself simple commands. "Walk to the front. Stand beside Gerry. Remember to breathe." I hoped the judge wouldn't ask me any questions that required thought. I was too tense. As I got up from my seat, a news anchor who used to interview me about astronomy reached back and squeezed my hand. Gail looked up at me, not able to hold back her tears, and softly said, "I love you."

I concentrated my entire being on trying to look composed. This was the first time these people had seen me since my resignation. I walked forward and stood beside Gerry. The judge turned to the prosecutor to introduce the case. Of course, the judge already knew all about it, and he, too, had seen the detailed Hopkins report. The prosecutor then began to summarize the phone calls in a brief, explicit way.

Many weeks earlier I had stopped seeing any coverage about my situation, because it upset me too much. Now, standing at the front of a courtroom packed with people, I heard a description of phone calls I'd made about child sexual abuse. Meanwhile, courtroom artists sketched the scene.

My reaction felt comparable to when Gail read me the *Post* story over my mobile phone. Although I felt the effect substantially less this time, I catapulted into a chasm of shame and humiliation. Nausea welled up in me. I feared I would throw up, or at least gag. I told myself to hold on.

Gerry had explained what would happen in court. Even so, since I pleaded guilty, I never expected the prosecutor to describe the calls. He did it with decorum; nonetheless, he did it. How can a loathsome, private matter be made so public? It was as if I were back in the middle bedroom and my buddies were eavesdropping.

At some point the judge asked me if I had anything to say. I steadied myself and murmured, "I deeply regret all of this." I was afraid if I said more, I'd be sick.

The judge then issued his ruling: a suspended sentence of two thirty-day terms, with no fine, and I was to continue my outpatient therapy.

It was over. Although I felt shaky, I also felt greatly relieved. But I was too ashamed to face the crowd. I looked the other way. Someone motioned for me to sit in the second row. I sat next to police officers, several of whom asked how I felt. "Not so good," I replied. One of them said, "Hang in there. You're a good man. A lot of us are pulling for you."

Moments later, an older police officer came up and whispered, "Follow me. Stick close." Leaving the packed courtroom was like moving through Macy's before Christmas. He took me down a side aisle, out the rear door, and then through a side door. We skipped down steps and through narrow corridors, passing police officers who nodded at me along the way.

When we reached the outside door, he pointed me to an unmarked car waiting at curbside with its motor running. As I ran toward the car, a camera crew that had just come around the corner did, too. I jumped into the car and we sped off, just as the cameraman arrived.

I thanked the driver and told him I was sorry to impose on him and the other police officers. And I said I was sorry about what brought me to the court. It turned out he was a detective who knew the case well. "I'm just sorry all this happened to you." he replied. "It must be hell for you and your family. I wish you the best."

We drove to Gerry Treanor's office, where Gail was waiting. Meanwhile, Treanor met with the press at the courthouse. He issued a statement from me that expressed my deep regret for making the calls and said that because questions would continue about the events that led to my resignation, I had authorized the release of a report from The Johns Hopkins Hospital that afternoon. I added that "In no way do I offer this report as an excuse for my conduct. Rather, it gives additional information, fills out the story, and provides a fuller context for my actions."

When we assembled at Gerry's office, Richard Marks called Tony Morella at AU to brief him on the court appearance. He explained that a copy of the Hopkins public report about me would arrive momentarily at Tony's office. Also, he told Tony that I would be on *Nightline* that night. Since it was the only interview I had given or planned to give since my resignation, he asked Tony to fax the Hopkins report and pass on word about the TV interview to the trustees. I felt strongly that I owed a direct apology and statement to the board and the university community generally.

The Hopkins report, released by authority of Dr. McHugh, said that a clinical staff of more than twenty professionals had conducted a thorough in-patient evaluation of me. The report explained that because people can engage in similar behavior for different reasons, they explored whether the phone calls indicated disorders such as pedophilia or "telephone scatologia," a compulsive craving to make obscene phone calls. Also, they investigated whether the calls expressed delusional thinking or hallucinations.

Although I did not understand their methodology until I read the report, the doctors had tested a variety of hypotheses. They had examined one possibility after another.

After the report discussed the numerous tests they had conducted with me, it gave a summary of the hospital's basic conclusions. It said they found no evidence that my phone calls were a manifestation of a general tendency to be antisocial, a paraphilic or sexual deviation disorder, or a mental illness involving delusions, hallucinations, or formal thought disorder. The Hopkins staff had studied the tapes in detail. The report further stated that I did not place the calls for prurient interest; rather, in a confused way I was trying to find answers to unresolved issues related to my own abuse. In this sense, the report said that to consider them to be obscene would be incorrect. The Fairfax County police department called them "indecent." The report said that was a more nearly accurate term. The report also said the person I called became a surrogate for my own victimizer.

It went on to say that I appeared genuinely remorseful about making the calls. It said that I was sexually and emotionally abused severely as a child. And it concluded by saying: "His prognosis, now that he understands how to deal with these issues constructively, and with his pain, is excellent."

After calling Tony, Marks drove us back to our hideaway apartment downtown. With the court hearing concluded, I decided to watch TV news for the first time in weeks. The local stations showed us walking into the courthouse while they described what happened in the courtroom. Seeing and hearing about myself didn't faze me this time, but seeing my wife on the screen made me shudder. Will this saga never end? What shame I've brought to innocent people.

As we sat down to a simple dinner, I asked, "Do you realize what I am about to do? I'm about to discuss my childhood experiences on live television! I feel like I'm about to have surgery without anesthesia."

Gail just looked at me.

"I don't know if I can do it. I truly don't."

But I knew I had to. At the end of ABC's *World News Tonight*, Peter Jennings promoted *Nightline*. "An exclusive interview . . . talking for the first time. . . ." or words to that effect. The local ABC affiliate promoted my interview on *Nightline* as the scoop of the day.

"Suppose I can't get words to come out or I choke up? This isn't like other interviews. This will expose the darkest, most hidden part of my soul."

My stomach was in revolt. Tumbling, exploding pains zigzagged through the middle of my body. We searched the medicine cabinet for anything that might help. There was nothing, so Gail dashed to a pharmacy.

While she was gone, I prayed. At first my prayer was rambling and disjointed. "Dear God, I don't know what I'm going to do. Please help me. I'm not sure I can do this. I feel so afraid. . . ." Then the words from the quietude of the Hopkins chapel came back to me. "Thy will be done." Just give me the strength. "Thy will be done." I prayed that my words on *Nightline* might reach others before they self-destructed as I had. I prayed that out of this bad, good would come.

Gail came back with antacid tablets. The instructions said to take up to eight a day. I took eight at once. But it was like holding an umbrella in a hurricane. My stomach remained a storm. I stuck the rest of the tablets in my pocket.

As we prepared to leave, I flicked out the lights, and Gail and I silently held each other in the darkened living room. Five minutes went by. Maybe ten.

"Bunny," I finally interrupted, "We've got to go." Downstairs, a limousine waited to take us to ABC.

As the car approached the studio, the driver called to us in the back seat. "I was afraid of that. Other press are watching for you at our front door. We'll try the back way." I looked at Gail and shook my head. We wheeled around the corner and headed toward a steel gate that was slowly rising. A camera crew rushed to the car, its bright lights illuminating the alley, as Gail and I dashed under the gate and into the bowels of ABC.

Dr. McHugh was in the green room when I arrived. I was glad to see him. He asked how I was. "Oh," I shrugged, "I'll be okay if my stomach holds out."

A secretary came in and said, "Excuse me, Dr. Berendzen, we've gotten several phone messages for you." This caught me off guard. Were they hate calls? Even though I'd received not a single such call or letter, I'd feared that I would. To have gotten even one before the TV program would have shaken me. Instead, several students and alums had called to wish me luck. One message I remember in particular. It was from Reverend David Eaton. "The Black pastors of Washington support you and are praying for you." In that tense moment, those gentle words helped to restore my soul.

The crew told us it was time to get our microphones on. Gail and I hugged good-bye.

A pretaped piece would precede the interviews with McHugh and me, I'd been told. That's all I knew about the format, and I had no idea what Koppel would ask. McHugh and I sat together in one room, looking at a camera. On *Nightline,* a guest doesn't see the interviewer. The guest can hear him in an earpiece, which feels as though it will fall out. The interviewer and numerous ABC personnel can see the guest every moment. The guest sees only the eye of the camera.

Koppel began the program by saying that in life we learn to wear masks, to conceal things, and to pretend to be in control. Then the pretaped part began with the theme, "Who is the real Richard Berendzen?" The introductory spot noted things I had accomplished at the university. Then some students spoke of their reaction to my plight. They were embarrassed and feared press about me would hurt their job prospects. That ripped at me, but it got far worse.

The piece interspersed brief, graphic descriptions of what allegedly I had said in the worst of the calls. I suppose I should have anticipated something like that, but I didn't. It hit me by total surprise. Beads of perspiration popped along my hairline; my heart raced. I felt ambushed and panicked and sickened. My feelings resembled those in the courtroom earlier, except this time it all was going into living rooms from Maine to Hawaii.

At the first commercial break, Dr. McHugh leaned over, squeezed my arm, and·said "How are you?"

I told him I was holding on. I should have added "barely."

I remember what he said next. "You'll be okay. Believe in yourself."

When Koppel interviewed me, I explained that I was now talking about things I had told no one and had intended to go to my grave telling no one. Circumstances had changed that. First I told one doctor, then two. Now I was telling the nation. I wanted others to learn from my experience. I pleaded with people who have been abused to discuss it with an appropriate person and to explore their own feelings, even if they don't think they harbor any feelings about the abuse. I said that if people are ever tempted to abuse children, they should consider the evil they do and the time bomb they plant. And I said I sympathized with any victim, male or female, anywhere, anytime.

When I spoke about the phone calls, I explained what I had learned at Hopkins—that I was trying to find a surrogate for my abuser, to find answers to questions left unresolved for four decades. I said I was "in effect talking to a person that I both trusted and loved, hated and despised all at the same time."

Koppel asked how I could resolve something or find answers by my speaking on a call. I tried to explain that these were conversations, not monologues. My interest didn't come from speaking but from listening. The prosecutor later told *The Washington Post* that it was "painful in hindsight" to see me trying to get information.

I added that two days before the court appearance, which was the soonest my lawyers would permit it, I had sent a written apology through the police department to the woman I had called. And I told Koppel that I wanted to state clearly that my childhood abuse did not absolve my adult behavior. Earlier that day, I had pleaded guilty to two misdemeanor counts of making indecent phone calls. The shame of that would live with me for the rest of my days. I told Koppel I was sorry for having intruded into anyone's life.

Koppel said to McHugh that many people were cynical about psychiatry and would wonder if it was being manipulated to excuse my behavior. Bristling, McHugh said Hopkins came to its conclusions after treating many hundreds of patients over the years. They had given me batteries of tests. Although no single test was definitive, the combination convinced them that I was not being deceptive or hiding anything. He said that as a child I had experienced "as severe a sexual abuse as you can suffer for a limited amount of time . . . as bad as you can get." Overall, he noted, my life had been one of "service and commitment."

For weeks, I'd wanted to explain the context of the calls and to answer the basic question of why I ever made them. Every amateur psychiatrist could have his or her own theory, but, with great pain, I had learned the true reason at Hopkins.

Never had I had an experience like this program. Before the nation, my soul was bare; my humiliation, obvious. The most intimate part of my life stood on public display.

I said I had failed the students as a role model, for which I was deeply sorry. I felt I had let down their parents as well, plus the alumni, the faculty, and the trustees. I said the students needed to know that I was vulnerable and fallible.

Even though I didn't identify my mother as the abuser and gave few details about my childhood, just getting that close to the topic shook me. My mother, now almost completely senile, was unaware of anything going on in my life. Even so, I still could not publicly break the code of silence. The prospect of doing so horrified me. My shame was too great.

After a commercial break, Koppel came back and said *Nightline* was getting many phone calls. One was from the head of the student government at AU, who called to say that the students supported me. What a sensitive, mature, and brave act. It brought my only smile of the evening.

Koppel concluded the interview by asking why I had agreed to do the program. I said that out of this bad, good must come. Surely, all this hurt had to lead to something worthwhile, it had to help someone. I wanted to say to other survivors, don't be as arrogant as I was and think you can control everything. Obviously, I could not. My message was to reach out, get help, and be aware of the long-term effects of childhood abuse. And I wanted potential abusers to understand the cataclysmic pain their wanton acts could cause.

When the broadcast ended, I sat numbed and bloodless. I hoped the program had benefited some viewers and had given the AU family a better understanding of recent events. I was convinced, however, that my life was truly over.

When I rejoined Gail, her pallor resembled a corpse's. We held hands and sat silently as the limousine returned us to our hideaway. We got our car and drove to a friend's home so I could see a videotape of the program. As we rode, I asked, "So, what do you think?" Gail and I always try to be candid and honest with each other. After a long pause, she replied, "I honestly don't know. The first part—the taped portion—about killed me. I kept thinking of you sitting there before the cameras. I don't know how you did it."

"Frankly, Bunny, I don't either. You do what you have to do. I felt so numb that I'm not sure what I said."

"You sounded fine but looked so pained. You didn't look your usual self. Heavens, how could you?"

"How do you think it went for Natasha and Debbie and your parents and all the AU people?" I then asked.

"Richard, the girls and my parents will be proud of you. What courage you showed! As for everybody else, I just don't know."

"Well, I know. I hope it helped somebody. But I am now truly dead. How can anyone discuss such personal, sordid matters over TV and then go on with life?"

"I don't know," Gail answered. "I do know this, though. Somebody better start talking frankly about child abuse. Before all this happened with you, I'd never even given this much thought. Somebody's got to break the wall of silence, the denial."

"Yeah, well don't talk to me about that. I just feel lifeless."

Our friends greeted us warmly at one-thirty A.M. They tried to reassure us. I wanted to see the tape for myself—except I didn't want to see it. After a few minutes of squinting at it, I said I'd watch the rest later. We thanked them and left.

We drove back to Nebraska Avenue and lingered outside in the dark night, as a cold breeze rustled the trees. In the coal-bin sky, no stars shone. There was no large cosmos. The limits of my world were finite, small, and contracting. Where was my world? Where was my base? Where was my future?

In eerie silence, we entered our dark house. Sparky, soundly asleep, didn't come bounding to greet us. By now it was two-thirty in the morning. We had risen at dawn for the court hearing. Was that part of today, too? Or was it in another lifetime? Gail went immediately to bed, as I sat alone on the sofa in the family room and pondered the void.

Seven

FACING THE FUTURE

The end had finally come. I had no plans, no goals, no schedule, and worst of all, no structure. For someone who had been too busy even for vacations, life without a plan was hell. Even at Hopkins, I had short-range goals: to get better and to get out. Then I had the hurdle of the court appearance. Now there was nothing.

To make a plan and focus on a goal, though, you must have hope and envision a future. I did not have hope, and I foresaw no future. I had love, but sadly, love was not enough. Gail loved me, believed in me, perhaps more than ever before, but you can't love someone out of a depression. I needed a goal, a structure, and a future.

The next morning, I woke in a mental fog. Where was I headed? I had no buoy. What shoals lay waiting in the haze? Did anyone know my course? Or care? Since the crisis, my former close colleagues and friends hadn't seen me at all until the night before on TV. And none had heard the embarrassing, highly personal findings from Hopkins until the day before. What was their reaction? I assumed we'd get calls. So I waited beside the phone.

Around lunchtime, a trustee called. "Dick, I was so proud of you last night. What courage. You must have helped lots of people." As we hung up, another trustee called. "I never dreamed anyone had such guts," he told me. "I'm absolutely on your side." A couple of other trustees called after that, but no university administrator did. Students and professors called, as did Gail's parents and Deb and Natasha.

People who called said I'd been "courageous" or "brave," which totally surprised me. That hadn't entered my mind. My goal had been to communicate with people I'd let down, and to try to help others. I had made it through the program through sheer determination, which isn't the same as courage. This hadn't taken bravery but resolute will. I'd gone into human autopilot.

That flight now had ended. Whether with a safe landing or a crash, I didn't know. The calls that day reassured me. The ones on subsequent days did so even more. I heard from a multitude of people, though still not from my closest colleagues. Mail began to arrive at ABC affiliates and at our house. Other people wrote to me at the university or at Johns Hopkins, which forwarded the letters. Our phone wouldn't stop ringing. The calls no longer came from investigative reporters but from students and alums and professors and people we didn't know at all.

Some people wrote to offer support; others, to share their pain. Pain, I learned, is a passport that takes us into other people's lives as nothing else does. Men and women who had been abused wrote to share their stories with me, and to say that healing is possible; I was not to lose hope. Their encouragement counted. I believed them when they said I could get better and find a meaningful life.

What truly surprised me were six people at the university who contacted me to say they had been abused. One man was a professor—a scholar and a fine teacher, respected by his colleagues and admired by his students. He described how my *Nightline* appearance had triggered powerful memories for him of abuse in his own childhood. I wondered if he had ever spoken to anyone before about this. Only at Hopkins had I ever spoken with men who had been abused, but this was a colleague, someone I thought I knew well.

A woman at the university wrote to say she had been abused by her father and had sought help after seeing me on television. No one knows exactly what percentage of the population were abused as children. Estimates vary widely, partly because it is hard to define "abuse." Would lewd or suggestive comments to a child constitute abuse? Obviously, intercourse and other direct sexual contact do. Where do you draw the line, however, for a child? In addition, people's reluctance to reveal sexual abuse in their childhood makes data collection even more difficult for the researcher. Some estimates go as high as one American woman in four abused or molested by her eighteenth birthday, and one man in six. Whatever the true figures are, all the statistics are startlingly high. Now, for me, the statistics assumed names and reality.

In the following week, as the press carried the Hopkins report, I heard from hundreds of survivors of childhood sexual abuse, young and old, male and female, ordinary citizens and national celebrities. I heard from people I did not know as well as from friends. I heard from the wives of abusers. I heard from survivors of childhood emotional and physical abuse.

Moreover, I heard from recovering alcoholics, from women who had been beaten by their husbands, and from men who had undergone unexpected bankruptcies. I heard from people coping with cancer and people who pulled through heart attacks and strokes. The common link once again was pain. In that pain lay the potential to form mighty human bonds.

By the end of that critical first week, I began to feel confident enough to venture out. Natasha and a friend were home from college. The four of us went to a small Ethiopian restaurant. Natasha, who was majoring in anthropology and African studies, wanted to eat there.

As we entered the restaurant, a man in a wheelchair grabbed my arm and said, "Hey!" I froze, unsure what might come next. "You've got guts. You're going to make it. Hang in there." He couldn't have known how much that meant.

The next night, we ventured farther. This trip, however, we neither chose nor wanted. We attended a funeral service for a special lady, Helen Palmer Kettler. For more than a year, she had fought cancer. Many months earlier, Gail and I had visited her in the hospital. As always, she had a lovely smile and, with a gentle Virginian grace from another era, had wanted to talk only about the university. We were saddened but not surprised when she died. What did surprise us was when her daughter called. "Will you please attend my mother's service? Shortly before she died, she asked me to be sure to call you. She knew the end was near and hoped you could attend her service." We would not have missed it.

Given that Helen had been a trustee, we knew that AU administrators and trustees would be there, too. In the funeral home, I bumped into Don Triezenberg, the vice president for development, whom I hadn't seen in many weeks. For the last sixteen years, I had seen him regularly. Time seemed to stand still. We agreed to meet for lunch the next week.

In the parking lot, I saw Ed Carr. I walked over to shake hands.

"It's been a hell of a time," I began.

"Yeah," he said.

"A lot has gone on. I'd like to get together with you."

"I'm busy now. We might be able to do it in two or three weeks."

"Well, Ed, I really would like to see you sooner than that."

He seemed reluctant. Nonetheless, a couple of days later, his secretary set the date for June 5th—one week after the funeral service.

I was anxious to meet with Ed for many reasons. He represented the university, and I wanted to reconnect with my institution, to share the experiences of the last few weeks on a human scale. I knew this time had been difficult for him, too. I was sorry for that, and wanted to apologize in person. And I wanted to thank him for having said to the press about me: "There is a professional man and a private man. The private man has a problem, and the professional man has a great record." So I was glad our meeting was set.

Meanwhile, Gail and I had invited some student leaders to the house. I had been deeply moved when Matt Ward, president of the undergraduate student government, called during my TV interview to say the students supported me. In addition, in the midst of it all, the student leaders had sent me a card with warm inscriptions: "Thanks for everything. We're with you. We love you." I wanted to thank the student leaders and to apologize personally to them. More than that,

I wanted to talk to them, face to face. I wanted them to know how sorry I was for embarrassing them and their school. And I wanted to answer their questions.

When the students arrived, several of them gave me hugs. As president, I'd gotten lots of warm handshakes, but rarely hugs. We sat in the family room and talked, just as I had in former days with students. Never before had the feelings been so intense, the warmth so great. The students represented the people I felt I had failed the most. Their graciousness and heartfelt words touched me unlike any others. One said he was proud of me for speaking out and was certain my words would help others. I described aspects of the Hopkins experience to them, like the sodium Amytal interview and the polygraph test. I felt like a teacher again, except that instead of explaining quasars, the brightest and most distant objects in outer space, I shared some of what I had learned about the darkest memories of my own inner space. As they left, one student paused. He softly said when the others were out of earshot, "I've been through my own hell. I understand what you've been through. I'm with you." He didn't explain and I didn't ask.

The next day I picked up my old friend and protégé, Don Triezenberg, for lunch. This would be my first conversation in person, since the crisis, with my closest AU colleague. We met, I'm sure, with every intention of being polite, reasonable men. After a few pleasantries, bottled-up feelings blurted out of me. I turned from driving and said, "Don, why during all this didn't you ever contact Gail, if not me?"

Don and I always had been direct with each other. I always appreciated his candor and welcomed his criticism. I did now, too. No longer his boss, I wasn't talking to him as my assistant, but as a man—my friend and colleague. I wanted an answer, an explanation.

He didn't give one. "It's been a hard time, a lot of confusion," he began slowly. Then his cheeks flushed with anger. "Why in the world did you, of all people, builder and protector of the university, make a bunch of calls that would put fund-raising and student recruitment at risk?"

"As well as me and my own family," I added.

"Well, if you want to put them at risk, that's your business."

"Wait a minute, Don. I'm profoundly sorry for hurting the university. God, I love the place. I didn't want to hurt it, but the calls weren't some fun event for me. I've spent many weeks now with therapists, real authorities in their fields, and I may have a bit more insight on this than you do."

"Well, you certainly jeopardized everything big-time. Why? Just for a kick? That's pretty irresponsible."

"Don, this wasn't a prank or something I did for a kick. You just don't understand. If you're willing, I'll drive you over to talk to the doctors. Maybe they can explain it better than I can."

At one point, Don said that after I had resigned, a local TV station told him they knew why I had stepped down. They had a story about the calls they were ready to run. I frowned, wondering how they had confirmed their story. Don responded, "No, they really were ready to air it. That's when Ed Carr went through that painful meeting, and finally issued the letter about your 'alleged personal improprieties.' "

The chronology then made more sense to me, and I regretted the tumult all this had caused for the people trying to steer AU. Even so, the press explosion still hurt.

Our acrimony flew back and forth on almost every issue. Civil wars are always the worst. Finally, I suggested that we'd have to agree to disagree. Truce. It cut me deeply to see how furious Don was with me. Even more, he was disappointed in me. I'd let him down. He had no understanding of the real nature of the calls or why I'd made them. We weren't communicating. In his eyes, I'd willfully cast aside university security for my own kicks. On this, his view and mine were polar opposites. It hurt to see a long and close association end.

Life, I was learning, could be wildly counterintuitive. I had assumed that my closest colleague, my alter ego for sixteen years, would understand the medical nature of what had happened—not forgive it or dismiss it, but at least understand it. And I had thought the young students I met, whose reputations and futures inextricably linked with AU's, would be my severest critics. Wrong on both counts.

My new self-education continued. Bill Holmes, the senior minister at the Metropolitan Memorial National Methodist Church across the street from AU, took me to lunch one day. As we sat in the corner of a restaurant populated by retirees, we ended up talking about theology and my ordeal. He gave me more than support; he gave compassion, feeling, and perspective. When he dropped me off at home, he shook my hand and said, "You've been through a lot. Before this, you had everything going for you. Your achievements, your family. All that is still in place. It may be hard for you to see this now, but you've been blessed. God *does* work in unusual ways. He can provide new insights and callings for people, and grace can come through intense pain and travail. You had talent. Now you have even more: You have grace. So rejoice! I'm happy for you. Really, I am."

I stared at him in bewilderment. I heard the words but didn't understand their meaning. I hurt so much, and he told me to rejoice! I had grace? What is that? I didn't need grace. I needed peace and self-respect and a job. But not grace.

I've always been suspicious of people who "find" religion or themselves when they face a crisis, but undoubtedly I had experienced something deeply spiritual in the Hopkins chapel. A door had opened there; now Bill Holmes opened it wider. Grace. That afternoon, I listened to the splendid old hymn, "Amazing Grace," one of my favorites. And I looked up "grace." The *Oxford English Dictionary* devotes nine columns to it! "The divine influence which operates . . . to regenerate and sanctify . . . to impart strength to endure trial . . ." Maybe now Holmes's words made more sense.

On June 4th, about two weeks after *Nightline*, I made my first foray into the downtown business area. A senior partner at KPMG, Peat Marwick, who was staff director of the city's budget commission, invited me to lunch. When my crisis hit the press, the mayor and I talked by phone, and I suggested his appointing Alice Rivlin to replace me as head of the budget commission. She had been director of the congressional budget office during the Carter administration. Reflecting the nonpartisan nature of the commission, I had asked her to cochair one of its committees with Frank Fahrenkopf, former chairman of the Republican national committee. So, the Berendzen Commission became the Rivlin Commission.

In my former life, a business lunch was as routine as the morning paper, but it now felt brand-new. I shaved, showered, put on a suit and tie, drove downtown, parked, and started walking toward the accounting firm. At a red light, a man I didn't know said, "You're Berendzen! I want to shake your hand. It's refreshing to see a man say, 'Yup, I made a mistake. I'm sorry.' I wish some others in this town would do that. I wish you well."

He handed me his business card. Reflexively, I started to give him mine. Then I stopped. Mine still said "President of The American University." He realized my awkwardness, said something polite, and went his way. My new nothingness rushed over me again.

I had no business card, no title, no secretary, no desk, no file, no office. It felt like everything that had defined me as a man was gone. This wasn't the first time I realized this, but it hit me hard as I stood amidst men and women with suits and briefcases on their way from offices to lunches. Messengers on bicycles, delivery boys, Federal Express drivers—everyone had a job and identity except me. In my suit and tie, I felt like an imposter.

Gail was equally marooned. She wrote in her diary:

"I, like Richard, have no definition. I used to be the wife of a university president. I was involved in so many things. I was interested in everything because everything seemed connected with my life at AU. I feel like I have nothing to do, to think about, or to plan for. Everything is unconnected. . . . Sometimes something will remind me of the way things used to be, and I will relive the horrors of the last several weeks in fast-forward, until I reach today. It is a horrendous mental journey."

The next night I had my long-awaited meeting with Ed Carr. He's a developer, and his office building in northern Virginia was so new that it lacked landscaping. I arrived at seven, and I think we were the only ones in the entire complex. It felt like we were two actors on an empty set. The sun was sinking, and the shadows lengthening. As we talked over the next three hours, night consumed the day.

Ed spoke first. "It's been a hard time. These past weeks have been difficult. . . ." He was more cordial than warm. I said how sorry I was for the discord and embarrassment I had brought to the university, and for the burden I'd placed on him.

He said he didn't know if his decisions always had been right, but when the choice was between the university and me, he had done what he thought was best for the school.

We talked about my tenure, and I said that I wanted to return to my faculty position after taking a suitable leave. A *Post* reporter was scheduled to interview me the next morning. Unless he saw a problem, I intended to tell her that those were my plans. For certain, she would ask. Although Ed was noncommittal, he didn't object. He added that a friend of his had said I could help AU greatly by returning to the faculty. Since he didn't understand the ins and outs of academic policy, he said he would have to consult with others. Despite his lack of giving an okay, he seemed receptive; he seemed neutral to positive. And he said nothing negative about my returning.

The most emotional part of the conversation came when we briefly discussed our respective childhoods. On this, he spoke openly and movingly. His situation had been radically different from mine. Still I felt a certain affinity and bond with him.

For some hour more, we had a frank, man-to-man conversation. Remarkable! There we sat in his spacious, largely unfurnished office, with the lights on and the windows bare. We looked out at blackness, while any external observer could have seen us clear as day. We *were* actors on a stage as we spoke our emotional and private dialogue. I, the former president, linked in this odd way with the chairman, who represented the institution.

It was a most unusual meeting—long and candid, emotional yet distant, bonding yet aloof. Even though I greatly appreciated it, I wasn't sure what we'd accomplished. We hadn't reached closure. The meeting had been neither positive nor negative. We had traversed a lot of ground, yet I wasn't sure where we'd gone. Or if we'd gotten there together.

Two days later, I had breakfast with Milt Greenberg, who had become the interim president at AU. Some ten years earlier, I'd hired him as provost, second in command to the president. He had served in that post during all my years as president, and I felt we had made a fine team. In addition, we'd become friends. Sometimes we referred to each other as brothers.

This would be our first conversation since the crisis. I felt empathy for Milt. Without warning, he had been catapulted into a maelstrom—first, to take over as interim president, and then to preside over a campus in trauma. When the press accounts broke about the calls, rumors reached me about wild theories explaining my behavior. Without facts or professional training, some individuals offered elaborate and preposterous analyses. Others spread stories about me that went far afield from the calls. None of these theories or stories had any substance; none was remotely close to true. In a few days they subsided. Nonetheless, it troubled me to see how some people reacted to crisis. Rather than wait for facts, they invented their own. Some people spread stories for their own gain, while "unnamed sources" simply distorted or fabricated facts. In times of sudden change, uncertainty, or shock, anxiety always can rise, and confusion abound. That, too, contributed to my remorse, for I realized that I had brought sadness and anger and apprehension to the university. After years of trying to bring it peace and pride, I'd inadvertently brought it discord and dismay. And now the leadership of the institution fell to Milt.

In April, after the press accounts had broken and while I was at the hospital, he had called an all-university meeting. In a statesmanlike speech, he explained the stages of grief and sought to reassure the university community. He also lauded my contributions and extended sympathy to my family and me. I didn't hear a tape of his remarks until much later, but when I did, I appreciated them—for myself and AU.

Over breakfast, we both started by saying this had been one helluva time. Then we chatted about my meeting with Carr. Milt said he liked the interview with me in that day's *Post*. This was the only print interview I'd given after the crisis, and I gave it because I felt I should respond to the major hometown newspaper, especially since its education writer asked for the interview. She wrote a fair and honest article describing my attempts to grapple with my transition. Milt said he found it moving.

In passing, I mentioned the part of the interview in which I'd said that I planned to take a year's leave and then return to AU as a physics professor.

"No! No, you definitely don't want to do that! You really don't," Milt shot back at me. He was aghast.

"I beg your pardon?" I stammered. His unexpected response dismayed me. "I've given this a lot of thought these past few weeks, Milt. Teaching is my profession and AU is my institution. I simply want to take a leave, heal, and let AU heal. Then I want to come home again."

"I'm telling you, you've been through great trauma and you don't want to do that. You don't want to return. You're going to plod around in McKinley Building teaching astronomy? No! You're confused. You don't know what you want. But you don't want that. No, you *must not return*. Absolutely not!"

I was flabbergasted. I asked him to explain, but he wouldn't elaborate. I left baffled. I tried to see the situation from the perspective of university officials, as I would see it if the roles were reversed. Certainly, all of this had caught them by surprise, and they had no guidelines to follow. Still, what was their attitude now? I didn't know and they wouldn't say. Was I being rejected or made to feel unwelcome? Were they paralyzed by fears of legal problems? Why not at least tell me what their concerns were?

Part of my anguish came from realizing the turmoil the university must be experiencing, and it hurt to feel estranged from men with whom I had worked so closely. This became another link in a chain of loss.

Emotionally, I was moving at least one step back for every two forward. Some days I seemed immobilized, and moved not at all. I began to understand that healing takes work as well as time. It doesn't just happen. I wasn't going to "get over it." I had to pursue it and tackle it. By early June, I wasn't sure this was even possible.

When to move? We began the difficult process of searching. Through the help of friends, Gail and I found an apartment we liked in Virginia, in a high-rise building located just across the Potomac. Best of all, it was close to Washington yet private and secluded.

Packing became our main occupation in June and July. Despite the charm of our new apartment, it was much smaller than the president's house. So we decided to move about a third of our possessions to Virginia, store another third, and discard or give away the remaining third. Even living things had to go. Gail gave away her spectacular seventy-gallon fish tanks. The apartment building did not allow dogs, so we found a new home for Sparky on a farm. We knew eventually he'd forget us and love the farm. He gleefully hopped into the pickup truck that came to get him. As it headed out the driveway, he looked back, his head cocked. His puzzled and worried look said a volume. It haunted us for weeks.

Our first joint step back into the mainstream came at a B'nai B'rith luncheon to honor a friend of ours. Months earlier, I'd agreed to be on the luncheon committee. After the recent events, Gail and I decided against going. Neither of us felt ready to attend a gathering with several hundred people.

Sometimes friends know better. Dear friends called to ask us to attend with them. When Gail hesitated, the woman insisted and said that she and her husband would drive us. We must sit at their table. No wasn't an option.

Gail and I had attended hundreds of events like this over the years, but never before with anxiety. This luncheon would draw political and business leaders, including members of the AU board—all people we hadn't seen since my debacle.

When we arrived at the hotel downtown, we reached the ballroom by descending a series of escalators in a vast atrium. I held my breath. Below I could see a crowd. At first, they were too far away to recognize. As we descended, we could recognize them, and the few who glanced up could recognize us. Would people stare? Would they shun us?

Hardly! Before we stepped off the escalator, people rushed up to greet us. Hands shot out to shake ours. Arms enveloped us in hugs. Beaming smiles surrounded us. "So good to see you!" "How are you doing?" "We've been so worried. . . ." We edged toward the ballroom, as more people dashed out to greet us. Once we got to the ballroom, others saw us and came from the far side of the hall. "Come sit at our table." "Stop by for coffee." "We're with you."

What an amazing outpouring of warmth, sensitivity, and basic kindness!

But the day wasn't over. When we returned home, we found that the postman had brought a carton of mail. Because many people didn't know where we were living then, some of the letters had taken circuitous routes to reach us. Today they arrived. What a diverse assemblage of writers! University presidents, survivors of child abuse, astronomers, recovering alcoholics, AU students and their parents, professors from other universities, business executives, AU alumni, an AIDS victim, AU professors, and people I didn't know.

That evening, I held Gail and said, "How fortunate I am—to have you, my daughters, and so many wonderful friends. And to get such support from people I don't even know. Maybe, just maybe, I can forge a new life out of the mess I've made. Anyway, I know I have few enemies and multitudes of friends. Thank God!"

Only two days later—on a sultry Saturday—that euphoria turned to melancholy and sadness. The time came for me to go to my former office to remove my personal belongings. Harry Schuckel, who as budget director had an office on the second floor, met us there and let us in. Only the three of us were in the building. To me, though, on that day that small building where I'd worked so long was filled with memories. The president's office building, the charming replica of a New England sea captain's house, once was where AU presidents lived. Given the hours I had worked, I effectively had lived there; I was there more than I was at the official residence. Much of my professional life had occurred in that house. From the creak of its floors to the musty smell of its attic, I knew that building well. Can inanimate and animate objects merge? That building had become part of me.

Over the years, Gail and I had had a tradition. Whenever I changed jobs or was promoted, we went to the new office with rags and sponges, cleanser and wood polish, to clean it until it shone. We arranged the furniture and shelved my books. Each time we had done this, we had brimmed with enthusiasm and hope.

Now it was just the opposite. My life rushed before me. I could hear echoes of student laughter, see professors' pride as they gave me their latest books, remember laborious meetings with administrators and trustees to resolve crises. I remembered Joan and Roberta politely and artfully handling complaint calls. Every memory brought melancholy but was too cherished to forget.

Books lined my study wall-to-wall. Some had been with me since high school and the days when I studied in the darkroom at home in Dallas. Others dated to my MIT days. Some were on higher education; others were on math, physics, or astronomy. Some were introductory; others were quite advanced. Which ones should I move to our apartment, which had almost no shelf space? Which ones to store? Which ones to discard? And how can you discard a book, especially an old friend? You don't discard friends just because they're old or you're crowded. But which ones will I need? Will I be a professor? If so, teaching what?

Returning to the president's office was perhaps my cruelest confrontation with my past. Memories from the middle bedroom brought their own horror, but that was a life I had survived. Now I was walking back into the life I had made. Everything I was, everything I had sacrificed so hard to attain, was symbolized by my office. Since I had made the phone calls there, the office was not only where I had reached my highest heights, but also where I had plummeted to my lowest depths.

I would reach for something to pack and suddenly remember a situation. It was like paging through a photograph album. There were no lifeless objects there; everything was filled with life, the life I once had lived and now must abandon.

We didn't finish on Saturday, so Harry graciously said he needed to be there Sunday anyway. The locks had been changed, and someone had to let me in. Harry did and then politely disappeared upstairs. He sensed my discomfort.

Books always have had a sacramental quality for me. Packing these books was not a chore, it was a rite of passage. It had to be done, but it hurt. For the most part we packed in silence. Gail had her own memories, and although this wasn't her office, it was certainly her life, too. Packing would have been easier if I had known my future. At that stage, on June 10, all I knew was that I had asked orally to return to teach. So far, I'd gotten no reply. We sealed carton after carton, unsure of our destination or our destiny, but painfully aware that we'd begun a long journey.

When we were ready to leave for the last time, Gail and I hugged, and she said she knew how hard this was. The empty office felt desolate, like a body without life. Or maybe that's how I felt. She went to the car and I stood there alone, with my memories ricocheting in a hollow chamber. I gazed at the bookless shelves, the barren desk, the cradled phone. I closed the door, took a deep breath, blinked hard, and left the building and my former self behind.

On May 18, before the court appearance and *Nightline*, Tony Morella, as university general counsel, wrote to Richard Marks, my attorney, that he'd been directed by the trustees to inform me of the

terms of my termination as president. At the end of the letter, he said
they would like to know my interests with respect to my faculty tenure
rights, which had been granted to me on September 1, 1974.

Procedurally, this was unusual. Faculty matters normally go
through faculty committees for peer review. Apparently the board
intended to take this matter outside usual channels. Instead of it
being professor-to-professor, it was to be lawyer-to-lawyer. On June
14, Marks replied in writing, noting that I had discussed my plans as
a faculty member with Carr and a few other key trustees. I requested
that the board approve a sabbatical leave for academic year 1990–91.
After that, I planned to resume full-time teaching responsibilities at
the university.

I assumed all would be fine with this request. It was straightfor-
ward and fit academic traditions. And I was an experienced professor
who, I felt, could contribute to his department and university. Any
other professor could have called a dean to check the status of his
request. In my case, though, unseen people were to deliberate while
I waited to hear from Morella, via Marks. So I waited.

Meanwhile, I had another special meeting at home. Just as I'd
invited student leaders over, I invited faculty leaders. I wanted to
apologize to them directly, too, and to answer their questions. I
thanked the officers of the university senate for sending me a statement of support many days before the court appearance. Their
thoughtfulness and sensitivity impressed me. What I'd thought would
be a one-hour meeting lasted more than two. What a pleasure it was
to reconnect with my faculty colleagues as we talked about professorial matters.

Many people reached out to us during those months. We were
invited to movies and to friends' homes for dinner. We'd never taken
time for friendships like this before. Our lives had been consumed by
official dinners and receptions, and we had sacrificed having friends
just as friends. Gail always had close women friends, but as a couple
we rarely socialized. Now we discovered the simple joys most people
take for granted. A few friends became a special part of our lives.
They diverted us from hurt, connected us to daily life, brought us
solace, and gave us hope.

Nonetheless, healing can take a serpentine path. Some nights we'd
come home from a happy evening with friends, and an hour later, Gail

would find me sitting alone under the pin oak trees. "Don't you understand?" I'd say when she asked if something was wrong. "They have a job, a career, a reputation, and a future. I don't. Why can't you see that it's over for me?"

And well-meaning people could leave me reeling. Shortly after the court appearance, a trustee and friend said to me, "You aren't planning on staying in Washington, are you?" When I replied that we were, he frowned and added, "Boy, if it were me, I'd move a long ways away. I sure wouldn't stay here." When I protested that we loved Washington, he replied, "Well, do what you think best. But I think you should leave town."

In a way, I knew he had a point. Washington lives on images of power or the perception of power. The warmest personal friendships sometimes last only until a person's term of office ends. And appearances count for a lot. In addition, Washington is the media capital of the world. My debacle would have attracted a fraction of the attention in most other cities. Even so, this now was our home, and we wanted to stay here.

Someone else—a gentle, well-intentioned man—said, "You know, you have brains, talent, personality. The only problem is the press attention. Why don't you change your name? Then you'd still have everything." So I was advised: Leave town and change my name.

Even though I was beyond my suicidal thoughts, I hadn't replaced them with anything positive. On some days I simply stayed at the dead end of my life. Gail didn't pressure me. She intuitively knew this was something I had to live through.

Then a jolting blow hit me. Word reached me that some key people at AU had decided I should never return to the university in any capacity. They were unnamed, and the information came second- or thirdhand. Marks had not yet heard back from Morella. I knew nothing directly. Was this just a rumor? How could I find out? This group, I heard, acknowledged that I had legal tenure rights but wanted to buy me out? Buy me out? End my career entirely at my own university, the one I'd tried to serve for sixteen years? Thereby possibly end my academic life? Occasionally, universities buy out or urge early retirement for a professor who is close to retirement. But for me, at my age? Unimaginable! This had to be a false rumor.

I felt I was at the bottom again, with nothing to lift me up. Feeling particularly morose, I tried to keep occupied. One day I drove to a store to buy more packing twine for our move. As I parked, a voice said, "President Berendzen?"

I turned, surprised and unsure of what might come next. A young man stood nearby. I smiled and corrected him: "Former President."

"Well, I graduated a few years ago and to me you'll always be President Berendzen. I just wanted to remind you of what you told us at my commencement."

"What was that?"

"You quoted Winston Churchill's shortest speech: 'Never, never, never, never give up.' I put that on my wall. It means a lot to me, and I hope you remember it."

That young graduate became the teacher, and I became the student. Moments like that made me want to try, really try, to make it to the other side of my trauma.

Gail received support in an extraordinary way. After our public travail, a small group of women decided to hold a luncheon in her honor, to show their continuing support. With the sensitivity and compassion that we men often fail to emulate, these women sensed her hurt and loneliness. When word of their proposed luncheon spread, other women asked to be included. The crowd swiftly became too large for a single home, so the event was shifted to a hotel function room. Like small streams merge to form a powerful river, what had been planned as a luncheon at a home ultimately overflowed a hotel ballroom.

Gail was the guest of honor at the lunch, and spoke publicly for the first time since our ordeal. This is what she said:

In the last two and a half months, I have learned many things. Briefly, I would like to share ten of these with you.

First—twenty-five years ago, when I married Richard, I loved him, admired him, and respected him. Now, today, having heard what I have heard, knowing what I know, I realize that I love, admire, and respect him even more.

Second, when all is said, what is fundamental is your faith, your family, and your friends. Especially at a time of crisis, they are absolutely bedrock.

Third, I have learned that loyal and sensitive people buoy

your spirit even on the roughest day and enable you to go on. If you ever know someone who might need support but you do not want to intrude, I urge you to overcome your doubts and reach out to them. Tell them what you are thinking. To them, silence might imply disinterest.

Fourth, I have learned that young people can be exceptionally insightful and compassionate. Students were among the first to express their concern and support for us. They were fair and objective. This gave me great hope, because students are the nation's future.

Fifth, on my long, daily drives in April from Washington to The Johns Hopkins Hospital, I learned that Baltimore's traffic is as bad as Washington's, that I-95 northbound has a remarkable amount of construction, and that the D.C. beltway is a mess every hour of every day.

Sixth, I found that during extreme stress my hair and my nails stopped growing. Apparently, when your heart is hurting, your body knows you don't need new nails.

Seventh, Washington, D.C. is blessed with many great resources. One of the least heralded yet impressive of these is Washington's remarkable core of women. They serve the city and the nation, often with little recognition. They care intensely about the community, about civic issues, and about each other. I have found that they bond. You here today exemplify exactly what I mean. I am proud and honored to know you.

Eighth, I have learned anew how much each of us can be the hostage of our own past. And from the hundreds upon hundreds of letters and calls we have received, I have become aware of how many people are living with pain—sometimes from their childhood, sometimes from their recent past. Whenever it occurred, that pain lingers on. And they are dealing with it. My heart goes out to them, and I salute their bravery.

Ninth, I discovered that many people do not know how to react to an emotional problem. For a stroke or heart attack, they know. But for an emotional problem, they are uncertain. Well, the pain there can be just as real and intense as with any physical affliction. In the midst of our travail in the press, one of our daughters said to Richard: "Daddy, if your body were hurting, people would send flowers. Your mind is hurting, so they throw bricks.'

And tenth, I have learned that from adversity can come strength; from pain, hope; from tragedy, insight. And, I pray, that from hurt and calamity can come healing and renewal.

When she finished, she received a standing ovation. Afterward, nearly everyone there came up to greet her. One prominent woman hugged her and whispered in her ear, "I was abused, too." Then she turned and walked away, her private pain once again tucked beneath her elegant composure.

I anxiously waited for Gail at home. Even before she arrived, I sensed what had happened, because about fifteen women called to ask for copies of her speech. Everyone told me how extraordinary she had been. I was—and still am—awed by the support women give each other. The spontaneity, genuineness, and depth of affection Gail felt that day was unparalleled in my experience. These women reached out to her because they knew she was in pain. I've been struck by how men and women respond differently to pain. Women try to support one another, while men often assume the other guy can handle it fine on his own.

I'll always remember that afternoon for another reason. It was the first time I had seen my wife smile, really smile, since our crisis had begun.

We spent most of July packing for our move to an apartment in Virginia. The city was sweltering, and the days seemed to blur into each other with a monotony as enervating as the humidity. My calendar, which used to be so crowded, now had single entries for entire days: "Pick up key for apartment." "Gail's mother arrives." Months before, my goals for a morning might have been to chair a meeting, give a speech, meet a donor. Now for a day it was: "Pack three cartons." I still worked by Management by Objective, but my objectives had changed.

Natasha, who was home, seemed almost oblivious to our packing. I kept saying, "Natasha, please give me your things to pack. I need to know what you want to take to Virginia, store, or get rid of." Days went by and nothing happened. Finally, when I told her the movers would arrive soon, her eyes moistened and she lowered her head.

"Daddy, I find this hard. I find this very hard," she said in a shaky voice. "AU is where I grew up. Where's my stuff going to be? Where is Brownie going to be?" We'd given this teddy bear to her when she was a baby. During their nineteen years together, Brownie had had operations, weddings, and a multitude of other adventures. Retired now, he was relegated to sitting on her bed, but he still symbolized many things to her.

I told her, "Natasha, you can take Brownie with you to school, or you can pack him and know he will be in Box Thirty-four at the warehouse. This house will become a memory—a good one for you, I hope. But you always will have a home with us wherever we are. You can come back to it any time."

Brownie went to college with Natasha. That small brown bear made us realize that it was harder for Natasha to detach from the house than for us. Even though she'd never felt totally comfortable in that house, she had grown up there. As a kid, she had roller-skated in the driveway; as a teenager, her rock band had practiced in the basement. The new apartment in Virginia felt as impersonal to her as a hotel room, and since she lived in a dorm at school, she felt she was losing the only home she'd ever known.

My first step toward resuming a professional life came in early July when a bank holding company asked me to do consulting on the Community Reinvestment Act, the federal law that requires banks to provide services to low- and moderate-income customers. Although I wasn't a professional banker, I had served on a bank board and believed strongly in the CRA. I was delighted to accept the assignment.

For the first time in three months, I had a place to go in the morning. Shave, shower, put on a suit—it felt simultaneously familiar and strange. Attaché case in hand, several mornings a week I walked out the door and went downtown.

They found a desk for me in a remote, windowless corner of the bank. It didn't matter. I got a pad of paper and some pencils from a supply cabinet, and started setting up meetings with people who headed housing projects and community development groups.

The people at the bank were terrific. A young man my daughter Deborah's age was the bank's compliance officer. What a splendid friend and colleague he became, as the two of us met with leaders of the poorest and most dispossessed people in the city. Women at the bank gave me hugs with tears in their eyes, and men shook my hand and said, "I'm glad you're with us."

It's easy to take a lot for granted, but I'll always be grateful for the kindness and support people showed me during those first weeks and months. A cab driver on M Street downtown honked, gave me a thumbs-up sign, and shouted in broken English, "Don't give up!" The doorman at the Mayflower Hotel said, "I admire your effort to help people. I'm praying for you." A waitress asked, "Aren't you Dr. Berendzen? I'm pulling for you."

One morning at the bank, my meeting ended by ten-thirty. I, who used to delight in efficiency, was disappointed that it didn't take longer. Now what? All I had to look forward to at home was packing more boxes. I couldn't stand the thought. So I did the next best thing to having a life. I imitated one.

I left the bank and said to myself, suppose I have a vitally important meeting five blocks away. I joined the professional current on the sidewalk, assuming the brisk, determined pace of the men and women around me. Intense in concentration, I walked with purpose and vigor. When I arrived at my destination, I stood in the lobby awhile, glanced at my watch, looked around as if expecting a colleague to join me, and then left and headed somewhere else.

After an hour or so, I tired of this charade and got on the subway with the tourists and retired people who use public transportation in the middle of the day.

Before boarding the Metro, I purchased a pocket-sized Brain Teaser booklet. On the subway, I tried the high school level math and logic questions. Years ago, I used to do these for fun. That day, something was off. I couldn't concentrate. I couldn't compute. My reasoning seemed murky. What is this? At first I was bemused; then, perplexed and even a bit frightened. Had the recent trauma done something to my thinking ability? What a horror! This is my life. My motor skills worked fine. I talked fine. Yet my analytical skills seemed befogged. I'd have to try this little test again later. At Hopkins, I'd done well on psychological exams of mental acuity. Did the trauma leave a longer term effect, or was I just imagining it? I didn't know.

I was a ship adrift in the fog. I didn't know where I was headed or if I was moving at all. The university still hadn't made up its mind about my tenure. I went aground on this reef every time I tried to unfurl my sails.

Then we got another jolt. Natasha was driving our Volvo when it spun on gravel, skidded over a hill, and went head-on into a massive willow tree, uprooting it. The underside of the sturdy car was demolished, but, thank God, Natasha managed to walk away unscathed. Gail got the call and dashed to the crash scene.

By the end of the day, the pressure and tension of the past few months coupled with the fear of almost losing our daughter became unbearable. My strong and stoic wife finally let herself go and dissolved. She cried more in a few hours than she had in the twenty-five years we'd been married. It brought a catharsis that was long overdue but frightening.

Natasha's accident exacerbated other pressures Gail had been feeling. It was the tremor that further fractured the fault lines. For days, she'd murmured that the scar from her operation bothered her. After the accident, it seemed to knot and sear through her skin. For two hours we sat on the sofa and I held her. Our only words were mine: "Let it out. You'll be okay. I've got you." I tried to be as strong for her as she had been for me.

Truth was, though, the accident had stunned me, too. We could have lost our irreplaceable daughter. So I'd lost my job, home, reputation, and privacy. Those were nothing compared with the terror of losing your child. Then, too, I was worried about my wife. I'd never seen her so low before. I resolved to be sturdy for her even if all else shook.

Then came the call.

"Richard," a trustee told me, "some key individuals in the AU community have considered your request to return to teaching after taking a leave. They're absolutely opposed to your coming back at any time or in any capacity. So they propose instead a lump sum payment for you to surrender your tenure rights as a faculty member."

By then, most of our things were packed for moving, and the rugs were rolled up. I sat on the hardwood floor, my back against the living room wall.

"What?" I stammered out. "You mean I can't even go away for a while and return? Why? I just want to return to my university and teach."

"Well, everybody respects the job you did. But this group is adamant about your not returning. Why don't you think about it? You don't have to respond right now."

"But I know my answer right now," I replied. "No! I don't want a lump sum. What I need is a career, one based on my education and experience, and I need security for my family. Damnit, I feel like I'm being cut off from my institution and even from my profession."

After we hung up, I turned off the light and sat on the floor in the dark, thinking how long a fissure line had stretched from a darkroom in Dallas to this dark room in Washington.

Later, Gail asked about the call. I told her, "Oh, it was just on-going negotiations with AU. We can talk about it later." I would tell her about it, but not tonight. Not with what she'd already been through.

A few days later, she went to see Dr. Berlin. She had talked to him at length about me, but little about herself. In part what prompted her to make the appointment was her upcoming trip to Dallas to check on my mother.

One of us went there several times a year. The time to do so had come again. We couldn't put it off any longer. I was enmeshed with AU negotiations and lawyers. So Gail decided to make the next visit. Since this would be the first time she would see my mother since learning the truth about my childhood, she was extremely apprehensive. Berlin helped Gail, and she and I discussed the trip at length. Finally she decided she was ready to go and, in a way, needed to go for her own sake.

My mother didn't even recognize Gail when she rang the doorbell. Gail explained who she was and why she'd come. She went into the house and checked that there was enough food and that nothing needed urgent repair. Everything looked in order, except my mother had adopted numerous stray cats. Gail talked to the neighbors who looked out for my mother, and then she left.

When Gail returned to the house the next day, my mother regaled her with stories from her past about places she had been and trips she had taken when she traveled the nation by herself. She has retold these stories for years. Sometimes her stories would jump decades, as she would rat-a-tat out her words in a jumble. She never talked about people. Except for Laddie, her beloved dog of her youth, she only remembered physical things—mountains and rivers, flowers and fields.

A dog barked outside. Gail asked, "Laddie was such a wonderful dog. Where did you get him?" This was the first time either of us had seen my mother since the Hopkins doctors had tried to talk to her. She looked blankly at Gail and replied, "Oh, I don't know where I got Laddie. But there was something else I felt I should tell you. It was important. What was it? I can't remember. It had to do with Richard." Then she got up to let another batch of cats through the front door. She never completed her thought.

On this trip Gail learned firsthand what I had perceived at Hopkins—that you can hate the sin and not hate the sinner. Both of us have felt rage toward my mother, but then there she was: a confused old woman. Her fury and passion long ago succumbed to time and age. Only her confusion remained.

By late July, Gail and I started moving lamps and dishes and other delicate items to the apartment. We drove them at night in Natasha's lumbering old Ford station wagon. As her first car, it was perfect for her. She could fit numerous friends in it, along with her band's instruments and huge speakers. One muggy night, we decided to move Tin Man. This full-body suit of armor has been part of our home for years. As a child, Natasha named it after the character in *The Wizard of Oz*. With any motion, the old leather straps that hold it together were likely to snap. We didn't trust it to the movers. So we carefully tried to take it to Natasha's car. But as we moved it, a strap broke and an arm fell. Then the other arm severed from the body, and the hand broke from it. We gathered up the parts and laid them in the bed of the car.

On our way to Virginia, we stopped for gas on Wisconsin Avenue in Georgetown. As I filled the tank, I looked in the window at the broken, disjointed parts of the once dignified suit of armor. It had stood so straight and true in our hallway. Whenever students came over, they were drawn to it and enjoyed trying on the helmet. Now it lay in parts in the back of a used station wagon, on its way to a new home and an uncertain future. "Bunny," I said to Gail in the front seat, "old Tin Man and I share a lot tonight."

About then a car screeched to a halt at the pump beside ours. It was filled with young men, who looked like they'd had a long night at the nearby clubs. One of them did a double take when he saw me. He pointed my way and the others stared. He cupped his hand to his head like a telephone receiver. His friends roared. As Gail turned her head away, a tear started down her cheek. I reached over and brushed the tear away, glared at the young men, and the three of us—Gail, Tin Man, and I—drove off in silence.

By the time we got the suit of armor into the apartment, it was late and Gail was tired. "Why don't we try to reassemble him tomorrow?" she asked. "No," I replied. "He's broken. By God, I want to get him standing tonight." Gail smiled as she lay down on the floor. "I knew you'd say that. Just let me sleep here, and wake me when he's upright." So for the next two hours, with bailing wire and duct tape, I put him together. Finally, I woke Gail.

"What do you think?" I asked.

"I can't believe it," she said with a grin. "He's standing again."

"Yes, and I will, too, someday. It just takes wire and tape and time."

On August 1st, I had dinner with Romeo Segnan, the physics department chairman at AU. A charming man, he exudes optimism. He was about to leave for a year's sabbatical in his native Italy, and I was a professor in his department. Only a few months earlier, while president, I'd given a guest talk in his astronomy class. Over a bowl of pasta, he asked me, "So, Dick, what are your plans?" Clearly, he was out of the loop. He seemed to know nothing about the university's negotiations with me. How odd. Normally, a chairman would be at the heart of a faculty matter. Even though this wasn't a normal situation, I had assumed he was abreast of it. I told him that I intended to remain a tenured faculty member, take a sabbatical, and then return to teaching. I added that all this was murky because the university and I were involved in negotiations. He didn't ask more, and I didn't elaborate. I assumed this was confidential and, besides, I didn't know much myself. I hadn't accepted the buyout, and the university hadn't approved my return.

More than he knew, I enjoyed meeting with Romeo. His upbeat spirit invigorated me, and I appreciated the colleagues I'd have on the faculty. Even though discussing teaching in his department with the former university president must have been awkward for Romeo, he couldn't have been more gracious. He seemed pleased that I might join him, and I was delighted by the prospect.

As August dragged on, I spent several days a week at the bank or at a friend's real estate development firm. Although my friend had no salary or office for me, he included me in his staff meetings. This helped my morale, but I still had bouts of depression. Even with something to get up to do, this life was surreal. I wasn't going to become a professional banker or real estate developer. I was an astronomer, an educator, a teacher, and a manager. Why couldn't I be in my rightful world—somewhere doing something worthwhile? On my gloomier days, I lurched back into depression. Oh God, I thought, not this! Did the black hole have me again? Please, oh please, no.

I had no job, no career, no prospects. About then, a new embarrassment hit another raw nerve. Natasha needed a cosigner for her apartment at college. Of course I'd sign. Then I got the application, which asked: Employer? Employer's address? Annual salary?

How could I reply? How could I back my daughter, who simply wanted to secure a student apartment? Every day brought a new indignity. And worst of all, I knew I had caused it myself.

My former thoughts of suicide didn't return. By then, I felt like I already was dead. "My blood is circulating, my heart is beating," I told Gail, "but so many aspects of me are dead."

"You're down now," she'd tell me. "After you heal, you'll be full of life again."

"If I can't even protect my own family, much less provide a future for you, then I effectively am dead. Besides, some people act as if I am already. If key people don't call or return my calls, if they don't include us in their lives, then I might as well be dead. For all intents and purposes, I am!"

Life, I learned, was quite capable of going on without me. I had resigned from committees, boards, and commissions, and they'd continued without missing a beat. It was like dropping dead from a heart attack, and then, as a ghost, watching Gail remarry and go on happily with her life. Intellectually, of course, I would want her to be happy with someone else, while at the same time, I would have the gnawing feeling that I had been easily replaced, that it could have been anybody, that it didn't have to be me. Then I'd think how petty and foolish I was. Of course life went on. I wanted it to. But could I be replaced that easily?

I knew that to heal and rebuild, I had to step aside for a time. Still, it was hard, for no manual exists for healing. No map shows the way.

One sweltering August night, Gail and I went out with a prominent couple from California I had met while president at AU. They were in town for a few days, and we offered them an evening tour of the monuments. When we dropped them off about midnight at their hotel, the man and I got out of the car and stood outside while the women continued talking inside.

He had seen me on *Nightline*. We talked about what had happened in my life during the past few months. Suddenly, without warning, he looked at me and said, "Now, Dick, I was sexually abused by a woman when I was a boy. It messed me up for several years. I got straightened out with help from doctors and therapists, but for several years I was very confused and wasted a lot of my life. It was sheer pain. I got nowhere professionally, and it hurt me personally, too." His abuser had not been a relative. "But if she had?" I asked. "Unthinkable, absolutely unthinkable!"

This was one of those rare moments I'd come to appreciate, of candid communication with another man—something that hadn't happened much since Hopkins and rarely before. More stunning still, I realized that the statistics I'd heard were true. Vast numbers of men—including truck drivers, professors, and professionals like my friend tonight—have been sexually abused as boys. Many of the abusers were women. This perversion knows no boundary of geography, race, creed, or income level. Its survivors are everywhere. You meet them every day.

Landmark days—New Year's Eve, an anniversary—offer an opportunity to reassess and to plan. So it was on my birthday on September 6. At fifty-two, I was proud of my achievements, disappointed by my failures, and quite aware that, even though I was just in my professional prime, lots of talented and ambitious young people were right behind me.

I felt like a fifty-two-year-old who had never figured out what he wanted to be when he grew up. I didn't know where to turn for guidance. As always, I had begun with books. I had scoured how-to and self-help sections of bookstores. They didn't help. I needed something else.

I remembered Gail's wise observation that "faith, family, and friends" are what ultimately pull you through. This trinity, in times of crisis, is fundamental. Upon it, you can rebuild. To do that, you must believe in yourself and have hope. Without hope, life has no tomorrow. Genuine belief that a tomorrow will come—a better tomorrow—gives hope. And hope makes life possible.

So, then, on my symbolic day, how could I tap into my faith, family, and friends, believe in myself, define myself more through relationships, and find hope? If weather is an indicator, my future looked bright. On a crisp and sunny morning on the sixth, Gail and I had breakfast with the ninety-five-year-old founder of the Wolf Trap Foundation and Farm Park for the Performing Arts. As we ate outdoors beside her home, her continuing vitality in spite of the many hardships she had weathered inspired me.

Afterward, we returned home, where I had delightful phone conversations with Natasha and Deborah. Then Gail and I had lunch with an old friend from California. We stopped by the National Cathedral for a quiet interlude in one of the small chapels. Then we drove to Chestertown, on the eastern shore of Maryland. An idyllic small town on the Chesapeake Bay, this is the home of Washington College, Maryland's oldest institution of higher education. Since 1962, the college has held the William James Forum. I was honored to be the kick-off speaker for the new academic year. Numerous times before, I had given talks about astronomy. However, this would be the first public address I would give since my crisis. How would it go?

Professors and student leaders greeted me. The college president came, too, as did visitors from the town. As usual, I spoke ad-lib. I didn't dwell on astronomical findings. Instead, I stressed the cosmic connection—how we humans are linked with a system far vaster than ourselves. How we are made of recycled stellar matter. Our very bodies came from star stuff, as Carl Sagan has put it. And as Harvard astronomer Harlow Shapley once said, "We're brothers of boulders, cousins of the clouds." In such a system, our day-to-day concerns shrink to infinitesimal nothingness. I refound my old love of astron-

omy; I was fortified by speaking about things far greater than ourselves. It truly did give perspective.

Who learned more that night—the audience or me?

By September I began to feel I had gained a foothold on optimism.
Although the cherry blossoms make springtime in Washington famous, for me fall is the best season. The days are crisp, the foliage
magnificent, and the beauty lingers, unlike the cherry blossoms,
which fall almost as soon as they bloom. But September always has
been the New Year for me—the start of the school year, the season
of rebirth, the time of new beginnings. This September, my usual
rhythm was off. For the first time since I was ill as a young child,
September didn't mean the new academic year for me. Whether as a
student, professor, or administrator, it always had been the same.
This year was different.

So, too, was my next talk. Instead of my usual themes of astronomy
or education, this one was on surviving childhood sexual abuse.
Never before had I given a speech on this subject. Never did I dream
I would. In the summer, the Department of Family and Community
Development at the University of Maryland asked me to be a special
guest speaker at a conference for therapists. It was open only to
professionals in the field, not to the press or the public. I wondered
if I was qualified to address such a group. They said I could provide
valuable insights, and urged me to synthesize my experiences for
them. Finally, I agreed.

I described the feelings I had as a child during the encounters with
my victimizer—the deep shame, the fear, humiliation, despair, sometimes excitement, and then the terrible burden of guilt coupled with
overwhelming confusion. Why was this happening to me?

Then I talked about my coping mechanisms. I said avoidance had
been my first line of defense. I avoided my abuser.

Control was next. I tried to learn how to control my feelings. If they
troubled me, I would deny to myself that anything serious even had
happened.

So denial became my next line of defense. It's the blank check on
which you write the cost of your sanity.

By intellectualizing, I refined my denial skills. I taught myself to
analyze the abuse rather than feel it. Thoughts are easier to control
than feelings; thoughts are a way to bring feelings under control.

"Well, she did this to me and it's terrible. But she does care about me and wants the best. . . ." Intellectualizing certainly helped me minimize my pain and create a world where I could live safely. It wasn't so bad. I still looked the same. No one knew.

Denial was when I told myself it hadn't happened at all. When feelings would surface, I repressed them. DON'T THINK ABOUT IT!

Sublimation made it easier to repress my feelings. Do something else. Work hard. The harder I worked, the easier it was to keep everything under control. I got good grades. I felt proud. I succeeded. I chiseled out a place for myself in the world.

To my surprise, the professionals really wanted to hear my perspectives. I did not reveal the identity of the woman who abused me, nor did I go into details about the abuse or my treatment at Hopkins. It was too soon; I wasn't ready. But I did discuss candidly my feelings as a child, my coping mechanisms, and some of what I'd learned since my crisis. Never have I had a more attentive audience. After the session, many participants stayed to talk with me privately.

That was a significant part of my own healing process. With the two talks I'd given, I began, just began, to feel worthwhile again. It came not from Gail saying I was a good man or Dr. Berlin reassuring me. It came with this affirmation from people I didn't know.

Throughout the fall, I continued my regular outpatient visits to Hopkins. By then I had examined and discussed exhaustively my abuse as a child, what prompted me to place the calls, and my ensuing public nightmare. The doctors and I explored every nuance of those issues. We agreed that they were resolved. In that aspect of my life, I felt whole, confident, and at peace.

My relationship with the university, however, remained unresolved. Initially, when I was told that I should accept a buyout for my tenure rights, I was stunned and deeply hurt. I attempted to fight it, but a strong and implacable group wanted me out. Reluctantly, I finally gave up hope of returning to teach at AU, and began instead to discuss the proposed settlement. This led to proposals and counterproposals, to long negotiations, and to acrimony.

Many trustees thought if my career were to be bought out, it should be for an amount in line with buyouts in other professions. When information about these private deliberations leaked—some of it misinformed—the campus quite understandably erupted. The larger university community—faculty, students, staff, alums—had known nothing about the buyout. The process relating to my faculty status had proceeded confidentially and unconventionally. Rather than follow the usual path through faculty committees, my faculty matters were handled exclusively in private by trustees, senior administrators, and lawyers. To confuse the situation more, someone then spread the rumor that I had demanded an endowed faculty position with a light teaching load, numerous graduate assistants, special travel funds, and a private secretary—none of which was true.

Oddly, even though these matters pertained directly to me, I became almost a peripheral player. Debates raged among trustees, administrators, professors, students, lawyers, and others. Many people were involved in determining my fate, but for a time I found that I had little to say about it.

I never expected this new upset for the university or me. Soon I found myself sliding back into the grips of depression. While the campus churned, I stayed all day in my darkened bedroom, terrified that I'd fall into that black hole, never to escape. By then I didn't care if I were bought out or went back. I just wanted it to end. I wanted peace to return to the university, and I wanted to escape the horror of the hole.

In the midst of it all, I received wonderful reassurances. Students wrote and called me to say they'd welcome me back. I shouldn't be bought out. They wanted me as a professor. Alums and staff and professors contacted me, too. For almost eight months, I hadn't been on campus. Since my disgraceful departure, I had had only a handful of direct conversations with campus people. These calls and letters, which came at that critical time, reassured me, and I thought I saw a way to restore comity to the campus. I stated publicly—not just confidentially for contract negotiations—that I wanted to go back and that I would not accept the purported buyout if it were offered to me.

Clearly, my relationship with the university presented the campus with an emotional, complex, and unique situation. The trustees as a group and the university community as a whole attempted to deal equitably and prudently with it. By early December, the matter was resolved. The university agreed that I could return to the faculty, starting in January of 1992. During 1991, I would be on administrative leave.

As the days got shorter in that fading, fragile light of fall, I finally had direction. And soon I found the beacon, the North Star, that showed me the way home. On the gravestone of a nineteenth-century astronomer is inscribed: "Stars have been my friends so long that darkness does not frighten me." I finally faced the future without fear. Uncertainty still abounded, but fear finally faded.

On my visits to Hopkins, I always stopped in the chapel before my appointment and then again afterward. One afternoon as I sat there alone, I thought to myself, "I now know who I am, where I am headed, and what I must do." It wasn't a thunderclap or lightning bolt. My epiphanies are plainer than that. I realized in the chapel that day that, for the first time since my resignation, I could make long-term plans.

Eight

RENEWAL

I focused on 1991. I would be on leave that whole year, so I had that time for mending and rebuilding. I decided to use it to renew and restore my mind, my body, and my spirit. I would immerse myself in my profession and prepare to be a professor again. I would read, take a trip, and spend more time with my family and friends. I would savor life. As I remembered the hurt I'd felt and the comfort I'd received, I resolved to try to help others who faced difficult times. My prayer that day was "Show me how." I had great faith that He would. I left the chapel and confidently headed home.

I walked in the door and told Gail I wanted this to be a memorable holiday season. I wanted to put up our Christmas tree at once, and I wanted to send Christmas cards. I used to consider them a waste of time. People were deluged with them and just threw them away. This year I wanted to thank people.

Our first task: to put up the tree. When we lived in the president's house, our trees always were live. After Christmas, we planted them in the backyard. They began to form a tiny grove. This year we were in an apartment. So we bought a "practical" apartment tree—an artificial one packed in a box. As I sat on the floor, bending the wire branches to look like nature, Gail attempted to untangle a massive jumble of Christmas tree lights. They dated back more than two decades. Some strands had been for six-foot-high giants. Now we needed one strand for a twisted, three-foot-tall fake tree. I looked up from my sad little tree with its bent branches and plastic fir. There stood Gail, herself a human tree entangled in a web of lights, some lit, others out. We both started laughing—at the silly sight, at ourselves, at it all. She dropped the lights and plopped to the floor, knocking the little tree over and entangling the lights even more. That brought yet another spasm of laughter. Whenever one of us stopped, the other one started again.

This went well beyond hilarity. It became a catharsis, a release, a purge. In a matter of moments, some eight months of pain were washed aside by a tidal wave of uncontrolled laughter. And the source of all this glee? Ourselves. To find seriousness in yourself, you also must find the humor, the absurdity, the incongruity. We'd had enough of anguish. Laughter is the final balm for healing. Pain can cauterize; humor can restore.

After the tree, I turned to the cards. I knew exactly what I wanted. That evening, I bought my cards—exquisite Ansel Adams winter scenes of Yosemite. For hours I wrote notes to people who had supported us during the year. I thanked them for being a part of our lives. I added my prayer that the pain of 1990, for anyone and everyone, was now behind us.

That year, 1990, had begun in the ugly downpour at the Jefferson Memorial. Like a twist in time, it sent me into a stunning, shattering confrontation with my past. I was rocketed from my paneled office in Northwest Washington back to a stark bedroom in East Dallas. The man recognized the boy that still lived within him. But more than that, 1990 isolated a secret shame, made me look at it, and taught me its true name. Child abuse—no matter why it is done or by whom—is sheer evil. I had to be brought down by it before I could rise above it. By the end of the year, I felt clear about my profession and my desire to try to help others.

Gail was surprised, to say the least, when she saw me at our kitchen table writing Christmas cards. She was wary about getting too excited. She had seen me slide back in the past few months. This time, though, I felt different. I had real determination. I remembered lines from the poem "If":

If you can . . . watch the things you gave your life to, broken,
And stoop and build 'em up with worn-out tools. . . .

I resolved to stop feeling despondent. For months Berlin had stressed that I would make it, that I had the strength to rebuild and assets to employ. Then, finally, the day came when I decided to go forward. The tools were always there, but it took awhile until I picked them up.

A few nights later, I went into the bedroom, where Gail already was asleep. In our twenty-five years of marriage, I have perfected a way to talk to her at all hours. Instead of waking her, I politely say, "Are you asleep?" or "You're not sleeping are you?" She rallies and props herself up to listen.

I think she sensed the resolve in my words as I told her my plans. In her sleepy eyes, I could see, "Wow, I don't believe I'm hearing this!" It was two A.M., and I ended by saying I wanted to invite people over for New Year's Eve. She got out of bed and put on her robe, and we sat in the living room and made plans, lots of plans.

"Let's invite some folks to join us to say good-bye to awful 1990 and welcome to 1991. Then, come January second, I'm going to get busy. I've got a year, and I'm not going to waste a minute of it. Do you realize how lucky I am to have that time? I want to use it well. I want to reimmerse myself in astronomy. I want to assist some community projects. And I want to read up on child abuse. I want to understand what's happening about this issue, what organizations exist. I don't know how I might fit in, but there may be ways."

Boom! I was making plans. You can't make plans unless you want to live. I finally did. Six or eight months earlier, my life felt so tentative that I didn't care. Now I wanted to go beyond "one day at a time."

We talked about people we especially wanted to see in the new year. I said I wanted to do more with Debbie and her fiancé, Seth. To talk more with Natasha. To spend more time with friends and each other. Our checklist got longer and longer as we talked deep into the night, finally falling asleep just before dawn.

In the twilight days of 1990, I set appointments for early 1991. I set them with people I knew well and people I scarcely knew. My calendar for early 1991 brimmed, just as it had in the past. This time, though, the meetings weren't for AU; they were for me. Where and how could I best serve during 1991? I planned to spend the first part of the year consulting and volunteering, and then to start preparing to teach. All the while I wanted to be learning more about child abuse.

Awful 1990 began in gloom, moved on to doom, and ended with hope. How could one year have contained so much? And how long would it take me to rebuild? I didn't know, but I did have confidence. That, after all, I'd lacked since April. Now I had it again. From my silent, private vigil in the Hopkins chapel in early December, I had emerged invigorated, optimistic, and ready.

After a late evening storm, with its jags of lightning and crashes of thunder, the sky can clear, and the blue return. So it was for me. "He restoreth my soul." Yes. Now it was up to me to restore the rest. And I would. Of that, I was certain.

At the stroke of midnight, as 1990 ended, Gail and I stood in our living room surrounded by friends, gazed across the Potomac at the nation's capital, kissed, and vowed to each other and to ourselves: "To life! Live it to the fullest." I resolved to remember the lessons of 1990 always, to rebuild, and to give back: to give back to students what I knew, to survivors what I felt, to the community what I'd gained. This was a new year and a new life.

On January 24, the Office of Exploration at NASA headquarters asked me to do consulting on the nation's plans for space exploration well into the next century. This was beyond cutting-edge science, beyond "where no one had ever gone before." This would entail real-world plans for other worlds' exploration. It involved astronomy, space science, biology, engineering, education, economics, foreign affairs, and public policy. It linked the public and private sectors, and their current budget concerns, to futuristic aspirations.

From its inception in 1989, I had had the privilege to serve on NASA's Exploration Advisory Task Force. Its nine members represented an array of backgrounds and perspectives. Chaired by Robert McC. Adams, the secretary of the Smithsonian Institution, the diverse group included Daniel Boorstin, the former Librarian of Congress, Stephen J. Gould, the Harvard paleontologist, and Jack Schmitt, the former Apollo astronaut and U.S. Senator. We deliberated about exploration, in particular a Presidential Initiative that proposed a long-range, continuing commitment for the United States to return to the Moon, this time to stay, and then to send astronauts to Mars. The Initiative even included a due date: human scientific outposts on Mars before the fiftieth anniversary of the first Apollo landing on the Moon. That is, by July 20, 2019.

On July 20, 1989, on the twentieth anniversary of the landing, President Bush announced the Initiative as a national goal. Our task force had been churning away when he preempted us. So our discussion shifted. Did the Initiative have a justifiable rationale? What benefits could it bring the nation? Would it be worth the cost? How could the Initiative—or even any planning for it—stimulate science, technology, international trade and cooperation, or education? Could we develop new products or technology or find new energy sources? Despite the costs, is such an ambitious endeavor feasible? It would entail great risk. Could we ensure safety for the astronauts? If we can't achieve our goals by the year 2019, when can we? Are we fated to remain forever on Cradle Earth, or is space truly the Ultimate Frontier?

Since I was a child, I had been fascinated by explorers and exploration. So I reveled at the task force meeting as ideas sparked. Despite the group's credentials and erudition, it did not reach a consensus. NASA asked me to try to make sense of the disparate issues and write a report summarizing them.

In 1990, I probed deeply into my own past and inner space; in 1991, I probed into the nation's future and outer space. Along the way, I remembered T. S. Eliot's words:

We shall not cease from exploration
And the end of all our exploring
Will be to arrive where we started
And know the place for the first time.

Most people don't realize that there are folks who get up every morning when their alarms go off, get dressed, and spend the day wondering if humans could survive on Mars.

"How was your day at the office, dear?"

"Oh, fine, we discussed whether people could live indefinitely in the low gravity of Mars. And if solar flares would kill them, without the protection of a thick atmosphere. Would they feel isolated so far from Earth for so long? What would happen if one of them went stir-crazy or had a heart attack?"

To explore Mars would be unlike any other undertaking in history. By far, it would be the largest peacetime effort ever made. Aside from the obvious problems of costs and technology, the Initiative would challenge the limits of our knowledge in numerous fields. In addition, it would entail risk and even danger. Still, humans press on. "No noble thing can be done," Montaigne, the sixteenth-century French essayist, argued, "without risks." And in a different context, I remembered President Kennedy: "We do these things not because they are easy, but because they are hard."

I loved puzzling out the challenges and weighing the options. Even more, I enjoyed the people at NASA. How wrong stereotypes can be. True, the engineers wore plastic pocket protectors and short argyle socks. However, the image of scientists and engineers absorbed only in technical pursuits but not in people did not fit reality. From my first day there, the professional staff stopped by to see me, one by one. "Sure glad you're with us." "Welcome aboard!" "Hope you can make some sense out of this mishmash." "Let me know if I can help." The support staff came to see me, too. One of them squeezed my hand and said, "I'm proud you're part of our team. God bless you."

The project immersed me in my profession at its most advanced, futuristic level. Everything pushed the limits of human thought and capability. For a man who had lived minute-to-minute for months, this contemplation was liberating.

On the Metro to the L'Enfant Plaza stop near my NASA office, I read astronomy journals and astrophysics texts to refresh myself on recent findings. One morning I noticed something extraordinary: I was reading arcane astronomy books like novels—fluidly, with ease. I remembered the concepts and anticipated the math. Then I remembered my frustration only months ago with a Brain Teaser booklet. Amidst people scanning magazines and paperbacks, I may have been the only one smiling over an astrophysics text—smiling not at it but at finding the old me.

Soon I was just as engaged with problems of our planet as I was with the challenge of leaving it and exploring elsewhere. In January, Gail and I became associated with an organization called For Love of Children, or FLOC. We'd become friends with Fred Taylor, the director, who impressed us with his devotion to children. Headquartered on Fourteenth Street in the grit of Washington, FLOC runs a learning center for youngsters with emotional and learning problems so severe they can't attend the D.C. public schools. As an experienced teacher and a returning professor, I offered to guest-teach there.

The Persian Gulf War had just begun. Rather than discuss astronomy as I'd planned, the principal asked if I would talk to the class about the war. Some of them didn't have access to a TV, much less an informed adult.

We started with the geography of the region. Where is Kuwait on the map? Why are our troops staging in Saudi Arabia? I took note of a quiet girl with a sparkle in her eye. When I joked with the class, she'd beam. When I asked a hard question, she'd frown deeply. To get her to talk, however, took some effort. Once past her shyness, she exuded curiosity. In every way but one she reminded me of other bright, eager students. The one difference was that her face and arms were deeply scarred.

After class, I asked a teacher what had happened to her. "Her mother poured scalding water on her when she was young." The scars were permanent—both those on the surface and those inside. Here the horror of child abuse was plain for all to see. I ached for the part inside—the private part no one could see. Even after what I'd learned at Hopkins, this girl's plight had a terror all its own.

About this time I got a call from Isaac Fulwood, Jr., Washington's chief of police. He invited me to a meeting at his office. I didn't know what he wanted, but I went.

I rode the elevator to the fifth floor of the municipal center and walked to the chief's office. Fulwood shook my hand firmly, shut the door, and said, "Thanks for coming. We want to talk to you frankly about a major problem." About half a dozen police officers and I sat at Fulwood's conference table.

With his eyes riveted on me, Fulwood began: "Washington is out of control." "Well," I responded, "I know from the papers that crime here is pretty bad. They say this is the 'Murder Capital of the Nation.' "

"No, no, I'm not just talking about the murder rate. I'm talking about devastating violence generally—about the abuse of children, about violence by children, and about domestic violence. We've got to save the children."

In graphic terms, he talked about mutilation murders and children who have been so badly abused that by fourteen they turn their rage on an eight-year-old. To my surprise, Fulwood noted that violence knows no gender boundary. Girls, he said, were becoming almost as violent as boys. Some young mothers turned on their babies. Children were abandoned and tortured. The descriptions of brutality were paralyzing.

Fulwood asked if I would pull together a group of knowledgeable people to propose solutions. I didn't know what could be done, but I contacted people who might have useful ideas. We started meeting regularly. We tried to find other cities that had set up successful violence prevention programs. We located only a few that had succeeded for a significant period of time. We solicited advice from professionals and listened to scholars, but I learned the most from talking to kids and local community leaders.

In an unmarked car, police drove me across the city, and I tried to absorb as much as I could. And I read voluminous documents.

From 1960 to 1990, the murder rate in Washington skyrocketed by 800 percent. Similar statistics apply to most large American cities. The United States has become the most violent industrialized nation on Earth. In fact, it is more violent than many Third World nations. And many of the perpetrators of this violence, as well as the victims of it, are young. This city—the nation's capital—now witnesses the consequences of youngsters growing up without parental guidance or love, without structure, discipline, values, or hope. And an inordinate number of the people arrested for violent crimes were abused as children. Many people arrested for nonviolent, self-destructive crimes were, too. *The New Yorker* reports that 78 percent of prostitutes have experienced forced sexual intercourse by the age of thirteen, primarily with someone close to the family or a relative, and most crack-addicted streetwalkers were sexually abused before the age of twelve.

I was moving in a world of incredible contrasts. I might spend the morning at NASA, assessing the feasibility of placing humans on Mars by the year 2019. Then in the afternoon, I might visit the Child Protection Division of Children's National Medical Center. I wished the ghastly, gruesome stories there were science fiction, but they weren't. A mother delusional from drugs ripped apart her baby's mouth because, while hallucinating, she thought she saw a mouse run into it. The public shudders at our daily dose of grim news stories. Yet, in fact, I learned that the worst stories often don't make it to the news. If individuals don't reveal all their pain, cities sometimes don't either. But in 1991, I learned about it in this city.

I also met an extraordinary array of dedicated people who quietly work every day to ease the pain, stop the abuse, and end the violence. Some of them were in private social service agencies, others in church-related programs, and still others in the District government. What they shared was intense dedication and almost total anonymity. They became my silent heroes.

Among this group were a number of police officers. Several nights a week, from nine P.M. until one or two A.M., they ran "Late Nite Hoops." And they held it in Anacostia, the epicenter of the Murder Capital. There, in one of the most dangerous places in America, they ran a basketball program. The players came from the streets, and the fans came from the neighborhood. Once or twice a week I would join them.

The program had many purposes. Sports offered a good way to teach hard work, self-discipline, team effort, and how to play by the rules. In addition, these young men really loved basketball. It provided an alternative to loitering on the street. It provided free entertainment in a neighborhood with little else but violence.

On my first visit I felt totally self-conscious, and probably looked like a narc to these men, many of whom came from halfway houses or had just been released from prison. But I was determined to get to know them. The police and I didn't want these games just to be about sports. With the games as the lure to get the men there, we wanted to talk to them about getting jobs or finishing high school, about AIDS, and even about going to college. Essentially, this was about options and about alternatives to crime. It was about careers and the future.

By my second or third visit, the ice began to melt. Some of the group and I would have a soda together and shoot the breeze when they weren't shooting baskets. Best of all, they weren't shooting each other.

My first night, I noticed girls about fifteen years old, with babies in strollers, others at their sides, and still others on the way. How shall we, as a society, educate and protect those children? How do we help the mothers? And how do we stop children from having children?

The guys played hard. They had few supplies. When a game ended, the teams would leave the court and pass their sweaty T-shirts to the next teams.

Only a few hours earlier I had considered the cost of astronauts' suits for space walks and lunar living. Now I wondered how to scrounge a few bucks for more T-shirts. In this remarkable nation, can't we do both? We need both and what they signify—one, world-class technological competitiveness, and the other, basic human decency.

At first, our conversations were awkward. The men responded, "I don't know" to every question I asked. In time, we actually began to talk. In four months, we found jobs for twenty-two of the regulars, and a few of them got into the University of the District of Columbia.

By anyone's standards, I had everything going for me—I was a middle-class white guy in his fifties with a solid education. Yet, months before, I had been on the edge of suicide and overwhelmed by despair. My problems evaporated when compared with theirs.

Many of them had been abused—emotionally, physically, or sexually. Now they were unemployed nineteen-year-olds with a seventh-grade education and no job skills. That crucible of anger and despair brews violence. Aside from the police, does anyone really care? Fortunately, many people had cared about me; I'd had superb support. Suppose I hadn't. Watching these guys night after night, week after week, let me understand the city, and the nation, as never before.

Police officers attended as volunteers. They tacked extra hours onto stressful days, starting at seven A.M. in the station house. Frequently command staff attended, including the chief. Patient and friendly keepers of the rules, these police volunteers became more than role models. They were like surrogate fathers to these young men. I doubt, however, if a single cop saw himself that way.

The Hoops continued until mid-May, when the small amount of funding for it ran out. As we drove there on May 3, one of the last nights, we passed boarded-up houses and buildings with barred windows. The inhabitants wanted to keep crime out; now crime caged them in. When we arrived, I greeted several guys I'd gotten to know. A cop offered me a Coke and a hot dog. This had become a community, and I was part of it. Then the incongruity hit me: That evening, on the other side of town, seemingly light-years away from Anacostia, AU feted its major donors at its annual President's Circle dinner. While I sat amidst drug dealers and worse, the wealthiest people of Washington met in genteel refinement at the AU dinner. That had been my community. In fact, I'd founded the Circle when I became president, to encourage support for AU. In 1990, I couldn't attend that dinner, for it came on the horrid night of my release from Hopkins. This year, I could have gone. I chose not to. I wanted to give the university and me more time to heal. Besides, the Hoops would end soon, and I didn't want to miss seeing the game and the guys.

Finally, on May 18, the Hoops held its last games. Each of the players got a plaque. To my surprise, I did, too. It hangs in my home now. With the loss of even modest funds, the program vanished into the night, just as the fellows who came to it did.

When I first started going to Hoops, Gail strongly objected. She feared for my safety. That first night, I wasn't too sure myself, as I wondered where some of the guys got the money for their gold chains and air-pump Nikes. I needed to go to the men's room. I found it at the remote end of the court, off to the side. When I walked in, it was empty. Then three muscular, unsmiling men entered. For a moment, I remembered Gail's concerns and headed out quickly. As I reached the door, one of them said, "Hey!" I froze. "You forgot your jacket."

How much I had to learn! Violence proved to be no problem at the games. The police simply wouldn't tolerate it. The message was out: No drugs or guns allowed. No one seemed to violate this.

Jolting moments did come, though. One evening quite late, as we walked to the car to leave, my foot slipped on something wet. In the darkness, I tried to make it out. It was red. I called an officer, who immediately said, "Oh, I'm sorry. A murder happened here earlier. I guess they didn't get everything cleaned up." A murder happened right here? God! I can get in the car and escape to tranquil Crystal City, Virginia. What about those who can't escape?

Can anyone break this cycle of abuse, neglect, despair, hopelessness, and violence? We all see the ingredients that explode into antisocial acts by youth, but why has it turned so violent? School yard fistfights of the past have transformed into 9-mm shootouts today. Why?

To find out and to understand the perspectives of youths-at-risk better, the group I'd assembled some months earlier decided to stop talking solely to each other and to start listening to the youths themselves. One day, Fulwood invited fifty or sixty young people from the roughest areas of the city to meet with us. They assembled late in the afternoon in the chief's conference room. Fulwood and another five police officers attended, along with two or three other people, including me. Fulwood led the meeting. He did so with the skill of a Hopkins specialist.

He said he needed to understand the violence in the District. So he asked the kids to explain it. The adults would listen, not make judgments. Everything was off the record. We wanted the truth. The kids should relax and just talk to us.

"Everyone has guns, so we have to have guns." "You know, a guy has to prove he's really a man." "I never leave my house at night, no way."

Fulwood picked a young man at random, and asked, "You, in the blue shirt, could you shoot that guy next to you?"

"Sure. Why not?"

"What might make you do it?"

"Maybe he has a watch or a stereo I want. Shoes I want. Maybe he looked at my woman wrong or maybe I'm bored, man. You know how boring it gets sitting around the projects? What am I supposed to do? Watch TV?"

"What about going to school?"

"No point in that."

"Do you have a job?"

"No."

"How do you make a living?"

"Hustle."

"So you could shoot him just to avoid boredom?"

"Sure, why not?"

"Aren't you afraid you might get shot?"

"Yeah, but so what? I'm gonna die anyway."

When the youngsters finished, one of the policemen said he wanted to say a few words. He had a slide show. It was tough love to the max.

"If you think violence is cool," he began, "take a look at this." He showed bodies at crime scenes and in the morgue, of kids the same age as those in the room. "Ugh!" "Look at that!" "Oh, man, they blew him away!" Everyone in the audience reacted to the graphic, soberingly real photos of the aftermath of violence. Some of the youngsters grimaced and looked away; some got through it by joking; others stared in fascination. After a few minutes, I left, feeling sick.

In the hallway I bumped into Fulwood and told him how jolted I'd been by the boy in the blue shirt. Fulwood looked at me and said, "You know where we ought to begin?" I shook my head, expecting to hear something about Head Start.

"We ought to find out how he was abused as a kid. I bet you anything that if we could get the true story, we'd find a fellow with a long record of childhood horror."

I nodded. This wasn't news, but I'd never before confronted it that way. It always had been filtered through TV, newspapers, or books, and the men I'd met at Hopkins were adults and not violent. Never had I met a kid who could shoot you in the head because it was Thursday and he was bored.

Why, if we have an agency like NASA, dedicated to space, don't we have an agency as determined and visionary dedicated to the well-being of children? As a nation, we undervalue the problems of children. They are our most precious resource; yet, statistics that should outrage us instead dull us. After reading story after story about abuse, we shudder and think, "That's too bad." With facts too brutal and horrid for us to face, we shake our heads and tune them out.

In the spring of 1991, I confronted these issues in ways I never had before as an educator or administrator. I found it simultaneously heartening and depressing, edifying and baffling. These vast problems certainly dwarfed my own. I met youngsters whose abuse far exceeded mine. Their courage impressed me; their quiet dignity inspired me. The word "respect" does not convey adequately my admiration for them, or for the people who work against all odds to save them.

About this time I met Douglas Besharov, the first director of the U.S. National Center on Child Abuse and Neglect, an attorney, and the author of *Recognizing Child Abuse: A Guide for the Concerned.* Gail noticed an essay he'd written in the opinion section of *The Washington Post.* She said it sounded like me. Written just after the war in the Persian Gulf, his editorial was entitled "Operation Domestic Storm." He wrote, "Now, what about the war at home, the struggle to deal with our pressing domestic problems?" He asked why we couldn't reorder our priorities and muster our will to take on the truly dangerous and seemingly intractable problems in our nation.

The essay, written a year before the LA riots, ended with perspicacity: "Up to now, our leaders have shown little appetite for taking the same kinds of firm steps against domestic problems that have had such apparent success on the military side. But if they don't, we should not be surprised that we can free Kuwait City but not Anacostia, Harlem, or East Los Angeles."

Impressed, I called Besharov's office. I wanted to meet this guy. Over lunch a few days later, we had a stimulating conversation about widely ranging topics. We talked at length about adult survivors and the scarcity of programs to serve them. He asked if I knew Dr. Jerry Wiener, chairman of the Department of Psychiatry and Behavioral Sciences at The George Washington University Medical Center. I didn't, but the three of us soon met together. We hit it off right away. Both Jerry and Doug shared my concern for survivors of childhood abuse, and we agreed that more services should be provided for them.

Out of that meeting emerged the idea of creating a new treatment, research, and training program—The National Center for Survivors of Childhood Abuse. We hoped to provide state-of-the-art treatment for long-term abuse survivors, as well as for recently traumatized children. The Children's National Medical Center agreed to collaborate. The GW Medical Center established an advisory board to help formulate this new initiative and asked me to chair it.

As we envisioned it, the center would assist not only survivors but also their families, particularly their partners and spouses. According to some estimates, 60 percent of child abuse victims don't remember the abuse until years later. The trauma resurfaces when many of them are married or in relationships. The trauma can overwhelm both the survivor and the partner.

We wanted the center to provide affordable treatment for anyone who needs it—children, adolescents, or adults. Although sensitive to the needs of any survivor, the center would be especially alert to male survivors. Relatively few programs exist for them, and male survivors are reluctant to ask for help. Of course, the treatment would be highly confidential; anyone could feel comfortable going. Also, the center would do research and attempt to understand both precursors and outcomes of abuse. It would provide education on prevention and remediation for the public, as well as training for medical, mental health, and social service professionals. And it would draw on the resources of a major university medical center and the Children's National Medical Center.

In addition, it would draw upon the extensive resources of the nation's capital city. This is the home of the U.S. National Center on Child Abuse and Neglect, the Child Abuse Division of the U.S. Justice Department, the National Institute of Health, the policy offices of Congress, and numerous other Federal agencies. Washington also is headquarters for many private-sector, nonprofit initiatives related to child abuse, like the National Center for Missing and Exploited Children, the Children's Defense Fund, the Child Welfare League of America, the Center on Children and the Law of the American Bar Association, and many others.

Any professional interested in child abuse—from practicing physicians to medical students, from social workers to law enforcement personnel, from policy makers to the press—could find at the new center, or within a few miles of it, extraordinary resources.

The center was to be the sort of place to which I should have gone years ago. Would I have taken that crucial first step? I don't know. Perhaps. If I had heard other male survivors speak about their experiences, I might have recognized something about myself and sought help. If I had known of a high quality center specifically attuned to the needs of male survivors, I might have gone. I hoped that this new national center would come into being and fulfill those needs.

In March, I met with a dean from AU to discuss my teaching assignment for January 1992. We met on neutral territory—in the lobby of a hotel. This was my first contact with a university representative in some time. Students, professors, alumni, and individual trustees continued to contact me, but my old administrative colleagues remained silent. By spring of 1991, I was used to it.

I was glad to meet with the dean. After a cordial chat, she said that I would teach a regular full load of three courses—two in astronomy and a third in modern physics. I said I looked forward to the astronomy, but that I'd never taught modern physics. Why couldn't I teach something I'd given before? She said the department needed modern physics taught and this was my assignment.

So, okay, I would immerse myself. I created my own review course to be a professor again. I called universities and publishers to locate the best current textbooks; talked to faculty colleagues across the nation about their courses; contacted observatories, planetariums, and NASA to obtain the finest up-to-date astronomical slides to add to my collection; went to the Library of Congress to read ten years' worth of books, journals, and science magazines; explored every foot of the National Air and Space Museum; retrieved my own former textbooks and old exams, and then plunged into the world I used to love so much.

At first, it was hard. I sat at the kitchen table long after Gail went to sleep, trying to remember concepts I used to know so well. I grew frustrated, and furious with myself. Had the years of administration dulled my analytical mind? Had the trauma?

My brain seemed stuck in neutral, but this was only temporary. By spring of 1991, I realized that in the trauma, my mind hadn't stopped. It merely had shifted to a lower gear for the steep, long pull. I couldn't accelerate it. Timetables can't be set for either grief or healing.

Gradually at first, then in a flood, I started to remember esoteric facts I hadn't thought about in years. I felt the pulse again.

Modern physics proved more of a challenge. The parts on atomic physics and relativity theory came back at once, but my quantum mechanics had grown cold. Some of it I hadn't used since I was an undergrad, more than thirty years earlier. So I started with a basic calculus text and moved up to post-graduate tomes.

To reach this nirvana took many lonely, painful weeks. At two P.M. or two A.M., I pored over my books. I worked problems in textbooks and gave myself exams from other universities. Was I a professor again, or was I a student, or is there a difference? I felt like Rocky Balboa preparing for a fight. He punched slabs of beef; I battled Legendre polynomials. In time I felt ready, even eager. I missed teaching. Sometime during 1991 I knew I was ready. So, naturally, I shared it with Gail. At the earliest light of dawn, I'd awaken her and ask, "You're not asleep are you? Let me tell you about the Laplacian operator in spherical coordinates. . . ."

Life had momentum again. Even with irregular beats and erratic pulses, it moved ahead. I had goals and looked forward to teaching. I felt centered, and from my renewed sense of self, I could focus on the future. I felt alive.

Hope. Out of the rotten bleakness of the past year, I finally, tentatively, and hesitantly let myself hope. Healing, which at first seemed like a maze with quick turns and countless barriers, now became a long uphill road.

Gail and I delighted in doing things we had never done before. One gorgeous spring day we drove to West Virginia for an outward-bound excursion with FLOC. Fred Taylor, the director of For Love of Children, had told us how inner-city kids found the program enriching and therapeutic. We wanted to see what the kids experienced, but we had no idea what we were getting into.

We turned from the highway onto a one-lane road and drove deep into the Appalachian woods. Eventually we parked in a clearing. Minutes later, an apparition appeared—a tall man wearing a helmet and a harness about his midsection. Fred greeted us and led us farther into the woods, until we came to the base of a tree, where a small band of people was looking up at a man on a tightrope. He stood motionless on a steel cable some sixty feet above a stream and boulders. He clung to a second cable, face-high. He slowly began to move, edging toward his destination—a tall, strong, secure tree with a platform. He still had thirty feet to go. Finally, he made it!

It looked like an amateur audition for the Flying Wallendas. The harnesses hooked to cables and the overhead wire gave security. Still, his foot could slip or a gust of wind could topple him, leaving him dangling like a bungee jumper who'd lost his bounce.

Fred handed me a harness and helmet, and asked, "Want to try it?"

"Sure," I replied.

I climbed the ladder and took the first step onto the wire. It swayed beneath me, and the people below suddenly appeared remarkably far away.

As I edged farther out on the wire, it began to sink as well as sway. Then I found that the upper cable—my stabilizer—wasn't parallel with the lower cable. The farther I would go, the more they would diverge. Toward the end, the upper cable would be well above my head. I felt the same as before the court appearance: queasy, shaky, fearful. I felt fear of falling; fear of the unknown; fear of doom. I hated trying to cross the wire, but told myself I must.

I inched sideways and looked dead ahead. Dread charged through me, the same feeling I'd felt when I heard "Come here." Mentally, I focused on the tree at the end—my refuge.

When I reached the end, I hugged the tree—not just for security but almost to thank nature for being strong, sure, and protective. When I looked back to survey the trek I'd just made, I couldn't believe my eyes. There, a short way out on the cable, stood Gail. Ever since her father died in a plane crash when she was a child, she has had a fear of heights. She dislikes escalators and won't ride on those glass-enclosed types that scoot up the sides of buildings. Yet there she was.

When she reached midway, she froze. Sheer terror enveloped her face. Her jaw clenched. Her fright turned into panic.

"Can you hear me?" I asked.

"Yes," she replied, in a fractured and feeble voice.

"You'll be all right. I'm right here. I'll talk you across."

From the middle of the cable, I heard a faint, "Okay." By now, Gail was undulating back and forth, as her feet swayed forward and her hands backward. Then the sway would reverse.

"I'm right here. Take a small step. Remember to breathe."

I talked and she edged. I counted her down—from ten feet to five. When she got to about three feet away, I said, "I could reach you now. You're almost here. You can make it on your own." Just as we had talked and walked together through other difficult challenges, we did there, too.

Moments later, she reached the tree and I swung her onto the platform and into my arms. The group below cheered. Standing atop that tree, feeling like part of the sky above, I saw a look on Gail's face that I hadn't seen for more than a year—not just relief and confidence but even triumph. She'd been there for me as I'd wobbled on a high wire last year. Even though my support today was minuscule compared with hers then, it felt good to be there for her.

And I thought of the inner-city kids facing such challenges—how they met them and conquered them. In doing so, they learned self-reliance and teamwork. To make it across on the wire, you must do it yourself. In parts of the Outdoor Learning Center—such as the fifty-foot-tall Giant's Ladder, with logs spaced many feet apart for rungs—everyone had to help each other. In doing so, they learned how it feels to trust others.

As we prepared to return home, I asked Fred what impressed the kids the most about their adventures. Was it rafting? Camping? The challenges? The wilderness? Instantly, he said, "The stars." These city kids have grown up under a cloud of haze with glaring streetlights. They've never seen darkness—true darkness—and imbedded in it, thousands of shimmering dots of light. "Their first night here is always the same," Fred went on. "They can't get enough of the sky." In the dark West Virginia woods, nature becomes the attraction. And the youngsters, so used to looking over their shoulders, learn to look up.

It reminded me of how I'd felt as a boy, lying on my back in the front yard in Dallas, awed and mesmerized by the grandeur above me. This silent, majestic canopy surrounded me. Perhaps my abuse made me more sensitive to it. I was drawn to its otherworldliness. In the fragile and mercurial world around me, it was stable. When I looked at the sky, I felt safe.

By July, the time had come for me to go to Dallas and see my mother. I had not been back for a year and a half. I knew I needed to go. Despite everything, my mother needed me. I was all she had. When I was a child, I wished her dead; now, I could not abandon her or else she literally might die. My past loathing had been transmuted into present-day practicality.

Gail and I knocked on the locked screen door. The wooden door was open. No one came. I knocked again. And again. Still no one came. But a half-dozen cats brushed by my leg as they rushed through a hole in the screen into the living room. Another dozen cats sprawled on the floor or crawled on the sofa.

I shouted, "Hey! Are you here? It's me, Richard."

Finally, from around the dining-room doorway, I saw her head, only her head, as she squinted at the door. "Who's there! Go away!" she shouted.

"It's me, Richard. Your son. Don't you recognize me?"

Slowly, she came into the living room, hunched over, holding a crutch—not for support, but as a weapon. "Who are you?" she demanded.

"I'm Richard, your son. Open the door."

"You are? You're Richard?"

She unlatched the door and we walked in. Cats curled around my ankles. One arched its back and hissed as another one clawed at my pants. In a red smock, my mother rushed up to hug me. I froze. "How are you?" I asked. She launched into a soliloquy about the cats.

"I don't know where they come from. I don't bother anyone. So I don't know about the cats. They're real nice cats. But I don't know. . . ."

As she babbled, I checked the house. The visiting nurse we'd arranged to stop in had done a good job. The place looked safe, even if decrepit. But the most decrepit part was my mother. Clearly, she no longer could take care of herself.

She looked pitiful. Never very tall, she now stooped to less than five feet. How could she ever have had such a towering, crushing impact on my life? I asked myself what the doctors had asked so often: *How do you feel?*

I felt sad for her. And I felt sad for the little boy who had never made it out of that house, whose childhood had died in the middle bedroom. The man now stood there. He had come through, but the boy never made it. I felt sad for him.

While Gail kept my mother busy, I slipped off to the middle bedroom. I wanted to see how I would feel. I walked down the hall and stood at the doorway. Nothing. I entered the room. Nothing. It just felt like a room. I didn't have flashbacks or feel pummeled from years before. The memories remained. They always will. But now they were only memories. There was no searing, panicking pain.

This was different from the way I'd felt after my father's death.

Then I had been at the mercy of memory, but now I was on higher ground. This was a private moment, somewhere between a poem and a prayer.

My mother—who once had seemed so intimidating, so terrifying, so controlling—had shed that persona like a snake slipping out of its skin. She now was weak and fragile, helpless and pitiful. But she was still my mother.

I tinkered around the house, fixing the stove and lights. The simple became complicated. "Mother, that light bulb is out. Do you have another one?"

"I don't bother anybody."

"I know, but do you have another bulb or should I buy one?"

"Maybe people came over and put them there or maybe they took them away. I don't know. Whatever anybody wants. I don't bother anybody."

My mother seemed to sense her vulnerability. As if to blunt the possibility of going to a nursing home, she muttered, "I'm not going anywhere. This is my home." She had repeated that endlessly, like a weary benediction, for her forty-six years on Fairview Avenue. Residence was perhaps the only real stability she could ever claim.

My doctors had said I should confront my mother directly about the abuse, and I did.

"Mother, you and I never had a conversation that we should have had years ago. Do you remember when you used to work in a dark-room? Do you remember the time you asked me to come over? Can you remember what happened?"

She was blank, silent.

I continued. "Do you remember what happened in the middle bedroom?"

"I don't know. Laddie was such a nice dog . . ."

"Okay, fine. But about the middle bedroom, things happened between us that shouldn't have happened."

She now was as cold and stony as she once had been fiery and mad. There was nowhere to go. My mother and I were at an impasse. Age and senility had stopped her. And I realized that I was trying to chat up a corpse.

Gail and I left Dallas, left my mother, left my childhood, and set off to be alone together in nature. We flew to San Francisco and drove north, past the wine country, past Mendocino, through the Avenue of the Giants, to the heart of the Redwood Empire. There, in a stretch of several hundred miles, stand the tallest and some of the oldest living things on Earth. To me, the redwoods are close to divinity. These trees were old in Marcus Aurelius's time, ancient when Columbus set sail, and now stand taller than the Statue of Liberty.

If man reached up to God and God reached down to man, they joined hands in these trees. Resplendent and majestic, soaring and sublime, to me they're metaphors for the aspiration of humankind and the grace of divinity. Their high, plush branches block the sun, and scant underbrush grows on the forest floor. The light that does get through is diffused and sparkles like diamond chips.

Late one afternoon, Gail and I drove off the main road, well into the forest. Then we walked along a narrow path, deeper still into an old growth grove. We stopped and stood silently, surrounded by towering trees. We'd seen no other people for miles. Our only companions were birds and redwoods. In the twilight, with a breeze rustling the treetops, I placed my hands against one of the giants, and touched history. This living thing had stood during sunshine and storms, fires and earthquakes. It had stood when the ancient Greek civilizations had existed, and while the Roman Empire had risen and fallen. Yet it still stood, straight and true. And it will do so long after I'm dead. It continues to stand, to survive, to endure.

In that transcendent moment, I felt linked to a system far older and larger than myself. It was like touching time.

We continued up the Oregon coast, enchanted by its rugged and extravagant beauty. Through the mist, we peered over sharp cliffs, down to the primordial coastline. If you blinked, you could imagine that you had returned to the Age of the Reptiles. Everything seemed jumbo-sized. The ocean beat against huge boulders, and in the distance the jagged, soaring peaks of the Cascade Mountains cut into the sky.

In Portland, we interrupted our trek through nature to find the house where I'd lived as a young child. Even after all this time, I recognized it. I remembered the sidewalk where I'd lain down, I was so tired. My mother stood over me. "What's the matter?" she'd asked.

I told her I was too tired to play. A child too tired to play? The doctor put me to bed and gave me giant-sized sulfur tablets. Thus began my three-year stint with asthma and rheumatic fever.

I remembered, too, the window from which I'd watched the kids play. I remembered the living room where my mother, in a mad tirade, slapped me against the wall and demanded that I sing. And I remembered her reading to me as my tight lungs wheezed and fever smoldered in my body.

I even remembered the day we left. I lay in the back seat, and my parents sat in the front. As my mother drove, she nagged at my father, "Damn you, Earl, for giving Richard this sickness! He'll get better when we get to Dallas. Damn you!"

Gail and I sat in front of the house for an hour and talked. Finally, I squeezed her hand and said, "Thanks for sharing this with me. We've got farther to go, but we've come a long way."

Then we crossed the Columbia River and drove on one-lane gravel roads through the wilderness, past Mount Saint Helens, and up Mount Rainier. Deer looked up as we rumbled by. Eagles soared overhead. In a full day, we saw fewer than ten people.

The crisp mountain air rejuvenated us. And so did the grandeur of the Olympic peninsula. Ripped from the rest of Washington by glaciers, this is a land apart, an almost indescribable place. We walked through a rain forest, with moss-canopied branches above us and ferns about us. We stood inside a hollow tree as water dripped around us. I thought back to Meyer 5 and watching the rain pelt down on East Baltimore. How much safer I now felt, how much more restored.

We traveled on to land's end, the westernmost edge of the forty-eight contiguous states. There on a ribbon of beach, between ocean and forest, lies a desolate, windswept stretch of sand and driftwood and massive off-shore pillars. Only the two of us walked the beach that day. Behind us, we could see menacing storm clouds, with occasional jags of lightning. The waves thundered against the boulders, tossing logs onto the shore as a child might toss a toy. As transfixing as it was, we knew we should leave. We weren't safe, exposed on a barren beach near water. Then the winds calmed, the dark clouds began to break, and the ocean became pacific. So we sat with our backs against a boulder, watched seagulls dive, the oval sun set, and gentle waves wash over our feet.

I reflected on our odyssey and felt a sense of closure. I had gone back to the middle bedroom and walked away. I left it behind. My past was just that—past. Only those four walls could have taught me that I now could close the door and walk away. I had to return to know that I could leave. No therapist could have told me that; no love could have convinced me. But my doctors, my wife, my family, and the support of hundreds of people had brought me to the threshold and given me the confidence to try.

The trip was more than a vacation. It wasn't about seeing sights, but about savoring nature, exploring my past, and finding myself.

Several days after we returned home, my older daughter, Deborah, married Seth Casner. Their love filled the hall and our hearts. I felt unparalleled pride. Natasha, for whom jeans are a persistent uniform, came down the aisle in a formal gown and heels. Who was this attractive young woman? And last, all eyes turned toward Deb. In her white resplendence, she and I slowly walked down the aisle. I kissed her cheek, squeezed her hand, and took my place beside Gail, as Seth took his place beside Deb.

In my toast after the ceremony, I described some trees Gail and I had discovered one evening in the redwood forest. They looked like two trees, but in fact they grew from a common base. An old tree had fallen, and they'd both sprung from it. They'd grown separately, yet side by side. Both climbed upward to the sky, separate while linked and mutually dependent. Out of one had come two; out of two, one. In that, I saw a strength and stability, a permanence and a linkage that I hoped Seth and Deb would share through all their years. As we raised our glasses, I said I hoped their love would last at least as long as the redwoods.

A few days later, Natasha left for Kenya, where she'd spend her fall term. She already knew Swahili but wanted to learn it better and to study Africa directly rather than through books and lectures. Most of all, she wanted to know the people.

Gail, Natasha, and I drove to New York, and waited anxiously at JFK airport for her flight to depart. For weeks she'd read about Africa, pored over maps, packed and unpacked her camping gear, and gotten shots. Now she was ready. But were any of us truly ready? We all were simultaneously excited and nervous as departure time approached. When other students in the program arrived, Natasha struck up conversations with several of them, and their anxious parents talked with us.

The gate opened. We hugged Natasha, and whispered "I love you" to her. And I added: "Have fun. Enjoy. Be confident. We're here for you." As Natasha boarded, Gail and I swallowed hard and waved.

"Give your children roots and wings," someone once said. In the summer of 1991, both of our daughters set off—one in marriage, one to Africa. We cheered and waved and smiled as they disappeared over the horizon. We were happy for both of them, but sad because nothing would be the same again. We all were moving into new, uncharted futures.

By early fall, my life had attained a certain emotional ballast. Although I was more confident and secure about the future, life lacked spontaneity. I had traveled from deep grief and despair back to the everyday world, but something was missing.

I began to understand how much work is involved in healing— conscious, deliberate, and demanding work. And its path is not a straight line. It's more like connected dots—some forward, some not.

Healing is a gift, undoubtedly so. Through healing we mend a broken heart, a shattered spirit, a crushed soul. Although time is the ultimate balm, healing takes more than just time. It takes determination, effort, and support. It takes willingness to fail and to try again. It takes personal resolve and other people's help. It can be frustrating and infuriating. In the end, it can bring satisfaction and peace.

I now see the elements that led to my healing. First and perhaps most crucial was my support system. Gail, Natasha, Deb, Seth, Seth's family, Gail's family, and our friends were the core. Even cousins and second cousins of mine, whom my mother had kept away from me when I was a child, rallied to me now. I anchored myself in their stability until I could find my own.

Strangers also were part of it. Even though we'd never met, they gave me support and even insight. Many people sent me books and articles. Someone sent a videotape of Bill Moyers's documentary about the hymn "Amazing Grace." Someone else sent cassettes of Bible readings. I looked in my dad's well-worn Bible. On the inside front cover, he had written "Mark 9, 1–23." It is a passage about a father who takes his son to Jesus because he is sick. Pleadingly, the father says, "If you can do anything, have pity on us and help us." Jesus replies, "All things are possible to him who believes." I played that passage on the cassette over and over. It became my inspiration, my lodestar.

Healing requires words. There is no way around a tragedy or trauma. The only way over is through, and the way you get through is by talking. Shakespeare understood this in *Macbeth* when he wrote:

Give sorrow words; the grief that does not speak
Whispers the o'er-fraught heart and bids it break.

I had never really confided in anyone except my wife, and clearly, before Hopkins I had never told her the real story about myself. I would not have gone down like a kamikaze pilot in my own life if I had started talking years before.

Friends help, but therapists are essential for anyone who has been profoundly traumatized. I could not have survived without the professionals at Johns Hopkins. My past was a minefield. Without them to guide me through it, I would have exploded.

The sad thing is that no one could have convinced me to start talking. I had no idea—and could not have been persuaded—that something from so long ago suddenly could take over my life. I want others to know what I learned—if you have been traumatized by abuse, you must find a way to understand and resolve it. Even if your life seems fine at the moment, unresolved trauma neither goes away nor diminishes over time. It can erupt at any time.

Even if the trauma never recurs, its initial impact can have long-term effects. Depression, alcoholism and other addictions, rage, insomnia, nightmares, and low self-esteem are some of the common shoals for people who carry too much emotional cargo. They should lighten the load by finding a supportive therapeutic environment—a safe place to feel terrible.

Galileo performed thought experiments. Aside from actual experimentation, he'd sometimes imagine an experiment rather than perform it. He'd carry it out in his head. In the past, I'd persuaded myself that I didn't need to share things with anybody. I could think my way through, imagine my way out. Now I know that is sometimes impossible.

I now believe that ways exist to transform almost any pain. Pain is part of life. The great metaphor still holds: Through the pain of childbirth comes life. And throughout life, we all will encounter pain again. Our challenge, then, is not to dread it, but to deal with it, to learn from it. Do we succumb? Turn bitter? Give up? Or do we find ways to overcome it and learn from it? "The mind is seldom quickened to very vigorous operations," Samuel Johnson noted, "except by pain."

I did not set out to transform my pain; I first had to deal with survival. Then, as I realized that I could survive, I knew that living would be worthwhile only if it had meaning and purpose. All this was incremental, but now I see that ultimately healing is about transformation and redemption.

Forgiveness is the second stage of healing. Having a support system and some therapeutic connection is level one. At this level, the trauma can be identified, articulated, and validated. It must be processed. By telling and retelling the story, it begins, at some point, to be diffused. You can't cry forever. It only seems that way. At some point, emotions subside. This may take a month or a year. There are no rules. Timetables are for trains and planes.

For me, forgiveness was perhaps the hardest part of the journey. I'm not sure if I'm completely there yet. My first task was to forgive the boy left languishing inside the man. Only once I was deep in therapy did I accept that what had happened to me had not been my fault.

Children are egocentric. When something happens, they truly believe they caused it. Children often blame themselves for being abused. Somehow, they think they must have provoked it. A child isn't capable of understanding the world in other ways. Over the years, those assumptions harden. This seems obvious but only to those who have never been abused.

Ultimately, liberation came when I truly realized that the abuse was not my fault. Children can experience pleasure during abuse. Our bodies, after all, are programmed to respond to stimulation. The nerves to the brain may not distinguish between "good touch and bad touch." But a child doesn't know that.

Humans also are programmed to survive. I gradually came to see that I had done all I could under the circumstances. I had few options. Finally, I could look far back at that little boy and say, "Hey fellow, it wasn't your fault. You're okay."

I also began to appreciate what a strong boy he'd been. He had survived and had more courage than I did now, in my darkest hour. If he could do it then, I could now. Shouldn't I fight to survive at least as hard as he did?

Forgiving my mother became more complicated. Forgiving is not the same as excusing. I can not excuse anyone who commits child abuse. In my mother's case, I realized that her mental illness made her do terrible things to me. I can't forgive what she did, but I can understand it now and let go of my hatred and rage. For me, forgiveness in the end meant remembering without malice. Before that happened, I had to release that rage. I could not think it away.

The rage that must have lingered inside me for years began to escape in the searing experience at Hopkins. The pressure broke. But it wasn't until I was alone at home one day and happened upon my mother's picture that I vented my full fury. Without that, I wonder if I ever could have found peace. People who are afraid to be angry may deny themselves the opportunity to heal. Just as healing requires forgiveness, forgiveness requires confronting your rage.

In time I realized that child sexual abuse resembles rape: neither are purely sexual assaults. Rather, they both are acts of violence and power. The cardinal word that describes them both is domination. In child sexual abuse, I'm convinced that the victimizer, enmeshed in personal ego-satisfaction, is not so interested in sex as in manipulation and domination. A person who has little influence in normal adult life finds a thrill, a release, in controlling someone who is totally inexperienced, docile, and frightened. So child sexual abuse actually is about the abuse of a child's rights and freedoms and self-determination. Sex is merely a means to an end. And the end is total domination.

I came to see that my mother had sought control. Yet during most of her life, events remained outside her dominion. As a child, she'd been at the mercy of a few male adults. She had to drop out of school to work in the fields. Her money from cotton picking helped feed the family. She had no say over her own money, education, clothes, or destiny. But she had resolved to set her own course. So she had left home and wandered the nation for years. The grasp on life she so desperately wanted always eluded her. Finally, she returned to Oklahoma and married my father, whom she could dominate. Her son provided the ultimate target. I was male, young, vulnerable, and powerless.

So her illness, her unquenchable need to dominate, and my pre-pubescent development all converged. In addition, in her warped mind, she confused her proper relationship to me. Love can be more than blind; it can be blinding. Blinded, bewildered, and mad—her need for domination overwhelmed her instincts to protect.

Finally I understood all this. Then I had to deal with myself again—for making the phone calls. As Oscar Wilde put it: "Misfortunes one can endure—they come from outside, they are accidents. But to suffer for one's own faults—ah—there is the sting of life." And oh, the calls stung. Even when I understood the compulsion behind them, I found it hard to accept that I actually had made them. I remembered well my insatiable curiosity to learn why abuse occurred in other homes. Nonetheless, that did not justify the calls. I always will regret having made them even though I now understand why I did.

For me, rebuilding my life did not truly begin until I convinced myself I had hit bottom. I had to know I had fallen as far as I would allow myself to go before I started to climb back. My prayer became "Please God, let me hit bottom." Eventually, I knew I had; I would allow myself to fall no farther. The fall had not been into a bottomless pit. It had been far and deep, and the pit dark, but the pit had a bottom and the walls could be scaled.

Ironically, once I plummeted to the bottom, I tapped into strength I didn't know I had. It lies dormant within all of us. The issue after a trauma is to find it in ourselves. For me, this took time, but until I found it I was the king of dread scenarios. Think of something encouraging for my future, and I'd find a way to wreck it. Eventually, I learned to stop forecasting worst-case possibilities; instead, I re-solved to look for the positive. It soon came in abundance.

Early one Saturday morning, Debbie came by. I didn't know why. She cleared her throat.

"Daddy, I'm pregnant."

What a wondrous, splendid thought! I was the first person she'd told after her husband. We hugged and I managed to say, "I'm so happy for you and Seth. And just think of all the fun Gail and I will have." When Gail came into the room, we didn't need to tell her. She'd already guessed.

By mid-fall, we'd settled my mother into a nursing home. Contrary to our worries, she almost immediately forgot the house. The nursing home became her new world, while her former life faded ever further into obscurity.

Once we sold the house, I went to Dallas to conclude the transaction and to retrieve the few things I wanted to keep. One of those was the Roman fort that I'd worked on with my dad. I hadn't seen it for decades, but I knew it was in the crawl space beside the attic.

I flew to Dallas for the Thanksgiving weekend. This became a meditative time for me. During the flight I thought about how much I had to be thankful for. That year, 1991, had brought immense transformation. In the quiet anonymity of my flight to Texas, I gave thanks for being so truly blessed. Great joy, like great grief, is silent.

Debbie and Seth, who were visiting in Dallas, volunteered to help me at the house. We went there Friday morning. This peculiar day was far too warm, even for Dallas. The leaden skies hung with a nearly opaque mist. An eerie breeze rustled the bare tree branches. With an extension ladder, Seth and I climbed up outside the house to reach the crawl space. Cobwebs hung from the rafters like tenement laundry. I inched through forty years of dust and debris until I found my fort. It was heavy and easily broken, but I still wanted to lug it out and ship it back to Washington.

That fort symbolized the one time my dad made a real difference. We worked on it together, and when he said, "Try linoleum cement," he gave me the key to its completion. Insignificant to anyone but me, those words were my "Rosebud." We tackled a problem together and solved it. My mother had nothing to do with it.

I dragged the fort to the ladder, and Seth and I angled it down. I also found a large box of my old schoolwork. As Deb waited below, Seth and I lowered the items.

The dust made it hard to breathe. With the electricity turned off, I could barely see. The space was hot, dark, and cramped. I was covered with dirt and wanted to go, but something prompted me to take a final look. Bending low, I brushed away cobwebs and rummaged through papers and trash between the rafters. My flashlight beam shimmered in the dust. From under old receipts, beside crumpled newspapers, next to a torn lampshade, the light reflected back from something. I noticed a small picture frame with its glass broken. As I picked up the frame, I realized where it was lying and where I was stooping: directly above the middle bedroom.

I brushed off the caked dirt and held the frame under the beam. It contained a prayer. Then I turned it over and saw, in my father's familiar handwriting, "September 6, 1959." He'd gotten this for my twenty-first birthday. Thirty-two years later, it finally arrived: "A Prayer of a Father."

> Build me a son, Oh Lord . . . strong enough to know when he is weak . . . Rear him . . . not in the paths of ease but under the spurs of difficulties. Let him learn to stand up in the storm . . . Then his father will dare . . . to whisper . . . "I have not lived in vain!"

As Seth lowered another carton down the ladder to Deb and late morning fog engulfed the house, I sat stooped over the middle bedroom amidst debris from decades past, and read my father's anthem to me. He'd cut it from a magazine, perhaps *Coronet*, and put it in a dime-store frame. At last, I'd broken through my father's emotional gridlock, and we communicated father-to-son for the first time. He had never been able to speak to me fully. He loved me and wanted the best for me, I was sure, but he never hinted at what he truly felt. Now, after his death, while rummaging through dusty remnants I would leave for the absolute last time, I stumbled across the most intimate words my father ever "spoke" to me. Maybe he'd known more about all that happened to me than I'd realized.

For my twenty-first birthday he'd given me a copy of Kipling's "If." Why did he give me that instead of this? How did it get in the attic? How did it escape my mother? It didn't matter. What counted was that my father, who could never get a word in edgewise when we lived in that house, now had the last word. His helplessness during so much of his life obscured his deep feelings. My father, I finally knew, had always held a prayer for me.

Crowded in the box of old schoolwork, I found a letter from my MIT days, when I was distraught over the breakup of my first marriage. I'd tried to keep it to myself; I didn't think it showed. I pulled out an old letter my advisor had written me, which praised my academic work, then added, "sooner or later, pick yourself up and start slugging it out. In this business, you are never down for a ten-count until you stop getting up. I'd like to see you enter Harvard in September."

He'd given me good guidance. His words applied as much that day in Dallas as they had all those years earlier in Cambridge. They echoed the message of Louis Pasteur from the last century: "My strength lies solely in my tenacity."

While in Dallas, I visited my mother, who had settled into a modest nursing home that seemed pleasant and friendly. Although in better physical shape than many of the other residents, her mental condition remained cloudy. She sat and stared at the other patients or the television. She focused on one person, then another. All the while, she didn't know where she was and would get lost finding her room twenty feet away.

The attendants had confiscated her crutch because she swung it at other patients. Sometimes as she watched TV, she would jerk and shake, just as she used to. I wondered if she still thought aliens controlled her through TV. My efforts to talk to her proved useless.

I'd ask, "Do you need anything?"

She'd reply, "Look at that."

"Look at what?"

"I don't know. I don't bother anybody."

"You're just pointing at a doorknob."

"I don't bother anybody."

"Debbie, your granddaughter, is in town. She could visit you."

"I don't think I've met her."

"Yes, and you have another granddaughter named Natasha."

"I do? I don't know a Natasha."

I found pity and relief in her pathos. She finally had reached a place in her mind beyond the rage and confusion that had bedeviled her for years. She would have moments of clarity. In a sporadic burst of lucidity, she remembered exactly who I was. She grabbed a male nurse, grinned, and said, "See my son. Isn't he beautiful? That's my son there. My son! He's big now, but he's my baby." The nurse smiled, winked at me, and my mother clapped her hands in a little pattycake.

She then quickly clicked back into dementia:

"I feel that in myself and what I always try to do. . . . And you know what I mean. . . . You meeting people here and some of them, but that's not what I am, because I never bother anybody. It's just a thing I have about me."

Her mind was on rewind, stopping and skipping over random bits of conversation from the past eighty years. Marooned in a world of wheelchairs and two-handed walkers, dazed and uncentered, she watched the world go by, with no idea of where she was or who she was.

When I got ready to leave, she took my arm and walked with me to the door. I tried to dissuade her. "I'm leaving now. Why don't you stay here. Just stay. You are not supposed to go outside. So when we get to the door, you have to stay."

I was unsure how much she understood until I had to pry her fingers from around my arm. Even though most of her thoughts were muddled, she knew I was going. And she hated it. The only force left in her drew her to me.

What happened in my childhood brought me confusion and pain then, and ultimately a calamity in 1990. Now I felt only the sadness, not the weight. I had extricated myself from it just as surely as I pried my mother's fingers from my arm. I could turn and walk away—away from her and from my past.

Tolstoy wrote: "All happy families resemble each other; each unhappy family is unhappy in its own way." While the form of my family's agony was unique to me, other dysfunctional families exist all around us. We just don't know it. At last I understood my mother well; I truly was at peace.

One of the most satisfying aspects of my healing came from helping others. Unknowingly, you mend by helping others mend. People had reached out to me when I faced tough times. They didn't just help; they got me through it. I owed it back.

A man I knew lost his job, so I invited him to lunch. At first he sounded decidedly upbeat, insisting everything was fine, just fine. I told him I was glad to hear that. Somehow, though, I had a hard time believing him.

"May I suggest what you actually feel?" I asked. "You wake up on Tuesday. It's ten o'clock and you're home with no place to go. You don't have a business lunch. You're worried about money, about your self-worth. You flick on TV and find yourself at midday watching some program you've never even heard of before. You get hooked on it, and then feel silly watching such fluff. Why not? You have nothing else to do. You open a can of soup and eat alone. Friends tell you to network—call your contacts. So you start taking people to lunch. Now comes the paradox: The guy who has no job ends up buying lunch for those who do. Sound familiar?"

He smiled. "That's it exactly. I'm going broke twice as fast." We talked another two hours, and I paid for lunch.

I found I could talk to other men with real openness and honesty, sometimes surprisingly so. Over lunch with a prominent government official, out of nowhere he brought up press accounts about my having been abused and, without a pause, he looked at me and said, "I, too, was sexually abused as a boy."

It stunned me. I asked if he'd thought of talking to others about it. He said after he'd done a cost-benefit analysis, he decided the risks outweighed the gains. He feared it would damage his career. A prime reason stems from society's suspicion that people who've been abused go on to abuse. This becomes especially difficult for men because many people assume that men are the most aggressive, persistent abusers. And they often are. This places an unfair burden on them, because the best evidence indicates that at least two thirds of the men who've been abused never harm anyone. As long as that shadow lies over the national consciousness, men remain reluctant to speak out.

We talked about that dilemma. The situation won't change until both men and women find their collective voice and say, "I was abused. It harmed me. But I got help and now it's resolved."

They may be met by silence; then, suspicion. Did they harm their kids? Do they have a stash of child pornography? People then face the burden of negative proof—proving that they will not do something. That's tough.

And if a man was abused by another man, the question then lingers, "Did he enjoy it? Does he like sex with men?" And if he was abused by a woman, will anyone understand that it truly constituted abuse? In its ignorance, society sees it as an act of sex rather than an act of violence, like rape. For men, secrets and silence still equal safety. This won't change until more men come forward. They must be encouraged to do so.

In mid-December, the advisory board of the newly forming National Center for Survivors of Childhood Abuse held its first meeting. Members and their spouses attended. In opening remarks, Louis Sullivan, the U.S. Secretary of Health and Human Services, recited the grim facts of abuse, stressed the need for improved services for survivors, and encouraged the center in its plans. After dinner, as chair of the advisory board, I thanked everyone for coming and asked each person—board members and spouses alike—to say why they were involved or what they thought the center should do. With one emotional and provocative recitation after another, we went around the room.

One of the spouses—Supreme Court Justice Anthony Kennedy, husband of board member Mary Kennedy—began by saying he was no authority on child abuse and felt out of place addressing medical researchers who were. However, he did have some thoughts on the issue. Extemporaneously, he delivered a cogent and compelling statement about the need for better treatment for survivors, better information for the public about the causes of abuse, and better education for members of the criminal justice system about child abuse in general.

After enthusiastic applause, the room erupted with spirited comments and discussion. In closing, I cited the data, gave a personal perspective, and pleaded for us to help those who, as children, had no one to help them. The meeting encouraged me that real assistance could be provided to survivors and their loved ones.

The next boost to my spirits came on December 21 at the JFK airport as Natasha returned from Africa. Her calls and letters had put our minds at ease. Even so, we waited anxiously as passengers disembarked. Suddenly, in the moving throng I saw her. "Where? Where?" Gail asked. "There," I said, "behind the woman in the caftan, next to the man with the beard." In ripped jeans and lugging two backpacks and a duffel bag, she came our way. Tan and tall and here, she looked great!

On our drive from New York to Washington, she regaled us with stories about her odyssey—living with the Maasai, sleeping on the ground under the stars, sailing on a dhow in the Indian Ocean, exploring Zanzibar, studying Swahili on the island of Lamu, fending for herself in Mombasa. Some of these adventures parents hear best after the fact.

When we stopped at a Howard Johnson's for dinner, two girls Natasha's age sauntered by with spike heels, long curved nails, teased hair, and fake leopard-skin coats. "Argh . . ." my polylingual daughter groaned. "Do you realize how revolting that is? There are people with real problems in this world. In this nation, where we have everything, you see that kind of phoniness." My daughter's returned!

Back on the highway, a relieved Gail went to sleep, and Natasha and I talked our way through New Jersey, Pennsylvania, and Delaware. By Maryland, she, too, dropped off. Her knowledge and self-reliance impressed me; her values and perspectives heartened me. I was deeply proud of her. Best of all, she was safe and home.

Our Christmas Eve, always a significant time, took new life that year. Deb and Seth unwrapped Natasha's gifts from Africa for the baby. She'd bargained and traded for them at street bazaars. Natasha, who lives for music, gave me a tape of her favorite pieces, which she'd spent hours editing. One side had music from her era; the other side, my era. It was a labor of love.

Gail and I gave each other the same thing for Christmas that year. In fact, it would be our joint Christmas, anniversary, and birthday gifts for several years to come. She founded Women of Washington, Inc., a nonprofit, nonpartisan organization to provide networking, mentoring, and professional growth opportunities for women. This had been a longtime dream of hers.

When I was president, she tried to link disparate groups that otherwise might never communicate with each other. She especially wanted to form an organization to assist women. She knew well from our travail that in times of personal crisis, women support each other. But, she reasoned, crisis is not the only time to bond. Women should reach out to one another, learn from one another, and support one another in their working worlds on a regular basis. She knew something else too: The women of Washington possess exceptional talent and ability. She felt that they would benefit from the opportunity to meet with other creative women of all ages and races and from diverse fields and backgrounds, and to hear thoughtful speakers. She wanted women to have a forum to exchange both ideas and business cards, to associate with successful leaders and inspiring mentors, and to be mentors to others.

To achieve these goals, she founded a new organization. Its lineup of opening speakers ensured that in the spring of 1992 it would start with a bang. They included Mayor Sharon Pratt Kelly of Washington, Children's Defense Fund president Marian Wright Edelman, and journalists Ellen Goodman and Judy Mann.

With 1991 closing and 1992 opening, I prepared to return to AU. On a crisp morning, I drove out to meet Romeo Segnan, the physics department chairman. He agreed to meet with me on December 27, during the winter break. I wanted to go then, before the spring term and with the campus nearly empty, to see where I'd teach. This would be my first time back since we'd moved my things from the president's office some nineteen months earlier.

I drove out Foxhall Road and turned onto Nebraska Avenue. On my left I passed the president's house, where we'd lived for a decade. It looked the same. Now, though, it no longer was my home. And that felt just fine. I entered the campus via the rear gate. The campus, too, looked the same. Why shouldn't it? It all looked familiar—the back path I used to walk from the house to my office, the building where I'd been dean. It was like seeing an old friend after a long interlude. Features were the same, memories remained; only nuances and my perceptions changed. I parked close to the McKinley building and walked directly to Romeo Segnan's office.

"Hi, Dick! Good to see you here." Romeo showed me the lecture hall I'd use and important professorial things—like how to unlock the projectors. And he showed me my office. I thanked him and said I was all set. I'd see him next on January 13 for the first day of class and my first official day back as Professor Berendzen. Romeo grinned. "Good, good, Dick! That's great. Call me if you need anything."

At seven A.M. on January 13, my alarm went off. I got out of bed, propelled by nervous energy. I dressed, ate breakfast, and stopped to hold Gail.

"Well, Bunny, this is it. I return—not just to AU but to my old life as a professor. I don't know what to expect. How will the faculty and students react? Will I encounter a phalanx of press like at the courthouse? I just don't know."

"Please call to tell me. Want to take a last look at your lecture notes? You have time."

"Are you kidding? I'm ready. I feel like a runner waiting for the starting gun."

On that crisp, clear morning, I again drove in the rear entrance, parked, and walked briskly toward my office, carrying three containers of course outlines, view graphs, and slides. On this first day of class, only a few people were out that early. From a distance, one person saw me. "Dr. B!" he shouted. I saw a member of the maintenance crew rushing my way—husky, smiling. I set down my containers to shake hands. Instead, he swung his muscular arms around me and lifted me to my toes.

"I'm so glad to see you. And how's Mrs. B? I've sure missed you."

Farther on, I passed two students, one of whom did a double take. I held my breath. After I'd passed them, he called out, "Glad you're back." No press lined the steps of the McKinley building; only two students stood talking. Thank goodness. Messages awaited me on my voice mail saying, "Welcome back," from staff and faculty members.

After a couple of minutes of uneasiness at the beginning of my first class, I began to feel the old adrenaline. The students seemed to respond. As the class shuffled out at the end, a student waited for me, shifting from one foot to the other. "Professor Berendzen, I sure admire your courage." As I thanked him, I thought how much I admired his sensitivity.

I went to my office to call Gail. "So far so good. Everybody's been super. And there's no press." Someone knocked at the door. A professor dropped by to welcome me. She gave me a warm hug and softly said, "I'm glad you're one of us." At the water fountain, I saw another professor. "Dick, this is great! We've got offices in the same building." For lunch, I went through the campus cafeteria line. As I approached the register, the cashier looked up. "Ohhhh! It's my buddy! You're back!" She almost knocked over the cash drawer as she jumped up to hug me.

So it went for the rest of the day, as my physics colleagues welcomed me and some twenty other professors and staff members dropped by my office or stopped me on the sidewalk. Hugs and handshakes. And many moist eyes, including my own. No one mentioned the events of 1990.

André Maurois wrote in *The Art of Living*, "Without a family, man, alone in the world, trembles with the cold." So it was when I was a child, and so it felt in 1990 when I seemed to have lost my professional family. A new warmth emerged in 1992 when I returned and was reunited with them.

As I drove out of the gate at the end of the day, I realized a simple maxim: You can resign from your job, but you can't resign from your family. For me, AU was family. I'd come home.

Two weeks later, on a bone-chilling day, I flew to Boston. My breath almost froze to my face as I got out of the cab in front of Boston University. BU's Center for Space Physics had invited me to be the first speaker in its spring lecture series. This, too, was a homecoming, for I had been a professor at BU in the 1960s.

I walked down the fifth floor hallway, by the astronomy department, with memories on all sides. I passed Room 522 where students had filled all the chairs and the overflow had sat on the floor. I passed my old office, where Gail called me on July 20, 1971: "You'd better come get me. Labor pains have started."

My old colleagues took me to lunch at the faculty dining room. "A few others may join us," someone mentioned. More? Who? In walked old faculty colleagues from the physics department and people from the beltway labs and from "across the river."

They all were males, middle-aged, and scientists. Like the NASA staff a year earlier, they showed their support in their own way: by being there and by including me as one of their own. For a male professional, that's high praise and strong support. It was their way of saying, "You were a good guy. You still are." I got the message and appreciated it.

In late 1990, I had resolved to restore my mind, body, and spirit. By spring of 1992, I had tended the first and last of these. So I decided the time had come to work on my body. I read up on nutrition and exercise. Then, for the first time in twenty years, much to Gail's delight, I started grocery shopping with her. I began studying labels.

Gail and I both stopped eating fried foods and, eventually, meat. We shifted our diet to low-fat, high carbohydrate, and high fiber, with lots of water. I dusted off our treadmill and discovered an exercise room in our building. The result: I shed thirty pounds, felt twenty years younger, and ruined my wardrobe.

By April and the second anniversary of my disaster, I truly felt like a new man. Bruised and battered, yes, but also stronger and I hoped wiser. I wouldn't call my fall a blessing. Yet from it, a new man was emerging. The entire debacle had given me exceptional opportunities to examine myself.

It was as if I'd watched my own open heart surgery. I saw through the protective skin, into my very being. Awake and in horror, I watched as a malignant tumor was torn from the deepest recesses. No neat excision with anesthesia, no elective surgery, this incision ripped me open with the ragged saw of humiliation and resurrected anguish. No manual told me how long the recovery would take, or if I'd ever heal. Still, as torturous as it was, the process did remove the tumor.

The spring term brought me more than renewal. I reveled in teaching and delighted in reconnecting with my old professional colleagues, both at AU and across the nation. Lunchtime conversations among the AU faculty members became mini-seminars on diverse topics, from current politics to ancient history, and almost anything else you can imagine. I felt like I was in grad school again.

Besides the faculty, there were the students. After all, the institution exists for them, and they always have been my greatest joy at any university. In spring of 1992 I got to know them as I never had before—not just through teaching but also through hours and hours of conversation outside of class. They came by "just to talk." At first a typical conversation would relate to my course or at least to AU, but it soon would expand to include their concerns and hopes. As the term went on, some of my students brought their friends by to talk. Then students I didn't know stopped by on their own. The events of 1990 never arose, but almost everything else did. They had questions of their own: What is education really for? Is it possible to make money and serve people? How can you achieve anything when you are continually discouraged? As a scientist, did I believe in God? What authors should students read for their own sake, not just for school? The Reverend Holmes had been right: Out of pain can come change and renewal. I knew that "through many dangers, toils, and snares, I have already come." I still wasn't sure about grace, but maybe it would "lead me home."

At the end of my astronomy course, we discussed the birth of the cosmos. We reviewed the arguments, pro and con, about the Big Bang Theory, which holds that the universe began in a titanic explosion fifteen billion years ago. This provocative and inspiring subject enthralled the students.

After my last class, I flew to Florida to address the National School Boards Association. Early Friday morning, April 24, I opened my hotel door to pick up the newspaper. In bold, black letters, the headline on *The Orlando Sentinel* boomed: THE BIG BANG. Beneath it was a multicolored map of the entire sky. The caption said a NASA satellite had found tiny temperature fluctuations that were relics from the original explosion.

My God! I couldn't believe it. If this finding proved true, it would be one of the most profound scientific discoveries of our century. Suddenly, we were with Galileo in 1609 as he became the first person to see the heavens through a telescope. This finding had almost no parallel. It would spark new research into the very earliest moments after the beginning and speculation about before the beginning.

The paper shook in my hands, I was so excited. The phone rang. "Professor Berendzen? We're a radio station in San Antonio. We got your number from your wife. Could we put you on live about the Big Bang?" I sat on the side of the bed, half dressed, trying to explain the inexplicable. Then I dashed downstairs to give my speech.

When I finished it, someone handed me a note: "Call ABC *Nightline*." As I once again sat on my bed, a producer politely but thoroughly grilled me. It was like a miniature PhD oral exam. After half an hour, he said, "Could you do *Nightline* on this tonight?" I explained that my return flight would put me in Washington at seventwenty. If they wished, I could do it. He said they had other people to interview. He'd know for sure by four o'clock.

At four, from a pay phone in the Orlando Airport, I called him. "Yes, we'd definitely like you on. The other guest will be the chairman of the astronomy department at Harvard." With the chatter of children all around me, I could barely hear. And I found I could barely speak, as my eyes filled. "Fine," I said. "I'll be home and ready by ten P.M."

Two years earlier I'd had to cancel the interview I wanted to do more than any other—about the Hubble Space Telescope, an instrument that might reveal details about the birth of the universe. The program was *Nightline*. Then, six hellish weeks later, I did the torturous interview about my calls and my abuse—again on *Nightline*. Now, to return to discuss the discovery of our age! And the other guest would be the chairman of my old alma mater.

The last time I was on this program, the prerecorded introduction seared my soul. This time, it raised my spirits. With Strauss's stirring *Also sprach Zarathustra* in the background, it captivated the viewer with sounds, images, and ideas. Ted Koppel began by quoting the first two verses of *Genesis*. When he came to me, I said he'd stopped one sentence short. The next verse says: "And God said, Let there be light. . . ." I then noted that the importance of the recent astronomical finding was that "this is the first light."

After a break, Koppel jokingly asked, "What earthly good is this discovery?" I replied, "It is simply the greatest story science has ever told." We consider biography, history, and geology to be important. This is the ultimate saga. Near the end of the show, he asked if this discovery would ameliorate or exacerbate the historic tensions between science and theology. I replied by paraphrasing Father Lemaître, a priest-astronomer whose theories anticipated the actual discovery in 1929 of the expanding universe. When asked how he could make his astronomical and his theological beliefs jibe, he reportedly said: "There's no problem as long as you keep to the proper set of questions. Science deals with What, Where, When, and How. And theology deals with Why and Who."

I went on to say that astronomers can describe in elaborate detail what happened one billionth of a second after the Big Bang. They can't yet say anything concrete about what happened one billionth of a second before the Big Bang, or if time originated then. Nor can they answer the fundamental question of Why?

The program ended. I took off the earpiece and met Gail in the green room. She gave me a smile and a kiss. A technician stopped me to explain his theory of cosmology, as did the makeup woman. Before I got out the door, two other workers wanted to talk. Only Koppel mentioned 1990: "This was sure a lot happier than the last time you were here."

"Sure was," I agreed.

The studio's limo drove us home. As we rode, we sat quietly. We communicated through the touch of our hands. We both understood the ironies and felt the moment. And I kept thinking of four simple words: "He restoreth my soul."

A day later, on a rainy Sunday afternoon, we attended a Greek festival. At the entrance, a friend rushed to us with her arms open wide. "Today was our big Easter service at church. And the priest based his sermon on the *Nightline* program you were just on!"

Someone grabbed my hand and said, "The priest is here. You've got to meet him." As we made our way through the crowd, person after person stopped me—no longer to wish me well or ask how I was, but to talk about cosmology and theology. In a crush of people, under a tent heavy with rain, we talked about origins and knowledge and faith. I was a professor again, but not the same as before. Something had changed.

A couple of weeks later, Natasha called. "Tell me about SS433," she began. "Does the redshifted radiation come from a jet ejected away from us due to a tilt of the accretion disk?"

"Whoa!" I pleaded. "How about a 'hello' first?"

"Sorry. I've got a final coming in astronomy. I was out sick when they discussed this material. And I'm nervous."

Indeed she had been out. Many weeks after she'd returned from Africa, where she'd been well, she suddenly came down with a mysterious sickness. She checked herself into an emergency ward in Boston. At first they thought it might be meningitis. So they gave her a spinal tap. Then they diagnosed the problem: malaria. Despite her antimalarial pills, she'd contracted it, and it had lain dormant until she returned. With medication and time, it went into remission.

Nonetheless, she'd missed classes. Once again, the ironies: My daughter taking astronomy at BU in Room 522, where I used to teach it, across the hall from where Gail called me before Natasha was born. For the next hour, my resolutely nonscientific daughter and I discussed neutron stars and mass transfer between close binaries. I assured her that she may have missed some classes, but she needn't worry. She talked like a science major. Parental pride comes from many things—your child's ability and accomplishments, spirit and values. Natasha has brains and heart. I am proud of both.

With my first term back as a professor now over, my life took another turn. Many months earlier, Gail and I had been asked to be plenary speakers at the eighth biennial National Symposium on Child Victimization. Entitled "Shattered Dreams: Childhood Recaptured," this multidisciplinary conference was for professionals and advocates in the field. The Children's National Medical Center cosponsored it with fifteen other organizations such as the National Committee for the Prevention of Child Abuse. Gail and I had discussed at length whether we were prepared to take that step. Unlike the University of Maryland conference, this one would include the press, and a few thousand people would attend from across the nation. Ultimately, we decided that, by May 1992, the time had come. Whether we had anything of value to tell top professionals in the field, we wondered. But we finally agreed.

That had been a long time earlier. Now we faced the challenge of actually preparing our talk. It would be *our* talk, not just mine or hers. We decided to try a new format. I would speak. Then, with no pause, I would sit and she would speak. Then we'd reverse, and reverse again—with me concluding the talk.

The audience gathered in the hotel ballroom. The head of the symposium greeted them and introduced us. She concluded by saying, "Today, Richard and Gail will tell us about their crisis, about the sexual abuse in Richard's childhood, and about their survival over trauma."

I began by noting that astronomers a few weeks earlier had announced perhaps the greatest scientific discovery of all time. They had detected the first light, the genesis moment, the embryonic universe itself.

"We see and know and ponder events from that remote past even now. We never escape from our origins, for events then influence today." The past, present, and future blend.

I reviewed the events of 1990 and described, in broad terms, the abuse in my childhood. I didn't identify the victimizer, although that astute audience no doubt could guess. I still wasn't ready to name my mother publicly. The shame was just too great.

Gail gave her perspective as the wife who suddenly had to confront both her husband's secret abusive childhood and his recent fall from grace.

The symposium organizers had asked us to emphasize survival techniques as well as the effects of child abuse. So I told about mine when I was a child and my more recent ways of healing. I told how 1991 had been a unique time for coping and mending, healing and restoring, growing and serving. I said that I'd learned that in confronting adversity, certain attributes were cardinal: faith, family, friends. I needed the right outlook and hope, acceptance and initiative, and service. Self-pity and victimization got me nowhere. And most of all, I learned how exquisitely fortunate, almost blessed, my life has been.

I concluded by citing the U.S. Advisory Board on Childhood Abuse and Neglect, which has termed those problems a national emergency. The board based this conclusion on these findings: first, that each year hundreds of thousands of children are berated and belittled, starved and abandoned, burned and beaten, raped and sodomized. Second, that the response to child abuse and neglect has failed. And third, that the nation spends billions of dollars because of this failure.

I quoted the board: "Not only are child abuse and neglect wrong, but the nation's lack of an effective response to them is also wrong. Neither can be tolerated. Together they constitute a moral disaster.

"All Americans should be outraged by child maltreatment."

Then I added my own views: "Indeed they should. Let me state it more bluntly: Child abuse is the most prevalent and yet least recognized evil in America today. It gnaws at the soul of our nation. America, wake up!

"Our nation faces challenges and needs on all sides. Every day's newspaper reminds us of that. But I will state unequivocally that there is no greater cause, there is no greater need, than to protect the children of this land. Beyond that, as a rational and compassionate society, we must care for the survivors. They neither need nor want pity. They deserve respect and support. Hundreds of thousands of children in this land scream in silent anguish. It is the loudest shout you will never hear. With the courage of legions of survivors, we should give that pain a voice. With their courage and our voice, a difference can be made."

Throughout our talk, the audience had sat in silence. Some people took notes. Others dabbed their eyes. As I ended, the group sprang to its feet with emotional applause. The head of the symposium thanked us and closed the session. Again, the audience rose to applaud. Several dozen people gathered in front of the platform. We shook hands, exchanged cards, hugged, and cried.

Whatever trepidation Gail and I had, vanished. We felt the warmth. We felt a real connectedness with survivors and those who aid them. We and they had communicated and linked, beyond the cognitive level. At last I felt I'd reached the affective feelings Dr. Berlin had stressed. We left the meeting rejuvenated and convinced that child abuse was an evil about which we must and would speak. To do less would be immoral. To know there exists such anguish and need and to do nothing, to say nothing, would be reprehensible. Our decision had been made for us. This trial run had confirmed what we'd wondered: Yes, we should speak out. And we would.

About this time, I had a unique opportunity not to speak but to listen. Sixty-five police officers gathered at the Police Boys and Girls Club in Northeast Washington to hear five authorities discuss child abuse. Police Chief Fulwood had asked me to bring in experts to talk to his force about this critical yet often overlooked problem. The police need to be able to identify child abuse and know what steps to take. The people I assembled provided both legal and medical insights. At the same time, we learned from the officers' real-world experience.

"What should we do when a parent says, 'My old man used to whomp me with a belt over anything. That's what made me a good person today. So damn right I take a belt to my kids sometimes. You're supposed to!'?"

Or, "How can a child learn good parenting skills when the child's mother is fifteen, the grandmother is thirty, and both of them are after the same sixteen-year-old male?"

Toward the end of the meeting, I told the group, "Lest you think abuse cases are rare or isolated, let me give you some data." The problems in the inner cities make a farce of the mythic American home, while the problems nationwide exceed reason or understanding. I cited the conventional overall estimates of one female in four and one male in six abused before age eighteen. These figures may be far too high, I suggested. Several officers shook their heads. "Not in this city, they aren't." I looked around the room and added, "If these numbers are close to right, then how many in this room were abused? Survivors sit around us every day."

The next day, Fulwood's office called to ask me to meet with him. When I arrived, he said, "Dick, I want training about child abuse for everybody on our force. Can you arrange it?"

I assured him that I'd try. "There's something else," he interjected. "Your comment about the large number of victims, and that many survivors may now serve on our force really hit me. That's got to be true! Think what that means for our operations. We place people in extremely stressful situations. What they face may link with problems in their own childhood. How do they handle it? How can we help?"

That evening I discussed this with other organizers of the National Center for Survivors of Childhood Abuse. Besides the D.C. police department, how about other police departments? Youth club supervisors? The clergy? School principals, nurses, and teachers? Day-care providers?

The list goes on. Every care provider for children should have comprehensive training about child abuse. This training should not be alarmist, but informative.

At the same time, we should care about survivors so that they can overcome their grief, move past their secrets, and lead fully productive lives.

A couple of weeks later, my focus shifted from the loss of childhood to the creation of it. My son-in-law Seth took a trip, and Deborah asked me to fill in at the childbirth class. About fifteen young couples ringed the room. I felt exorbitantly old. The instructor took us through every stage of labor, step by step. She discussed the benefits of breast-feeding, and analyzed the pros and cons of laying a baby on its back versus its stomach. Then we all sat on the floor. Deb, like the other women, lumbered down, one joint at a time. We faced each other, and she pushed on my hands. I cupped her hands as she held an ice cube. Then she cupped mine. And all of us practiced focusing and panting. The very full women did fine, while I hyperventilated.

During a break, I commended the instructor on her masterful delivery. She thanked me and asked what I did. "Professor," I said. Of what, she wanted to know. "Astronomy. You consider the birth of babies. I consider the birth of the cosmos. We're in the same business." She laughed, and said she was glad to see a granddad at a class.

She couldn't have been as glad as I was to be there. Deb's pregnancy moved from being an abstract concept to a coming event. I got to share her excitement and trepidation. As she focused, breathed, and pushed hard against my hands, I felt the force of her mock labor and my real love. Here was my daughter, whose life I'd helped create, planning for the birth of new life.

On July 1, six of us—Deb, Seth, Seth's parents, Gail, and I—all packed into the doctor's office to "see" the baby. I'd never seen a sonogram before. Suddenly there it was: flickering images on a black and white screen. The technician said, "There's a hand, and here's the spine." I remembered the first time I'd ever seen Saturn through a telescope. Pictures became real. The fetus became a baby, my grandchild.

The technician slowed the scan again, as we focused on one critical spot. A pulsing core locked my eyes to the screen. My heart skipped a beat, as we watched the baby's little heart pound. Seth's mother beamed and called out, "Mazel tov!" This child was loved and welcomed even before he arrived into our Judeo-Christian extended family. The technician moved on. We counted all ten fingers and one foot. We couldn't see the other foot. "Not to worry," Deb said, who was fighting hard to think positively. "If need be, he could hop on one foot! At least the rest looks good."

The best was yet to come. The technician froze the frame. Before us was the full face of a beautiful baby, with one eye open and a tiny fist against its chin, like a lilliputian version of Rodin's "The Thinker." Deb cried out, "He looks just like Seth! Exactly!"

As one daughter waited to give birth, we celebrated the other's twenty-first birthday. Deb prepared for motherhood; Natasha prepared for grad school. On July 20, I thought back to sitting beside Gail as she focused and breathed and pushed. I remembered "If" and the poem in the attic. And I remembered my twenty-first birthday.

Young and divorced, I was alone in Boston. Well, not quite alone, for my mother had moved there before the divorce, and she was still there. I could not get rid of her. Reluctantly, I agreed to have dinner with her on my birthday. This was a special day for her, too. She was so confused I wasn't sure she quite understood the event. She chattered in nonstop non sequiturs. I tuned her out that night, just as I had a decade earlier. As she rambled, I picked at my food, blocked out my childhood, grieved for my fallen marriage and faraway Debbie, and resolved to pick myself up. If turning twenty-one signified that I was a man, then by heavens I'd act like one. But, oh, how I ached that night.

For Natasha's coming of age, we wanted to give her something special. "If" was out: I'd given it to her years ago. We thought of clothes and jewelry and trips. We considered books and poems and sayings. Of course, we sent her letters and routine gifts. But we wanted something unique.

We bought a small meteorite the size of your thumb, mounted it in a silver band, and hung it on a silver chain. Its indented iron surface, with dabs of ocher rust, contrasted smartly with the shining silver, Natasha's favorite metal.

Around her neck would hang a shooting star, a piece of debris from the formation of the solar system. This asteroidal chunk may be as old as the Earth, and it is not of this planet. It's the oldest and most unusual thing she'll ever hold. By comparison, the Rocky Mountains are infants, and diamonds, ordinary. This is the stuff of origins—the origin of the solar system and maybe even life on Earth. This is an object from another place and time; she carries with her antiquity and our never-ending love.

Deb's due date and Natasha's birthday happened almost to coincide. For Deb, the days dragged on, as nature moved at its own pace. Two weeks past the projected arrival day, the doctor agreed to induce labor. On the big day—August 5—I woke up early. We assembled our gifts for Deb and the baby, and for the last time I checked the cameras. We were ready. Was Deb?

At five P.M., Gail and I entered the Columbia Hospital for Women, the same hospital where Gail had her hysterectomy. I remembered well pacing the floor and waiting. This evening, though, our wait was filled with happy anxiety.

In high spirits, Deb sat up in her bed and joked with Seth and me as we waited for the nurse to begin the IV. When I had an IV in my hand at Hopkins, I'd nearly fainted. I worried about Deb, who hates needles anyway. The nurse pulled up a chair beside the bed, and Seth and I shot to opposite sides of the room. He sat down and I leaned against the door. "Fine pair of male supporters I've got!" Deb laughed. We feebly explained that we didn't want to be in the way.

After three tries, the nurse found a vein. Deb's are like faint threads. All the while, we heard the rhythmic thumping of the baby's heart, as a device recorded the fetal heart rate. The time had come. The nurse said that all of us except Seth now must leave. As my daughter faced her greatest ordeal, there was no way I could help— except for her to know that I was there. I would always be there. I squeezed her hand and kissed her forehead. Then we all left the room.

Gail and I walked outside the hospital on that crisp, clear evening. The bright sun cast long shadows against a gold-colored backdrop. We looked up at Deb's window and said silent prayers.

When we reentered, we learned that Deb hadn't responded to the IV and they had decided to perform a cesarean. The clock advanced: The birth could end within an hour, and we could see Deb and the baby soon thereafter. Seth would stay at her side.

Nervously, the grandparents chatted in the lobby. Deb had told us to bring plenty of reading material because she might be in labor for hours. I'd dutifully brought a thick astronomy text, which stayed in my attaché case.

By now it was nine P.M. One grandparent after another sauntered to the drinking fountain. We weren't that thirsty. The fountain happened to be in the hallway to the delivery area. On my turn at the fountain, the double doors swung open and a beaming Seth emerged, outfitted in a blue medical smock. He grinned and gave a two-thumbs-up sign.

"Maxwell Berendzen Casner has arrived! He and Deb are doing great. Want to see them?"

Moments later, we cautiously peered into the recovery room. Deb was lying under a mound of sheets, wearing a blue hospital cap, and holding a small bundle. Seth held her left hand. She looked tired and slightly groggy but also radiant. Close to her cheek lay a tiny face, the same one we'd seen on the sonogram. Now it was real. And well and perfect. My child's child!

No reading prepared me, no conversations indicated fully how this moment would feel. No grandparent could have told me. To hold my own infant daughters brought emotions beyond description. Now to hold my grandchild touched yet other feelings. I felt pride and joy and love.

The nurses transferred Max to the nursery to be weighed and checked further. And Deb drifted off, looking relieved and happy. As our contingent crowded beside the nursery window, a nurse told us the weight: nine pounds, five and a half ounces. No wonder Deb had seemed "full with child."

Moments after seeing Deb, I called Natasha. Suddenly my daughters had changed: One was a mother, the other an aunt. I had the ponderous title of granddad, and our family now stretched across generations.

For an hour, we grandparents stood beside the glass and admired Max's silken skin and ruddy cheeks. His eyes opened just a crack, then shut, then opened again. These were some of his first looks at the world. I thought of all that he would discover—warm sunlight and cold rain, the good times and special friends, and all of life.

Whether the baby was a boy or girl, Deb had picked the same middle name, and Seth had agreed. She said she was proud of her last name and didn't want it to end. Since I have no sons, that could have happened. But not now with Max.

The next day, Gail and I returned with Rubrim lilies, Deb's favorite flowers. Deb had a tough day. The cesarean made for no labor but a grueling recovery. By evening she felt better than she had previously but craved sleep. The rest of us counted down the minutes outside the nursery window. At exactly seven-forty-three P.M.—on the first day anniversary of Max's birth—we all sang "Happy Birthday," as he lay sleeping on the other side of the pane. Startled, a visiting childbirth class chimed in with us.

When I held my own infant daughters, I wanted to make life good for them. As I held my grandson, I wanted to make life safe for him. Max deserved no less, just as all children deserve this and more. They deserve what Max has in abundance—support and love from all sides. Even before he was born, he was cherished. Now he is loved by relatives that span generations.

In Max I see an exemplar for infants everywhere: nurturing parents, an elaborate support system, and family members united to ensure him a safe, protected, fulfilling childhood. That, after all, should be every child's birthright—freedom from pain, fear, and abuse, and the right to joy, laughter, and love.

In his sleep, one day after his birth, little Max's dreamlike smile said it all. From birth onward, this child and all children have the right to keep that smile.

IF

If you can keep your head when all about you
    Are losing theirs and blaming it on you;
If you can trust yourself when all men doubt you,
    But make allowance for their doubting too;
If you can wait and not be tired by waiting,
    Or being lied about, don't deal in lies,
Or being hated, don't give way to hating,
    And yet don't look too good, nor talk too wise;

If you can dream—and not make dreams your master;
    If you can think—and not make thoughts your aim;
If you can meet with Triumph and Disaster
    And treat those two impostors just the same;
If you can bear to hear the truth you've spoken
    Twisted by knaves to make a trap for fools,
Or watch the things you gave your life to, broken,
    And stoop and build 'em up with worn-out tools;

If you can make one heap of all your winnings
    And risk it on one turn of pitch-and-toss,
And lose, and start again at your beginnings
    And never breathe a word about your loss;
If you can force your heart and nerve and sinew
    To serve your turn long after they are gone,
And so hold on when there is nothing in you
    Except the Will which says to them: "Hold on!";

If you can talk with crowds and keep your virtue,
    Or walk with Kings—nor lose the common touch;
If neither foes nor loving friends can hurt you;
    If all men count with you, but none too much;
If you can fill the unforgiving minute
    With sixty seconds' worth of distance run—
Yours is the Earth and everything that's in it,
    And—which is more—you'll be a Man, my son!

        —RUDYARD KIPLING
        (who was abused as a child)

Appendix A

TOLL-FREE HELP: NATIONWIDE NUMBERS FOR CHILD-ABUSE AND NEGLECT SERVICES

800-531-HUG-U	Adult Survivors of Child Abuse
800-448-3000	Boystown National Hotline
800-843-5200	California Youth Crisis Line (in CA only)
800-I-AM-LOST	Child Find (missing children)
800-551-1300	Child of the Night (runaways)
800-248-8020	Child Quest International (missing and abused children)
800-4-A-CHILD	Childhelp USA Child Abuse Hotline
800-FYI-3366	Clearinghouse on Child Abuse and Neglect Information
800-477-2627	Colorado Outward Bound School (for survivors of child abuse)
800-999-9999	Covenant House Hotline (crisis line for runaways and others)
800-221-2681	Family Service America, Inc., Hotline

800-272-0012	Kevin Collins's Foundation for Missing Children
800-872-5437	Missing Children Help Center
800-843-5678	National Center for Missing and Exploited Children
800-826-7653	National Center for Missing and Exploited Children (TDD for the hearing impaired)
800-782-SEEK	National Center for Missing Youth
800-222-1464	National Child Watch Campaign (missing children)
800-222-2000	National Council on Child Abuse and Family Violence Helpline
800-851-3420	National Criminal Justice Referral Service
800-227-5242	National Resource Center on Child Abuse and Neglect
800-KIDS-006	National Resource Center on Child Sexual Abuse
800-231-6946	National Runaway Hotline
800-621-4000	National Runaway Switchboard
800-442-HOPE	National Youth Crisis Hotline
800-421-0353	Parents Anonymous National Office (for overwhelmed parents)
800-627-3675	Red Flag/Green Flag Resources (sexual abuse and domestic violence)
800-826-4743	Vanished Children's Alliance
800-786-4238	Voices in Action, Inc. (for incest survivors)
800-HIT-HOME	Youth Crisis Hotline

Appendix B

ORGANIZATIONS FOR ADULT SURVIVORS OF CHILD ABUSE

The following organizations provide information for adult survivors of child abuse:

Adult Survivors of Child Abuse
   (ASCA) Treatment Centers
10251 E. Artesia Boulevard,
   Suite 215
Bellflower, CA 90706
(310) 866-5810
(800) 531-HUG U

Childhelp USA
5225 Wisconsin Avenue, N.W.
Washington, DC 20015
(202) 537-5193

Colorado Outward Bound School
945 Pennsylvania Street
Denver, CO 80203
(800) 477-2627

Echoes Network, Inc.
1622 N.E. 8th Avenue
Portland, OR 97232
(503) 281-8185

Giarretto Institute
232 E. Gish Road
1st Floor
San Jose, CA 95112
(408) 453-7616

Incest Resources, Inc.
46 Pleasant Street
Cambridge, MA 02139
(617) 492-1818
(requests by mail only)

Incest Survivors Resource
   Network International
P.O. Box 7375
Las Cruces, NM 88006-7375
(505) 521-4260

National Child Rights Alliance
  (NCRA)
P.O. Box 422
Ellenville, NY 12428
(413) 773-7116

Survivors of Incest Anonymous,
  Inc. (SIA)
P.O Box 21817
Baltimore, MD 21222
(301) 282-3400
(requests by mail only)

Survivors United Network
3607 Martin Luther King Blvd.
Denver, CO 80205
(303) 355-1133

Voices In Action, Inc.
(Victims of Incest Can Emerge
  Survivors)
P.O. Box 148309
Chicago, IL 60614
(800) 786-4238
(301) 282-3400

Appendix C

ORGANIZATIONS THAT COMBAT CHILD ABUSE

NATIONAL ORGANIZATIONS CONCERNED
WITH CHILD MALTREATMENT

Action for Child Protection
4724 Park Road, Unit C
Charlotte, NC 28209
(704) 529-1080
  Responds primarily to inquiries from professionals and institutions involved in child protection.

American Academy of
  Pediactrics
141 Northwest Point Boulevard
P.O. Box 927
Elk Grove Village, IL 60007
(800) 433-9016
  For professional and public educational materials contact the Publications Department. For information on child abuse and neglect, contact the AAP

Committee on Child Abuse and Neglect.

ABA Center on Children and
  the Law
1800 M Street, N.W., Suite 200
Washington, DC 20036
(202) 331-2250
  Responds primarily to inquiries from professionals and institutions involved in child welfare and protection.

American Association for
  Protecting Children
American Humane Association
63 Inverness Drive East
Englewood, CO 80112-5117
(303) 792-9900
(800) 227-5242

APPENDIX C

Professional publications and public inquiries regarding child protective services and child abuse and neglect.

American Medical Association
Department of Mental Health
515 North State Street
Chicago, IL 60610
(312) 464-5000

Responds to inquiries and provides publications relating to child abuse and neglect.

American Professional Society
on the Abuse of Children
(APSAC)
332 South Michigan Avenue
Suite 1600
Chicago, IL 60604
(312) 554-0166

Responds to inquiries from professionals involved in combating child maltreatment.

American Public Welfare
Association
810 First Street, N.E., Suite
500
Washington, DC 20002-4267
(202) 682-0100

Addresses program and policy issues on the administration and delivery of publicly funded human services.

Association of Junior Leagues
660 First Avenue
New York, NY 10016
(212) 683-1515

For legislative information, contact Public Policy Director; for individual Junior League programs and child abuse and neglect information, League Services Department.

Boys and Girls Clubs of
America
Government Relations Office
611 Rockville Pike, Suite 230
Rockville, MD 20852
(301) 251-6676

1,200 clubs nationwide serving over 1.6 million boys and girls. Offers child safety curriculum.

C. Henry Kempe Center for
Prevention and Treatment of
Child Abuse and Neglect
1205 Oneida Street
Denver, CO 80220
(303) 321-3963

Offers a clinically based resource for training, consultation, program development and evaluation, and research in all types of child maltreatment.

Child Welfare League of
America
440 First Street, N.W.
Suite 310
Washington, DC 20001
(202) 638-2952

Responds primarily to inquiries from professionals and institutions specializing in child welfare.

Childhelp USA
6463 Independence Avenue
Woodland Hills, CA 91367
Hotline: (800) 4-A-CHILD or
    (800) 422-4453
Provides comprehensive crisis counseling by mental health professionals for adult and child victims of child abuse and neglect, offenders, parents who are fearful of abusing or who want information on how to be effective parents. The Survivors of Childhood Abuse Program (SCAP) disseminates materials, makes treatment referrals, trains professionals, and conducts research.

General Federation of Women's
    Clubs
1734 N Street, N.W.
Washington, DC 20036-2920
(202) 347-3168
10,000 clubs nationwide. Provides child abuse and neglect prevention and education programs, nonprofessional support, and legislative activities. Programs are based on needs of community.

Military Family Resource
    Center (MFRC)
Ballston Center Tower Three
Ninth Floor
4015 Wilson Boulevard
Suite 903
Arlington, VA 22203
(703) 696-4555

Recommends policy and program guidance to the Assistant Secretary of Defense (Force Management and Personnel) on family violence issues and assists the military services to establish, develop, and maintain comprehensive family violence programs.

National Association for
    Perinatal Addiction Research
    and Education (NAPARE)
11 E. Hubbard St.
Suite 200
Chicago, IL 60611
(312) 329-2512
Provides a network for exchange of information and ideas regarding prevention and intervention in the problems caused by substance abuse during pregnancy.

National Association of Social
    Workers
7981 Eastern Avenue
Silver Spring, MD 20910
(301) 565-0333
Addresses social policy on family violence, legislation, and program support advocacy. Responds to inquiries from professionals and institutions involved in child welfare and protection.

National Black Child
Development Institute
1463 Rhode Island Avenue,
N.W.
Washington, DC 20005
(202) 387-1281
Provides newsletter, annual
conference, and answers public
inquiries regarding issues facing
black children/youth.

National Center on Child Abuse
and Neglect (NCCAN)
Administration on Children,
Youth and Families
Administration for Children and
Families
Department of Health and
Human Services
P.O. Box 1182
Washington, DC 20013
Responsible for the federal
government's child abuse and
neglect activities. Administers
grant programs to states and
organizations to further research
and demonstration projects,
service programs, and other
activities related to the identification, treatment and prevention of child abuse and neglect.

Clearinghouse provides selected
publications and information
services on child abuse and
neglect.
(703) 385-7565 or
(800) FYI-3366/394-3366

(outside the Washington, DC
metropolitan area)

National Center for Missing and
Exploited Children
2101 Wilson Boulevard
Suite 550
Arlington, VA 22201
(703) 235-3900
(800) 843-5678
Toll-free number for reporting
missing children, sightings of
missing children, or reporting
cases of child pornography.
Provides free written materials
for the general public on child
victimization as well as technical documents for professionals.

National Center for Prosecution
of Child Abuse
1033 N. Fairfax St.
Suite 200
Alexandria, VA 22314
(703) 739-0321
A program of the American
Prosecutors Research Institute,
promotes the prosecution and
conviction of child abusers by
offering information and practical assistance to prosecutors
involved in child abuse litigation. Publishes manuals on legal issues and provides
technical assistance, referral
services, and training seminars
on child abuse litigation for
prosecutors.

National Child Abuse Coalition
733 15th St., N.W., Suite 938
Washington, DC 20005
(202) 347-3666

Monitors federal policy and legislative changes in the area of child abuse and neglect and publishes a monthly newsletter summarizing recent developments in the federal government that impact on child protection professionals.

National Clearinghouse for
  Alcohol and Drug Information
  (NCADI)
P.O. Box 2345
Rockville, MD 20850
(301) 468-2600

Gathers and disseminates information on alcohol- and drug-related subjects, produces public awareness materials on substance abuse prevention, prepares topical bibliographies, and distributes a wide variety of publications on alcohol and drug abuse.

National Clearinghouse on
  Family Violence
Health and Welfare Canada
940 Brooke Claxton Bldg.
Tunney's Pasture
Ottawa, Ontario, Canada K1A
  1B5
(613) 957-2938
(613) 957-2939
(800) 267-1291

Collects and disseminates information on all aspects of family violence, with a special emphasis on material development in Canada.

National Committee for
  Prevention of Child Abuse
332 South Michigan Avenue
Suite 1600
Chicago, IL 60604-4357
(312) 663-3520

68 local chapters (in all 50 states). Provides information and statistics on child abuse and maintains an extensive publications list. The National Research Center provides information for professionals on programs, methods for evaluating programs, and research findings.

National Council of Juvenile
  and Family Court Judges
P.O. Box 8970
Reno, NV 89507
(702) 784-6012

Focuses on improving the court system's handling of juvenile and family court matters. Primarily responds to professional and institutional inquiries.

National Council on Child
  Abuse and Family Violence
1155 Connecticut Avenue,
  N.W., Suite 400
Washington, DC 20036
(800) 222-2000
  Provides services to
strengthen public awareness
and education, professional development and organizational
development in family violence
prevention and treatment programs.

The National Court Appointed
  Special Advocate Association
2722 Eastlake Ave. E., Suite
  220
Seattle, Washington 98102
(206) 328-8588
  Provides support to local
court-appointed special advocate programs with training,
legal research, fundraising, and
public awareness services.

National Crime Prevention
  Council
1700 K Street, N.W., 2nd
  Floor
Washington, DC 20006
(202) 466-6272
  Provides personal safety cur-
ricula, including child abuse
and neglect prevention for
schoolchildren and model prevention programs for adolescents. Educational materials for
parents, children, and community groups are available.

National Criminal Justice
  Reference Service (NCJRS)
National Institute of Justice
P.O. Box 6000
1600 Research Blvd.
Rockville, MD 20850
(301) 251-5500
(800) 851-3420
  Provides information on all
aspects of law enforcement and
criminal justice, answers inquiries, conducts computerized
database searches, distributes
publications, and makes referrals.

National Educational
  Association (NEA)
Human and Civil Rights Unit
1201 16th Street, N.W.
Washington, DC 20036
(202) 822-7733
  Offers training to NEA members. Sells child abuse and neglect training kits and
supplemental materials to professionals and the general public.

National Exchange Club
  Foundation for Prevention of
  Child Abuse
3050 Central Avenue
Toledo, OH 43606
(419) 535-3232

Provides volunteer parent aide services to abusive and neglecting families in 37 cities.

National Mental Health Association Prevention Clearinghouse
1021 Prince St.
Alexandria, VA 22314
(703) 684-7722
Offers a network to connect experts with those in need of assistance and to facilitate communication among professionals involved in primary prevention.

National Network of Runaway and Youth Services
1319 F Street, N.W., Suite 401
Washington, DC 20004
(202) 783-7949
Provides written materials, responds to general inquiries regarding runaways and adolescent abuse, and serves as a referral source for runaways and parents.

National Organization for Victim Assistance (NOVA)
1757 Park Road, N.W.
Washington, DC 20010
(202) 232-6682
Provides information and referral for child victims as well as crisis counseling.

National Runaway Switchboard Metro-Help, Inc.
3080 North Lincoln
Chicago, IL 60657
(800) 621-4000 (toll-free)
(312) 880-9860 (business)
Provides toll-free information, referral, and crisis counseling services to runaway and homeless youth and their families. Also serves as the National Youth Suicide Hotline.

Parents Anonymous
6733 South Sepulveda Boulevard
Suite 270
Los Angeles, CA 90045
(800) 421-0353 (toll-free)
(213) 410-9732 (business)
1,200 chapters nationwide. National program of professionally facilitated self-help groups. Each state has different program components.

Parents United/Daughters and Sons United/Adults Molested as Children United
232 East Gish Road
San Jose, CA 95112
(408) 453-7616
150 chapters nationwide. Provides guided self-help for sexually abusive parents as well as child and adult victims of sexual abuse.

Victims of Child Abuse Laws (VOCAL)
12 North Broadway
Suite 133
Santa Ana, CA 92701
(714) 558-0200

Provides information and support to individuals falsely accused of child abuse.

CHILD ABUSE AND NEGLECT RESOURCE LIST

SEXUAL ABUSE

National Coalition Against Sexual Assault
P.O. Box 21378
Washington, DC 20009
(202) 483-7165

The National Coalition Against Sexual Assault was founded in 1979 to lead a national movement to promote awareness about sexual violence and advocate for services for survivors. Members include rape crisis centers, counseling services, educational programs, women's shelters and concerned individuals.

National Resource Center on Child Sexual Abuse
106 Lincoln Street
Huntsville, AL 35801
(205) 534-6868
1-800-543-7006

Their toll-free number serves requests from the general public on information on child sexual abuse. The National Resource Center publishes the *National Directory of Child Sexual Abuse Treatment Programs* and has developed methods to increase professional awareness on issues including male survivors of sexual abuse, case management, and sexual abuse allegations in child custody litigations.

EDUCATION/PREVENTION

Clearinghouse on Child Abuse and Neglect Information
Box 1182
Washington, DC 20013
(703) 385-7565
1-800-394-3366 outside metropolitan Washington DC
This Clearinghouse, a component of the National Center on Child Abuse and Neglect, is a major resource center for publications and public awareness and child abuse. Their database provides bibliographies, program directories, and public awareness materials. From this database and other resources, the Clearinghouse develops publications on a variety of subjects including sibling abuse, cultural sensitivity, sexual abuse prevention and treatment, and substance abuse.

National Center for the Prosecution of Child Abuse
National Prosecutors Research Institute
1033 N. Fairfax Street, Suite 200
Alexandria, VA 22314
(703) 739-0321
The National Center for Prosecution of Child Abuse aims to improve the investigation and prosecution of child abuse through court reform, professional specialization, and interagency coordination. It provides training, technical assistance, and an information clearinghouse for child abuse prosecutors and others.

DRUG AND ALCOHOL ABUSE

Office for Substance Abuse Prevention
National Clearinghouse on Drug and Alcohol Information
P.O. Box 2345
Rockville, MD 20847-2345
1-800-729-6686
This Clearinghouse provides information and referrals on substance-abuse issues. Answers questions and supplies information over the phone.

APPENDIX C

VOLUNTEER OPPORTUNITIES

National Court Appointed Special Advocate (CASA) Association
2722 Eastlake Avenue, Suite 220
Seattle, WA 98102
(206) 328-8588

The CASA Association is a network of trained community volunteers speaking up for abandoned, neglected, and abused children in court proceedings throughout the United States. To become a volunteer, contact your local CASA program or the National CASA Association listed above.

SELECTED BIBLIOGRAPHY
ON CHILD ABUSE

Adams, C. and Fay, J. *No More Secrets: Protecting Your Child from Sexual Assault.* San Luis Obispo, CA: Impact, 1981.

Armstrong, I. *Kiss Daddy Goodnight.* New York: Hawthorn, 1978.

Bass, Ellen and Davis, Laura. *The Courage to Heal: A Guide for Women Survivors of Child Sexual Abuse.* New York: Harper & Row, 1988.

Bass, Ellen and Thornton, Louise (eds.). *I Never Told Anyone: Writings by Women Survivors of Child Sexual Abuse.* New York: Harper & Row, 1983.

Barker, N. (ed.). *Child Abuse and Neglect.* Dubuque, IA: Kendall/Hunt Publishing Company, 1989.

Bear, Euan with Dimock, Peter T. *Adults Molested As Children: A Survivor's Manual for Women and Men.* Orwell, VT: Safer Society Press, 1988.

Besharov, Douglas J. *Recognizing Child Abuse: A Guide for the Concerned.* New York: Free Press, 1990.

Bolton, Frank G., Morris, Larry A., and MacEachron, Ann E. *Males at Risk.* Newbury Park, CA: Sage Publications, Inc., 1989.

Butler, Sandra. *Conspiracy of Silence: The Trauma of Incest.* San Francisco, CA: Volcano Press, 1985.

Childhelp USA. *Survivor's Guide.* 6463 Independence Avenue, Woodland Hills, CA: Childhelp USA.

Cicchetti, D. and Carlson, V. (eds.): *Child Maltreatment: Theory and Research on the Causes and Consequences of Child Abuse and Neglect.* New York: Cambridge University Press, 1989.

Clark, R. and Clark, J. *The Encyclopedia of Abuse.* New York: Facts on File, Inc., 1989.

Crewdson, John. *By Silence Betrayed: Sexual Abuse of Children in America.* Boston, MA: Little, Brown, 1988.

Davis, Laura. *The Courage to Heal Workbook: For Women and Men Survivors of Child Sexual Abuse.* New York: Harper & Row, 1990.

Finkelhor, David. *Child Sexual Abuse.* New York: The Free Press, 1984.

Finkelhor, David (ed.). *A Sourcebook on Child Sexual Abuse.* Newbury Park, CA: Sage Publications, Inc., 1986.

Forward, Susan and Buck, Craig. *Betrayal of Innocence: Incest and Its Devastation.* New York: Penguin Books, 1978.

Fraser, Sylvia. *My Father's House: A Memoir of Incest and of Healing.* New York: Harper & Row, 1989.

Garbarino, J. and Scott, F. *What Children Tell Us: Eliciting, Interpreting, and Evaluating Information from Children.* San Francisco, CA: Jossey-Bass, Inc., 1989.

Gil, E. *Outgrowing the Pain: A Book for and About Adults Abused as Children.* New York: Dell, 1983.

———. *Treatment of Adult Survivors of Childhood Abuse.* Walnut Creek, CA: Launch Press, 1988.

———. *The Healing Power of Play: Working with Abused Children.* New York: Guilford Press, 1991.

Grubman-Black, S. D. *Broken Boys and Mending Men: Recovery from Childhood Sexual Abuse.* Blue Ridge Summit, PA: TAB Books, 1990.

Helfer, R. and Kempe, R. (eds.). *The Battered Child.* (4th ed.). Chicago: University of Chicago Press, 1987.

Hunter, Mic. *Abused Boys: The Neglected Victims of Sexual Abuse.* New York: Fawcett Columbine, 1990.

Justice, B. and Justice, R. *The Abusing Family.* New York: Plenum Press, 1990.

Kempe, R. and Kempe, C. *The Common Secret: Sexual Abuse of Children and Adolescents.* New York: W. H. Freeman and Co., 1984.

Lou, Mike. *Victims No Longer: Men Recovering from Incest and Other Sexual Child Abuse.* New York: Harper & Row, 1990.

Meadow, R. (ed.). *ABC of Child Abuse*. London: British Medical Journal, 1989.

Miller, Alice. *Thou Shalt Not Be Aware: Psychoanalysis and Society's Betrayal of the Child*. New York: New American Library, 1984.

Mrazek, P. and Mrazek, D. "The Effects of Child Abuse." From *Sexually Abused Children and Their Families*, edited by P. Mrazek and C. Kempe, Pergamon Press, 1981.

Nasjleti, M. "Suffering in Silence: The Male Incest Victim." *Child Welfare* 49:5, pp. 269–275, May 1980.

Purdy, A. *He Will Never Remember: Caring for Victims of Child Abuse*. Atlanta, GA: Susan Hunter Publishing, Inc., 1989.

Ratner, Ellen. *The Other Side of the Family: A Book for Recovery from Abuse, Incest, and Neglect*. Deerfield Beach, FL: Health Communications, Inc., 1990.

Rush, Florence. *The Best Kept Secret: Sexual Abuse of Children*. Englewood Cliffs, NJ: Prentice-Hall, 1980.

Sanford, L. *Strong at the Broken Places: Overcoming the Trauma of Childhood Abuse*. New York: Random House, 1990.

Wyatt, G. and Powell, G. (eds.). *Lasting Effects of Child Sexual Abuse*. Newbury Park, CA: Sage Publications, Inc., 1988.

NATIONAL CENTER ON
CHILD ABUSE AND NEGLECT

The National Center on Child Abuse and Neglect (NCCAN), which is part of the U.S. Department of Health and Human Services, constitutes the largest resource center in the nation on all aspects of child abuse and neglect. It was established to help professionals improve services to children and families in turmoil and to draw public attention to the problems of child maltreatment.

NCCAN is responsible for a variety of activities that include conducting research; collecting, analyzing, and disseminating information; providing assistance to states and communities in developing programs and activities related to the prevention, identification, and treatment of child abuse and neglect; and coordinating federal efforts to combat child maltreatment.

The information component of NCCAN is the Clearinghouse on Child Abuse and Neglect Information (P.O. Box 1182, Washington, D.C., 20013 [Tel: 800-394-3366]). Established primarily as a major resource for professionals concerned with child maltreatment issues, the Clearinghouse maintains a number of databases including documents, audiovisuals, program directories, public awareness materials, and information about national organizations.

ACKNOWLEDGMENTS

M any people helped in producing this book, and I am deeply
grateful to them. I especially thank Laura Palmer, a person of
exceptional insight. Long before I met her, she had explored lingering anguish from the Vietnam War, and then the suffering and courage of people with AIDS. With me, she explored the trauma and
aftermath of childhood abuse. With a keen sense about other people's
pain, she understands despair and how people overcome it. She
entered my life as a stranger; she continues in it as a close friend.
Thank you, Laura.

Kris Dahl, my agent, skillfully guided the manuscript of this book
through the labyrinth of publishing. She and her superb assistant,
Dorothea Herrey, appreciated from the outset the importance of treating the book's subject matter with candor yet decorum. I thank them
both.

No author could be more fortunate than to publish with Villard
Books. The staff there artfully blends professionalism with personal
care. Diane Reverand sets the lodestar at Villard. With astute sug-
gestions, she supported my efforts throughout. In addition, the re-
markable Villard/Random House staff—Dennis Ambrose, Richard
Aquan, Melanie Cecka, Wanda Chappell, Jacqueline Deval, Alex
Kuczynski, Sharyn Rosenblum, and many others, including Shelley
Garren and Chris Stamey—helped greatly. I thank them all.

Besides the people who helped produce the book, I also thank
those who stood by me during my darkest days. They made the book
possible. The people mentioned below—and many others—gave me
help and hope when I needed it most. I will treasure their support
always.

At The Johns Hopkins Hospital, I saw firsthand the skill and
dedication of health-care professionals. I saw doctors and nurses
and therapists and orderlies and technicians and counselors work
together as a harmonious team. They met me at my lowest ebb.

Unlike any people I had known before, they delved into my inner being, even into my carefully concealed childhood. They broke down my protective barriers and helped me understand the linkage of my present with my past. They pulled me through my toughest times and gave me hope. With gratitude, I thank Dr. Paul McHugh, Dr. Fred Berlin, Dr. Martin Malin, and everyone else at Hopkins who helped me so much.

One good result from a bad time is that you can see with dazzling clarity who your friends are and at the same time learn how very many you have. I wish I could acknowledge them all, for so many gracious and caring people showed Gail and me genuine friendship. Their insights aided me, their laughter encouraged me, their warmth sustained me. I am honored to know them.

Thank you to Tara Sonenshine and Gary Friend, Lou and Ulysses Auger, Lou and George Economos, Deborah Szekely, Jeanne Oates, Goli Kashani, Carole Hurwitz, Beth Peters, Joan Leach, Roberta Goldstein, Richard Marks, Judy Berman, Gerry Treanor, Donna Pieper, David Lloyd Kreeger, Nabil Koudjeti, Carol Shamieh, Sue Block, Florencia Quito, Paul Vassalo, David Eisner, Bishop James K. Mathews, Scott and Mary Ann Nordheimer, Nancy Dickerson Whitehead, Jeanne Bradley, Joyce and Calvin Cafritz, Barrett Prettyman and Noreen McGuire, Eric Dyson and his mother, Rolanda Jackson and her grandmother, Scott Simms and his mother, Rosemary Williams and her parents, Debbie Toll, Allan Ostar, Chuck Fisher, Chong Yim, the Reverend Bill Holmes, Father John Whalen, Marion Wright Edelman, Earl DeLong, Jehan Sadat, Lynn Bandfield, Michael Leapley, Ron Eisenberg, Brian Keane, Justice and Mrs. William Brennan, Ellen Ratner, Beverly Silverberg, Alan Fleischman, Stan and Judy Bromley, Jane Littlefield, the Reverend Neal Jones, Mark Craig, Richard Reeves, Susan Eisenhower and Roald Sagdeev, Fred Taylor, Ike Fulwood, Tom Blagburn, and many caring trustees at The American University and their spouses.

I heard from friends whom I had not seen for twenty, thirty, and even forty years. They demonstrated that true friendship is timeless. Thank you to Mike Mendillo, Dick Hart, Owen Gingerich, and other professional colleagues, and to Carl Jackson, Don Morris, Austin Lewis, and other childhood friends.

After the press reported about the abuse in my childhood, hundreds upon hundreds of survivors of childhood abuse, and of other misfortunes, contacted me. Never before have I experienced such an outpouring, most of it from people I did not know. These men and women, young and old, from across this nation and from other nations gave me strength and showed me courage.

Other people did likewise. Complete strangers reached out to Gail and me. They urged us to hold on, or said they were praying for us. How could I ever repay such kindness?

Throughout my hardest days in 1990, some several hundred members of The American University wrote or called us. Among the first to do so were students. And I heard from students' parents and faculty members and staff members and alums. There is no way I could thank them adequately, but I want to express my deep gratitude. Likewise, I want to thank my students as well as my fellow faculty members for being such splendid friends and colleagues since I returned to full-time teaching. They could not imagine how much they mean to me.

In a time of crisis, the most basic human institution—the family—comes together. My extended family rallied to my side. For their loving and generous spirit, I thank Ben and Claire Edgar, Mark and Lorna Edgar, John Fournier, Nita Hayes, Ida Quaglini, Mark and Rena Harrison, Kay Wilson, Bea and Jerry Casner, and my son-in-law Seth.

With humility, I say here what I say in my heart: Thank you, Deborah, Natasha, and Gail, for coming into my life and for being who you are. You are the bravest and most supportive people I have ever known. I cherish you and love you.

Finally, I give profound thanks for those life-sustaining words: "He restoreth my soul."

ABOUT THE AUTHORS

From 1980 to 1990, RICHARD BERENDZEN was president of The American University in Washington, D.C., where he currently is a professor of physics. An educator, astronomer, and administrator, he frequently gives lectures and interviews about education, trends in society, and science. He is chairman of the Advisory Board for the National Center for Survivors of Child Abuse. He and his wife live in Arlington, Virginia.

LAURA PALMER is the author of *Shrapnel in the Heart* and *In the Absence of Angels* with Elizabeth Glaser. She lives in New York City.

The author will donate a portion of his profits from this book to organizations that combat child abuse or aid survivors of child abuse.